I0797436

MOSES MALONE

MOSES MALONE

The Life of a Basketball Prophet

PAUL KNEPPER

University of Nebraska Press • Lincoln

The University of Nebraska Press is part of a land-grant institution with campuses and programs on the past, present, and future homelands of the Pawnee, Ponca, Otoe-Missouria, Omaha, Dakota, Lakota, Kaw, Cheyenne, and Arapaho Peoples, as well as those of the relocated Ho-Chunk, Sac and Fox, and Iowa Peoples.

For customers in the EU with safety/GPSR concerns, contact:
gpsr@mare-nostrum.co.uk
Mare Nostrum Group BV
Mauritskade 21D
1091 GC Amsterdam
The Netherlands

Library of Congress Control Number: 2025013229

Designed and set in Lyon Text by L. Welch.

For Brodie
Forge your own path like Moses

CONTENTS

ILLUSTRATIONS

PREFACE

During a morning walk around my neighborhood in Austin, Texas, in June 2023, I listened to French phenom Victor Wembanyama on *The Old Man & the Three* podcast a week before he was selected first in the NBA draft. I was struck by the nineteen-year-old's maturity and sophistication as he espoused his philosophies on basketball, celebrity, and life.[1] Then it hit me that Wembanyama was the same age as Moses Malone when Malone became the first modern player to jump directly from high school to professional basketball in 1974. The similarities end there.

Wembanyama moved away from home at age fourteen to play for a youth-club team, where a staff of twenty-five people oversaw his physical and emotional development. He turned professional a year later and began working daily with a weight trainer, physician, and orthopedist. By the time he declared for the NBA draft, he'd been named Most Valuable Player of the top league in France and competed with the French national team.[2] Wembanyama had extensive experience with the press, watched countless hours of NBA film, and expressed himself more eloquently in English, his second language, than most native speakers his age.

Malone, by comparison, grew up in a poor African American neighborhood in Petersburg, Virginia, with little exposure to the outside world. His primary concerns were his next meal and a clean outfit for school. Moses didn't have access to NBA film or elite coaching. He taught himself the game on the Virginia Avenue School playground. When the Utah Stars of the American Basketball Association (ABA) drafted him out of high school, no support system was in place as he adjusted to life as a professional athlete in nearly all-white Salt Lake City, nor were predecessors available to advise him as he embarked on his historic journey.

Moses endured the backlash that comes with being a pioneer. His decision to skip college was threatening to coaches and administrators, who thrived on the labor of young athletes, and the NBA, which valued the NCAA as a free farm system. Several coaches, executives, and members of the media criticized Malone's decision, suggesting he was likely to fail. Some made ignorant remarks about his intelligence, often rooted in racist stereotypes.

Moses silenced his doubters by earning a spot on the All-Star team in his rookie season. His success prompted other prospects to consider skipping college, and ABA and NBA executives began scouring high school gyms for talented teenagers. A year after Moses joined the ABA, Darryl Dawkins and Bill Willoughby were selected out of high school in the first round of the NBA draft.

Dawkins was a hulking man-child with a colorful personality. He produced a fourteen-year NBA career highlighted by backboard-shattering dunks, though he earned a reputation as immature and undisciplined and never fulfilled his potential. Willoughby failed to find his niche while playing for six teams over eight seasons. Some coaches found him difficult to manage. Both became cautionary tales for future athletes, and NBA teams shied away from high schoolers.

Moses appeared to be an anomaly. The jump from high school to the pros was extremely difficult. It took twenty years for somebody else to try.

By the time Kevin Garnett made the leap in 1995, the basketball landscape had changed drastically. Cable television and sneaker companies infused billions of dollars into the game. Garnett, and the prep stars who followed him, were more prepared upon arrival thanks to greater exposure to the NBA, elite prep schools, and participation in national AAU and sneaker-company tournaments. Once in the league, they received financial and emotional support.

Garnett researched the careers of Malone, Dawkins, and Willoughby when contemplating his decision to turn pro and consulted with Willougby. His best friend moved to Minnesota with him when he was drafted by the Timberwolves, and numerous assistant coaches and team personnel were on hand to assist him with the transition on and off the court.[3]

Garnett was followed to the NBA by high schoolers Kobe Bryant and Jermaine O'Neal a year later. Kobe's father, Joe "Jellybean" Bryant, played professionally in the NBA and Italy and guided Kobe through the process. Kobe's agent steered him to a successful Los Angeles Lakers franchise, and his parents lived with him in L.A. Mrs. Byrant cooked her son's meals and coordinated his social life. Bryant and O'Neal spoke regularly about their shared experience.[4]

Kobe signed a $10 million deal with Adidas before wearing a Lakers uniform. A year later, the sneaker company inked another prep-to-pro prospect, Tracy McGrady, to a $12 million contract.[5] Nike ponied up $90 million for LeBron James when he made the leap in 2003.[6] Those youngsters were set financially even if they failed. If Moses had flamed out after a few seasons, he wouldn't have had enough money to live on or a skill to fall back on.

Malone overcame the obstacles to produce one of most distinguished careers in basketball history. In addition to his groundbreaking jump, he won three MVP awards and is widely considered the greatest offensive rebounder ever. And yet, for reasons discussed as follows, a definitive biography was not written about him until now.

There was no flash to Moses's game. He didn't soar to the basket like Julius Erving or Michael Jordan, showcase the wizardry of Magic Johnson, or put on dazzling shooting displays like Stephen Curry. He wasn't known for a trademark shot like Kareem Abdul-Jabbar's skyhook or Hakeem Olajuwon's "Dream Shake." Even among dominant big men, he wasn't a behemoth who overpowered his opponents like Wilt Chamberlain and Shaquille O'Neal.

Moses's superpower was his relentless drive. His greatest skill was the yeoman's work of battling for offensive rebounds. Those qualities don't make for *SportsCenter* highlights or generate YouTube clicks by younger generations of fans.

Malone's legacy is hurt by the devaluation of the offensive rebound. During his prime, teams played through a big man, with the objective of shooting as close to the basket as possible. The easiest way to do that is by grabbing a rebound near the rim. Moses ranks first all-time with 7,382 offensive rebounds (ABA and NBA combined). Number two on that list is Artis Gilmore at a distant 4,816.

Basketball has since moved away from the hoop with the proliferation of the three-point shot. Deep shots lead to long rebounds, resulting in fewer scrums under the basket. Coaches deemphasize offensive rebounds in favor of transition defense. The game has also become less physical, with an emphasis on quickness over strength. Executives no longer seek players with Malone's skill set, and younger fans cannot identify with his style of play.

Prior to the player empowerment movement of the twenty-first century, most players of Malone's caliber spent their whole career with one or two teams. Among his contemporaries, Magic was always a Laker, Larry Bird only wore Celtic green, Erving played all eleven of his NBA seasons with the Philadelphia 76ers, and Kareem split his career between the Milwaukee Bucks and Lakers. Moses suited up for nine franchises during his twenty-one-year career and didn't play more than six seasons with any club. Consequently, he's not associated with one team or embraced by a fanbase as much as other superstars.

Perhaps the biggest factor in Malone's relative anonymity is that he wanted it that way. Shy by nature and self-conscious about his speech impediment, he avoided the media. Some of the game's fiercest competitors on the court, such as Jordan and Bryant, flashed billion-dollar smiles off it, which led to endorsement deals that made them more appealing to fans. The public only saw Moses's scowl, resulting in misconceptions about him as a person.

Before the internet, sportswriters created the mythology around the legends of the game. Since Moses kept his distance from reporters, he was portrayed as gruff and unintelligent and didn't receive publicity or praise commensurate with his accomplishments. Due to his death at the age of sixty, he never had the opportunity to reshape his image as a beloved elder statesman, like his rival, the once notoriously standoffish Abdul-Jabbar.

Some of the reasons Moses is underappreciated are what make him such a compelling figure. "There were plenty of players with bigger hands, faster legs, a higher leap, a more accurate shot," said Pat Williams, former general manager of the 76ers. "By all objective standards, Moses shouldn't have been one of the best in the game—but he was. I spent many hours watching him play, and I concluded there's only one explanation for his greatness: Moses Malone had *attitude*. The man never quit. He thrived on intense competition and physical contact. The rougher it got, the better he played." Williams concluded that "Moses Malone was the hardest-working player in the history of the sport."[7]

Fans don't fantasize about being a "blue-collar superstar," though Malone's unparalleled work ethic and searing intensity were more relatable than gravity-defying dunks. There's something heroic about the humble warrior who loves to compete with no regard for fame.

As a result of Malone's reticence, there's much that was previously unknown about this misunderstood and complex individual, from his sharp wit to his devotion to teammates and friends. Charles Barkley refers to Malone as "singularly the greatest influence in my career," and Erving speaks of his "brilliant basketball mind."[8]

Once we gain a greater understanding of Moses the man, we can take a fresh look at the player, an indomitable force who discarded Hall of Fame centers like sparring partners. For a five-year period when icons named Kareem, Dr. J, Magic, and Bird graced the hardwood, Moses Malone was the greatest basketball player in the world.

ACKNOWLEDGMENTS

So many people have contributed to this book in ways big and small, from sources I interviewed, to public relations employees and school information directors, to librarians who assisted with research, to those who shared photographs with me, and to friends and family who lent support. I'm grateful to all of them.

A few sources deserve special recognition. Ed Gholson and Kevin Vergara showed me around Petersburg and were there to answer any questions I had about Moses. It's easy to see why they were two of his best friends, and I'm grateful to have them in my life. Floy Johnson gave me a tour of Fonde Recreation Center and shared many fascinating stories about Moses. Tony Dale is another dedicated friend of Moses who assisted me in numerous ways.

Shoutout to Petersburg! One of the great joys of writing this book was speaking with so many kind people from Moses's hometown. Clinton Bufford was a great resource for life on St. Matthew Street and the Heights in general. Bernard Wilson connected me with several of Malone's high school teammates, and Treska Wilson-Smith helped put me in touch with other sources.

I received a few no-look passes from authors Theresa Runstedtler, Bob Kuska, and Pete Croatto. Kuska introduced me to Larry O'Brien's papers at Springfield College. The curator of that collection, Jeffrey Monseau, was a pleasure to work with. I'm grateful to Leah Nash and Sandra White for everything they do to honor Moses's legacy and for welcoming me to the golf tournament that bears his name. Michelle Souli provided genealogical information regarding Malone's family, and Fred Cantor was a source of encouragement early in the process.

Writing a book is a long and arduous endeavor. I appreciate all my family and friends who encouraged me and humored me with questions about how it was progressing. That starts with my wife Stacey, whose many roles in this project included cheerleader, sounding board, advisor, and editor. I'm so fortunate to have her by my side. I'm grateful for my son, Brodie, who brings me immense joy and inspires me to write, and my loving parents, Barry and Jane, who have always supported me. My brother, Gregg, is a pillar in my life and everything you could ask for in a sibling. Thank you to Sam, Jordyn, Scarlett, Elle, Margo, Robbie, Elba, and Alina for your love and support. Special thanks to Aaron Marcus for reading a draft of this book and providing valuable feedback.

Lastly, thank you to Rob Taylor for believing in this project, Taylor Martin for all of her assistance, and the rest of the people at the University of Nebraska Press who helped bring this book to life, in addition to my copyeditor, Joseph Webb.

MOSES MALONE

1

The Heights

The rickety house at 241 St. Matthew Street had asphalt siding and a tin roof covered with tar. The paint on the front of the house had chipped away long ago, and the slightly sloped front porch appeared to be on the verge of collapse. The interior was equally shabby. Plumbing was spotty, and one of the bedrooms had a hole to the outside world where a window had once been. The living room consisted of an oil stove, an old couch slanted to one side where the springs sunk in, and an orange crate that served as a table. Three portraits hung on the wall: Martin Luther King Jr., President and Mrs. Kennedy, and Jesus Christ.[1] This was the home of Mary and Moses Malone.

Mrs. Malone was born Mary Hudgins on July 28, 1928, in Chesterfield, Virginia, the oldest of Jannie and Oscar Hudgins's nine children. She came up hard. Her father, who lost his right arm in a shotgun accident, was a wood worker whose annual income was $460, according to the 1940 census.[2] Mary left school after fifth grade to help keep the family afloat.[3]

The Hudgins suffered a tragedy when Mary's mother died at age thirty-four. Oscar didn't have the means to care for all his children and sent the boys to live in an orphanage. Mary was sixteen years old and tended to her younger sisters. She cooked, cleaned, ironed their clothes, and sent them off to school.[4] She remained the matriarch of the family in the decades that followed, caring for her father in the later years of his life and attending graduations and other special events for her nieces and nephews.[5] When her brother William was murdered, she looked out for his son Mario.[6]

On January 22, 1955, Mary married Moses Malone in Chester, Virginia. Moses was born in nearby Drewryville in 1930 and worked a factory job at the Continental Can Company.[7] On March 23, 1955, their son, Moses Eugene Malone, was born with the help of a midwife in Chesterfield County, Virginia. He weighed seven pounds.[8]

When Moses was about two years old, Mary kicked his father out of the house. The elder Moses was drinking too much, and she didn't want her son to be exposed to that behavior.[9] Moses's father was not a part of his life going forward. Mary and the younger Moses moved to East Bank Street in the Blandford neighborhood of Petersburg before settling in at the house on St. Matthew St. around 1965 in a Petersburg neighborhood called the Heights.

Mary earned about $59 a week working at a home for the elderly. She later landed a job packing meat at a supermarket for $135 a week. "I always saw to it that Moses had food on the table and a shoe on his foot," she told writer Ira Berkow. "We never had much savings, never more than $25 in the bank, and that was in case he got sick, and I'd have enough to get him to the doctor."[10] Moses had two pairs of pants for school, which Mary washed nightly.[11] Holiday and birthday gifts were modest or nonexistent. One exception was an organ Mary purchased for Moses for Christmas when he was six. He cherished that organ into adulthood, and it instilled in him a lifelong love of music.[12]

Ms. Mary, as she was known in the Heights, packed a strong personality into her slender 5-foot-2 frame. She was sweet but tough, a disciplinarian who always spoke her mind. And she was very protective of her baby. The boy was picked on often. He was painfully shy and an easy target due to his stutter and lanky build. Kids teased him for not wearing a winter coat and snowshoes in the cold weather, luxuries Mary couldn't afford.[13] Ms. Mary unleashed her wrath on any child who made fun of her son.[14]

She nicknamed Moses "Teeny" as a baby because he was so skinny. The name stuck and caught on in the neighborhood.[15] Neighbors and friends remember him as a quiet kid who kept to himself. He never got into fights or trouble with the law. When comfortable with the people around him, he opened up a bit and liked to crack jokes.

Despite the absence of Moses's father, the Malones were surrounded by love. Mary's nephews James and Harold lived with them for a while, as did her father for the final years of his life. Mary had other siblings, nieces, and nephews nearby, including sisters Laura and Naomi, who lived in the Heights. Moses was particularly close with Naomi and her daughter, Diane, who was the same age. He also spent a lot of time with his uncle Charlie Hudgins.

The Malones built a community at the Morning Star Baptist Church on St. Mark Street, which they attended regularly.[16] They also enjoyed the emotional support of the proverbial village that raised Moses and the other children. Originally known as Delectable Heights, the Heights was a poor, Black neighborhood within walking distance of downtown Petersburg. Money was tight, though those who grew up there look back on their childhood fondly.

Wealth is relative. Moses's neighbors were all in a similar financial position, and most didn't venture far from the neighborhood. Corporate dollars did not flow through Petersburg. The white middle class lived more comfortably than Black folks, but the contrast wasn't as stark as in many larger cities. The Malones weren't bombarded with images of wealth on social media, cable television, or in movies, the last of which they couldn't afford to attend. They didn't realize how poor they were.

The Heights was a small neighborhood, so everybody knew each other, and families looked out for one another. "We didn't have much, but we had each other," said Roger Pegram, who grew up a block from Moses.[17] If you needed a teaspoon of sugar or a couple of dollars for groceries, your neighbor helped you out. Parents sat on their front porches while young kids played hopscotch, tag, jump rope, and marbles in the yard. Adults had a license to scold or even smack any child who stepped out of line, and bad behavior was sure to get back to one's parents.

The Heights could be rough. Johnny Byrd, whose convenience store was a few houses down from the Malones, was held up numerous times, and residents had to be wary of wild dogs roaming the streets.[18] However, the children felt safe in their familiar surroundings. Guns and drugs hadn't infiltrated the neighborhood yet. Fights were common but settled with fists, and if two kids threw punches in the morning, they'd be playing together again by the afternoon.

Moses delivered the local newspaper, the *Progress-Index*, for a while and, like many boys in the Heights, earned spending money by caddying at the Country Club of Petersburg in walking distance from the neighborhood.[19] But most of the time he was free to play with his friends. "I didn't like him to do no work at all," Mary told Frank Deford of *Sports Illustrated*. "I know how hard I come up, so I didn't want him to."[20]

Entertainment options were scarce. Sometimes the boys messed around with sticks or hit golf balls in the woods. During the summer months, Moses cooled off at the Bunker Hill swimming pool on Jefferson Street.[21] In his spare time, he drew pictures of buildings or the schoolyard, and every year he attended the Southside Virginia Fair that came through town.[22]

Mostly, boys and girls who had outgrown their parents' front lawn spent their leisure time at the Virginia Avenue Elementary School schoolyard. Virginia Avenue, the street the school was on, ran parallel to Moses's street, one block over, just a short walk up High Pearl Street.

In elementary school, Moses played baseball and football. The local schools fielded football teams that competed against each other. Moses, who was tall for his age, emerged as a reliable target at wide receiver for the Virginia Avenue School. He enjoyed watching football on TV and was a devout Dallas Cowboys fan in the heart of Washington Redskins country.[23]

Moses first picked up a basketball at age thirteen. "I thought basketball was a sissy's game—too easy," he said years later. "When I first was introduced to basketball me and couple of my buddies, we'd come around the playground, and we had a little rubber kickball. I threw the rubber ball up, and it went into the hoop. I said, 'This might be a game I wanna try.' All of a sudden, I left football, left baseball, and I really started loving the game."[24]

Virginia Avenue Elementary School was the site of some of the best basketball games in Petersburg. Initially, the older players didn't welcome the young Malone. He was tall with long arms but lacked coordination. "He had no hands," said David Pair, a friend from the neighborhood. "We'd pass him the ball and it would hit him in the chest." The guys laughed and kicked him off the court. Moses would stand by the fence and watch them play.[25]

Foreshadowing his professional career, the boy went to work. Every day after school, he played ball on Virginia Avenue. When most of the guys went home in the evening, he stayed there practicing his shooting, rebounding, and moves around the basket until the early morning hours. There were no lights in the schoolyard, so he relied on the dim glow of a lone streetlight. Don Wall, a friend who lived across the street from the school, fell asleep every night to the repeated *bang bang ching* of Moses dribbling the ball then shooting it through the metal nets. Rumor spread through the Heights that Teeny slept with his basketball.[26]

The competition at the schoolyard was fierce. When a team lost, it might be a long time before its players had a chance to play again. Sometimes the boys played for orange juice, a rare treat for Moses. The more he played, the more his love of the game grew, and he'd hoop with anybody at any time. Phyllis Jones and Janet Pegram, two girls from the neighborhood, played Moses two-on-one to 20. Moses would spot them 18 points and still win.[27]

When the weather didn't cooperate, Moses and the other boys moved their games to the Harding Street Recreation Center. Originally called the Harding Street Community Center, the venue had hosted legendary acts such as Sam Cooke and James Brown. Over the years, it morphed into a community recreation center where kids from different neighborhoods tested their skills on the basketball court.[28]

Roger Pegram was a high school football star from the Heights a few years older than Moses. He and some friends put together a team to play in a basketball tournament at the Harding Street Rec Center. Roger's younger brother, Curtis, was a close friend of Moses, and they formed their own team. Roger couldn't believe what he witnessed as James and Moses's squad beat his team in the championship game.

"We never knew Moses could play ball," he said. "We'd be at the school yard, all the older guys. All the other guys would get up and play, but Mo never participated. Never knew he could play until we played in a tournament at the Rec. And we were just so shocked how Moses played. You could just tell how talented he was—for a guy who you never seen him play basketball. Never seen him play!"[29]

Malone's rate of improvement was staggering. When asked years later by *Playboy* magazine how long it took before his hard work paid off, Moses said, "Only about a year—one of my years was worth five of anybody else's. When I was 14, I was going up against much older guys and puttin it to em."[30]

In the summer of 1968, not long after Moses picked up the game, he visited his cousins James and Harold, who had moved to New York. "There was this playground tournament up about 165th Street and Amsterdam

Avenue," Moses recalled years later. "There were these three fancy city dudes, and they were using their flashy behind-the-back and between-leg stuff to beat everybody. My cousin looked at them and said 'Hey, I know a guy who can beat you all.' They said, 'Who?' and he pointed at me. So, I found two guys who couldn't even play. One was from New York and the other was from my hometown in Petersburg. We played to 32, and my team won, 32–20. I got 30," he said. "Then this girl came over and said, 'Hey, you're kind of cute.' 'I was kinda shy. I turned away.'"[31]

Moses and Mary had few possessions, the most prized of which was an old Bible, dog-eared and coverless, that had been passed down by Mary's father. When Moses was fourteen, he wrote on a piece of paper that he would be the best high school player in the country his junior year and tucked it inside the Bible.[32] It was a preposterous prediction. Sure, the boy was tall for his age, but his skills were far from exceptional, and he had never even played organized basketball.

The other ballers at Virginia Avenue were vital to Malone's growth. They challenged him daily, instilling in him a competitive drive. He patterned his game after the older guys, some of whom took him under their wings. David Pair only stood about 5 feet 9, though he was on the high school wrestling team and would become a state judo champion. He showed Malone how to use his body to gain position under the boards. Sometimes he just kept Moses company while the boy practiced his free throws.[33] Baby Head was a 5-foot-10 guard who, according to his brother Leroy, could shoot like Stephen Curry. The Cole brothers, Baby Head, Leroy, and Bozo were regulars at Virginia Avenue, and Moses grew close with Baby Head in particular.[34] Gut Johnson played football for the high school and looked out for the younger kids in the neighborhood. He took a liking to Moses, and the two would play one on one, full court, until well past midnight.[35] Some of the older boys Moses befriended were into gambling and drinking on the street corner, but he stayed away from those activities.

Malone formed a spirited rivalry with a boy from St. Mark Street known as "Jimmy Snake." Jimmy was a street kid who didn't have much use for school or organized ball. He grew to about 6 feet 6 and jumped high enough to touch the top of the backboard. "He looked like a giant," said Ricky Hunley, a football star from the Heights who went on to play in the

NFL. "He used to wear Moses's skinny ass out cause Moses didn't carry the weight that Jimmy did." Moses and Jimmy were always placed on separate teams to keep the games fair.[36]

While some of the older kids provided guidance, for the most part Moses taught himself the game. Petersburg wasn't a basketball hotbed. There wasn't an Amateur Athletic Union (AAU) scene or expert coaches working with the kids in the Heights.

Moses and his friends watched their favorite players on television then emulated their moves on the court. They'd call out their hero's name as they went up for a shot, drove to the basket, or swatted an opponent's offering. Moses's idol was Spencer Haywood, the superb forward best known for paving the way for players to leave college early for professional basketball. "Haywood to the hoop!" Moses would yell as he drove to the basket. "Haywood with the shot!"[37] Morris Fultz, a friend from the Heights who played high school ball with Moses, pretended to be Julius Erving. Mo Howard went by Lew, for Lew Alcindor of UCLA. Ronald Robinson idolized another UCLA standout, Sidney Wicks.[38]

Before and after runs at the playground, the boys sat around and daydreamed about what they would do when they grew up. "I'm going to be a millionaire," said one kid. "I'm gonna play in the NBA," said another. "We didn't take it too serious," said Fultz. "But Mo was serious. He said he was going to be like Spencer Haywood."[39]

David Pair was a big Wilt Chamberlain fan. He had a poster of the Big Dipper hanging in his house. Moses asked Pair, "How come you like Wilt so much?"

Pair replied, "Because he's the best."

Moses said, "Someday I'm gonna be the best."

Pair said, "Okay, when you're the best I'll put up your poster." Not many years later, Pair hung a Moses Malone poster on his wall.[40]

2

Chuck Taylor All-Stars

Clint Bufford lived two houses down from the Malones on St. Matthew Street. He was a few years older than Moses and played for Peabody High School's basketball and football teams. One day during the 1969–70 school year, Peabody's assistant basketball coach, Pro Hayes, drove Clint home from practice. They passed the Virginia Avenue School, where Moses was playing ball.

Hayes spotted the lanky eighth grader, who by then was about 6 feet 1 or 6 feet 2, and asked Bufford about him. "What's his name? What grade is in? Does he play organized ball?" At that time, Moses was attending Peabody High School. Virginia Avenue Elementary School ran through seventh grade, and there was no junior high or middle school. Bufford called Moses over to the car. Hayes asked him to practice with the varsity team in the evenings after school. The boy demurred. Hayes persisted, pointing out that it would be beneficial to play against strong competition on an indoor court instead of the concrete schoolyard.

The next day Moses practiced with the varsity team. Hayes was impressed, but the boy didn't return. The coach asked Clint to talk to him. Clint thought maybe Moses was self-conscious about his long, skinny legs. He'd never seen his neighbor wear shorts; it was always jeans or overalls. He convinced Moses to return to practice. Moses showed up for a few days, but then he quit again.

This time Coach Hayes went to the Malone home. He told Mary that her son had potential and sealed the deal by offering Moses a pair of Converse Chuck Taylor All-Stars, the premier basketball shoe on the market worn by most NBA players. Mary couldn't afford to buy Moses basketball shoes, opting instead for the cheapest tennis shoes she could find. Hayes told Moses that the Chuck Taylors were his so long as he showed up for practice every day. If he stopped coming, he had to return them.[1] That was the start of Moses's career in organized basketball.

Petersburg is a small city in southeast Virginia at the fall line of the Appomattox River, best known as the site of a nearly yearlong siege at the end of the Civil War. General Robert E. Lee and his troops eventually lost the battle, opening a pathway for the Union to Richmond, the capital of the Confederacy, twenty-five miles north of Petersburg. Lee surrendered at Appomattox weeks later, bringing an end to the war. Petersburg had a population of about thirty-seven thousand people during Moses's childhood. Tobacco was the leading industry until the city's biggest employer, Brown & Williamson Tobacco Company, left town in 1985.[2]

Despite its location in the heart of the south, Petersburg had a longstanding free Black community residing predominantly on Pocahontas Island.[3] Yet the city was not immune from discrimination. Moses, who was born the same year that Rosa Parks refused to surrender her bus seat to a white person in Montgomery, Alabama, and fourteen-year-old Emmett Till was lynched in the Mississippi Delta, lived the earliest years of his life in a city under the scourge of segregation.

There were "Whites" and "Colored" restrooms, water fountains, and waiting areas at the Petersburg bus station. Courtrooms used separate Bibles for Black and white folks, and the public library had different entrances and reading rooms for the different races. Black people were allowed to buy food from Woolworth's and W. T. Grant but couldn't sit at their lunch counters.[4]

Wyatt Tee Walker, pastor of the Gillfield Baptist Church, served as head of the local NAACP and spearheaded a vibrant civil rights movement in the city. He helped organize protests and sit-ins by students from Virginia State University and Peabody High School at Petersburg Public Library, housed in the McKenney Building, in 1959 and 1960, which resulted in integration of the facility. That led to demonstrations and eventually an end to segregation at the Blue Bird and Century Theaters, Spiro's Department Store, and the Trailways Bus Station, as well as other locales.[5]

Walker met Martin Luther King Jr. at an interseminary meeting while in seminary school, and the two became friends. Dr. King was so impressed by Walker and the movement in Petersburg that he recruited his friend to be executive director of his civil rights organization, the Southern Christian Leadership Conference (SCLC) in 1960. "The fact that Dr. King selected me to lead the SCLC is proof that Petersburg played a big role in the civil rights movement," Walker told the *Progress-Index* in 2009. "The SCLC used the local model of the movement that we had in Petersburg and applied it to the entire South. That was a critical strategy."[6]

Segregation was illegal by the time Moses finished elementary school, though the separate races continued to reside in different communities and attend different schools. "We were kind of isolated in our own neighborhood," recalled Francine Cole, who grew up on Virginia Avenue. "It's amazing that there are some neighborhoods that are white, maybe ten minutes, fifteen minutes from where I grew up that I didn't know existed until, you know, later on."[7]

In 1954 the Supreme Court ruled in *Brown v. Board of Education of Topeka* that racial segregation in schools was unconstitutional. The following year, the year Moses was born, the Court provided guidelines for the integration of schools, stating that states must do so "with all deliberate speed."[8] Fourteen years later, as Moses entered eighth grade at Peabody High School, the Petersburg school district had still not integrated.

Virginia state officials furiously resisted integration. Senator Harry Byrd authored a document signed by close to one hundred members of Congress in 1956, known as the Southern Manifesto, which rejected the Court's decision in *Brown* on the grounds that it violated states' rights. Byrd advocated a policy called massive resistance, a multipronged approach to prevent Virginia schools from integrating, or at least delaying the process as long as possible. State officials withheld funding, and in some cases, closed schools entirely if they were on the verge of integrating. The public schools in Prince George County, located about twenty minutes from Petersburg, closed for five years from 1959 to 1964. In other instances, state and local governments issued vouchers to white students to attend private schools rather than share a school with Black children.[9]

When the courts struck down such policies in the late 1950s, Petersburg and other localities adopted a "freedom of choice" plan, whereby students of all races could pick which school they attended. In practice, the burden of transportation and admission hurdles designed to discourage

Blacks from applying or being accepted to predominantly white schools maintained the status quo.[10] In 1963 Petersburg High School admitted five Black students. That number increased steadily over the next handful of years, and by 1969 three hundred Black students were enrolled at the predominantly white high school, but just one white family at the Black school, Peabody High School.[11]

Finally, in December 1968 Judge Robert R. Merhige Jr. ordered full integration of the Petersburg schools. The district's elementary schools integrated for the 1969–70 school year, and the high schools were set to follow in the fall of 1970, with the Black high school, Peabody, becoming a junior high school, and the white school, Petersburg, serving as the high school for all students. Merhige paid a price for ordering the integration of Petersburg and other school districts. His family dog was bound and shot (though it survived), and segregationists burned the cottage where his mother-in-law lived.[12]

Many white families sent their children to private schools, some as far as forty-five minutes away. Several Black families were angry as well. For the Black community the issue wasn't so much integration itself as the way it was implemented. Why didn't they have a say in the matter? And why was the white school the high school and the Black school the junior high school? They argued that Peabody was a superior school in a nicer building than Petersburg High School.

Peabody High was a source of pride and connection for Black residents. Opened in 1870, it was the first publicly funded Black high school in Virginia.[13] Several of the current and future Peabody students wanted to attend school there because their parents or siblings did. Gonzell Phillips was the tenth of twelve children. His eight oldest siblings attended Peabody. The teachers were familiar with his family and always joyously welcomed the next Phillips brother or sister to the school. A few of the teachers even came to his home to visit his siblings.[14] To take away the Black people's high school was to erase their history. Instead of following in their parents and siblings' footsteps, they were forced to attend a school whose marching band's favorite song was "Dixie," the unofficial anthem of the Confederacy.[15]

Black students met with civil rights attorney Harry Marsh III and attended school board meetings to urge the board to make Peabody the high school. On Oct. 3, 1969, about nine hundred Peabody students marched from the school to the courthouse, passing Petersburg High School along the way, in protest of the integration plan.[16] About a year later, early in the first integrated school year, Black students rioted, smashing windows at Petersburg High School. From the window of the basement classroom where she was confined, Cindy Ruffa, a white student, watched groups of young white men who were not students approach the school with chains in response to the riots.[17] The principal locked down the school and canceled classes for two days.

Black kids also looted stores and started fires on Sycamore Street downtown. They targeted Rucker-Rosenstock and Woolworth's, department stores owned by white people, which had back doors where they could sneak out. There is no evidence that Moses participated in the looting. Ms. Mary wouldn't have tolerated that. But some of his friends did, and the controversy over integration had to leave an impression on him.[18] More than fifty years later, some of his classmates are still bitter about not graduating from Peabody High School.

The integrated Petersburg High School consisted of grades ten through twelve, so Moses remained at Peabody Junior High School for ninth grade. He had sprouted to about 6 feet 6, and Baby Head and Bozo pushed him and Morris Fultz, another tall kid from the Heights, to try out for the school team. Moses began the season on junior varsity, coached by Pro Hayes. He, Fultz, and another kid from the neighborhood named James Walker walked to and from practice together every day.[19]

Robertnett "Pro" Hayes grew up in Petersburg and graduated from Peabody High School. He served three years in the army during World War II, then earned his bachelor's degree and a master's in industrial management from Virginia State University. Hayes began teaching at Carter G. Woodson High School in Hopewell, the town next to Petersburg, in 1951 and led the school's basketball team to six state championships in seventeen years, including five consecutive from 1955 through 1959. In 1968 he was hired as an industrial arts teacher and assistant basketball coach under Carl Peal at his alma mater, Peabody High School.[20]

Hayes was married but never had children. He treated the boys at Peabody and Petersburg High School like his own and became a father figure to many of his players. The boys knew they could talk to him about personal problems. If Hayes found out that a student didn't have lunch one day, he took care of it.[21] He imparted life lessons to his players, many of which didn't resonate with them until years later. "Be honest. Treat people the way you want to be treated. Remain patient. Don't lose your cool."[22]

Hayes's players laugh at the hypocrisy of those last two points. The coach was far from patient and rarely kept his cool. Hayes was a disciplinarian whom former players describe as a "Bob Knight type." "I can remember one day at practice, Pro threw an apple at one of the guys running up and down the floor," recalled Mark Thompson. "He wouldn't do what Pro wanted him to do. Pro threw an apple. Pro threw chairs. Pro throw the clipboard. Pro throw anything he could get his hands on. Pro throw the ball at you. Pro gonna get one of the balls off the rack and throw that at you."[23]

Hayes ran up and down the sideline during games, exhorting his team on, and vociferously argued any call against his players. His favorite target was his twin brother, a referee who often worked the Peabody and Petersburg games. Coach Peal often had to encourage Hayes to calm down so as not to receive a technical foul.[24] Pro got away with his tirades because the boys knew that he cared. For Moses, who didn't have a father at home, Hayes became an important figure in his life.

The boys also respected Coach Hayes's knowledge of the game and appreciated his attention to detail. If they messed up a play in practice, they would run it over and over until the team operated like a well-oiled machine. He taught the basics—setting a pick, boxing out, executing different types of passes—and emphasized defense. As the assistant coach, he diagrammed the plays for the varsity squad.[25]

Moses thrived under Coach Hayes as a freshman on the junior varsity team, averaging 25 points per game. In February he was called up to varsity, along with sophomore Morris Fultz. Malone scored 30 points in his first varsity game against Manchester High School, though it was a game days later that convinced Coach Peal that the young man was special. Petersburg was facing its archival, Hopewell, led by senior center Mike James. James stood about 6 feet 8 and had such an enormous wingspan that teammates called him Spiderman. He was being heavily recruited by colleges across the country and appeared to be a huge mismatch for the 160-pound freshman Malone. To Peal's surprise, Moses didn't back down and held Spiderman to 13 points.[26]

Next up was the Central District Basketball Tournament. Petersburg faced Midlothian in the first round, which had beaten it twice during the regular season. Peal's squad hadn't been able to match Midlothian's size. Moses was the difference. He led the Crimson Wave to victory, with 26 points and 19 rebounds. Petersburg lost in the second round to Hopewell. Malone averaged 12 points and 12 rebounds over six varsity games in his freshman year, laying the groundwork for what would be a historic high school career.[27]

The Crimson Wave was a young team in 1971–72, Moses's sophomore year, returning just one starter from the previous season. Malone had grown to about 6 feet 8½, though the coaches weren't certain exactly how tall he was because their measuring equipment didn't reach that high. He still weighed about 170 pounds. The *Progress-Index* referred to him as a "towering toothpick" and "skinny giant."[28]

Moses, Fultz, and Michael Howard overwhelmed teams inside, and Malone began making a name for himself in Virginia with extraordinary performances. He posted 34 points, 20 rebounds, and 10 blocked shots in a win over Dinwiddie High School in January 1972. A few nights later, he tallied 26 points and 18 rebounds against Prince George High School.[29]

Moses averaged 22 points per game for the season and was named to the All-District and All-Regional teams, rare feats for a sophomore. That season, he told teammate Bernard Wilson that he was going to be a professional basketball player. Wilson didn't believe him, but he didn't discourage him either.[30]

Coach Peal's squad went 16-2 during the regular season, with the losses to Hopewell and Colonial Heights. It won its first playoff game, then fell to a Hopewell team that went on to win the state championship. The loss was devastating to the Crimson Wave. Hopewell was the main rival, and Coach Peal's players felt like they let a potential state championship slip away. Their time would come. Moses would not lose another high school basketball game.

3

Visitors from the Moon

It was raining at one in the morning when Hal Miles and some of his friends had just left a house party in the Heights. Miles drove past the Virginia Avenue schoolyard and noticed a solitary figure on the basketball court. He pulled over to get a better look. Through the raindrops, he saw Moses practicing free throws—barefoot. He had placed his only pair of Chuck Taylors under a cardboard box so as not to ruin them in the rain.[1]

Basketball players are assessed by various attributes such as athleticism, quickness, strength, and skill. The great ones possess an additional quality: hyperfocus. They play basketball at every opportunity, and when they're not playing, they're thinking, talking, watching, dreaming about it. That hyperfocus includes an extraordinary competitive spirit and unquenchable desire to be the best. Anybody who crossed paths with Moses in high school saw that he approached the game differently than even his most dedicated teammates. It meant something more to him. Moses Malone was going to be great.

Moses knew it too. Ten years later, he told Ira Berkow of the *New York Times*, "The Lord made some people to be engineers. He made some people to be doctors. He made me to be a great basketball player. He say, 'Moses, whatever you do, be sure you be great at it.'"[2]

Moses viewed basketball as his way out of poverty and refused to allow anything to interfere with his path to greatness. He was an extremely proud young man who followed his own agenda and wasn't easily swayed by others. By remaining true to himself, he avoided the pitfalls of the streets that swallowed up some of his peers. He never drank or smoked cigarettes or marijuana. He rarely attended clubs or house parties, choosing instead to work on his game, and didn't mess around with girls until his senior year in high school.

Moses was kind to all but didn't trust many and kept a small circle of close friends. He confided in guys like Baby Head and Pair from the neighborhood. He also became tight with Nathan "Panther" Dickerson, the manager of the basketball team, and James Mitchell, who went on to fame as a local DJ who went by Mitch Malone.[3] For Moses, friendship was sacred; his friends were like family.

Malone remained painfully shy. His stutter wasn't severe, but it was compounded by a guttural voice that was difficult to understand. He was also self-conscious about his damaged front teeth and extraordinary height. In his first year of high school, he bought chips for lunch every day and ate alone outside behind the school.[4] If someone wasn't in Moses's inner circle, he kept his distance. When he didn't like something someone said or did, he'd just stop talking. He was never rude or confrontational. On the contrary, his fellow students remember him as somebody who always said hello in the hallways. He was simply quiet and looked down when he spoke, unwilling to make eye contact with even family or close friends.

Malone was a bit of a clown in school, mumbling jokes under his breath.[5] Sometimes he'd stick his head into a random classroom and greet the teacher: "Hey, Mr. or Mrs. So and So, what's going on?" His smile and the way he had to duck his head under the doorway made the other students laugh.[6]

One spring afternoon, Malone asked Ollie Jarvis, the high school baseball coach, if he could be the batboy for the baseball team that evening in its game at Thomas Jefferson High School. Coach Jarvis agreed. Players and fans laughed at the sight of the 6-foot-10 kid retrieving the Petersburg bats. Moses only lasted a couple of innings, then made his way to a nearby basketball court and played pickup ball with some of the Thomas Jefferson kids.[7] Basketball was always on his mind. Even at practice, he'd act like a big kid, cracking jokes or tugging on teammates' shorts.[8] But once that ball was tossed, he flipped the switch. It was laser focus.

Moses was the centerpiece of a Petersburg team that expected to win a state championship in his junior season. Still rail thin, he had topped out at 6 feet 10, with astonishing quickness and athleticism for a young man his height. He ran the floor like a guard and could match many of their skills. If a teammate showcased a crossover dribble in practice, Moses duplicated it.[9] Players weren't allowed to dunk in high school games in Virginia at the time, so Moses demonstrated his aerial displays in practice. For his signature dunk, he'd leap above the rim, pin the ball to the backboard, then slam it in on the way down.[10]

Malone still weighed less than 200 pounds, though was surprisingly strong for his size. One day during practice, the basketball and wrestling teams engaged in a playful argument over use of the water fountain. The wrestlers claimed it for themselves, but Malone decided he wasn't going to wait until they were done before taking a few sips. Two of the wrestlers waited for Moses in the hallway outside the wrestling room. When he walked by, they grabbed him and threw him inside. "And that's when I realized that Mo wasn't a regular guy," said one of the wrestlers, Hal Miles. "In that situation right there, it took five championship wrestlers to get Mo down. It took five of 'em."[11]

Moses's greatest basketball skill was rebounding, particularly on the offensive glass. From a young age, he had an incredible knack for determining at what angle the ball would come off the rim and a relentless drive to get it. His post moves were unrefined. He'd often throw the ball toward the rim, retrieve it, and go back up from a better position.

Malone was part of a huge frontcourt for the Crimson Wave. The two starting forwards, Morris Fultz and Michael Howard, were each about 6 feet 6. Both could jump. Howard was an exceptional all-around athlete who also excelled on the pitching mound. The point guard was a 5-foot-7 speedster named Stanley Taylor. Opponents remember him for the burgundy-colored tassels he wore on his socks during games. Stanley was the emotional leader of the team, who pumped teammates up before games.[12] The other starting-guard spot belonged to Ronald Walker, a rugged defender who also played running back for Petersburg's football team.[13]

Bill "Buck" Nunnally, a 6-foot-4 forward with a massive wingspan, came off the bench, along with Gonzell Phillips, Ronald Robinson, and Bernard Wilson. The Crimson Wave's depth, combined with Coach Peal's exhortations to "run, run, run," made their grueling practices more difficult than the games. The team was a responsible group of young men who were committed to a common goal of winning a championship, though they didn't spend much time together off the court. Once practice ended, they'd return to their own neighborhoods and hang out with other friends or maybe chase girls.

The teammates developed chemistry through years of playing together. They knew each other's strengths and weaknesses, what spot on the court Mike Howard liked to shoot from or when to toss the ball to Fultz on a fast break. Moses and his teammates sought out competition anywhere they could find it. During the offseason, some of them played pickup ball with the soldiers at the Fort Lee Armory. The coaches also scheduled scrimmages against college teams from Virginia State University and Randolph-Macon College.[14]

Moses continued to work late into the night at Virginia Avenue School and still enjoyed mixing it up with his buddies at the Heights, but he'd outgrown those games. The same guys who determined a few years earlier that he wasn't good enough to play with them now insisted that he could only play if he confined himself to the perimeter, far from the basket.[15]

Not long after the schools integrated, Moses and other Black kids began playing ball at Lee Memorial Park in the white neighborhood of Walnut Hill. Named after Robert E. Lee, the commander of the Confederate army, it was the only park in Petersburg with lights. Moses and his teammates competed there with kids from other cities in pickup games and summer leagues. The top ballplayers from Hopewell joined them, and guys came down from Richmond to play.[16]

It was there that Moses struck up a friendship with Hopewell forward Ed Gholson. Hopewell was Petersburg's main rival, but Moses and Gholson bonded over their love of the game. Moses saw in Gholson a kind and loyal friend. He welcomed him into his inner circle. Gholson would help take care of Mary when Moses left Petersburg for the pros, running errands for her and mowing her lawn. He and Moses would remain close friends for the rest of Moses's life.[17]

Crimson Wave head coach Carl Peal was a strong Black man with light blue eyes. "If you've ever seen pictures of Coach Peal, he had muscles coming from everywhere," said Ed Robinson, who was teammates with Moses on the 1973–74 team. "I wasn't scared of Mo [Moses]. I was scared of Coach Peal. Cause I looked at him, I thought man he could break me in half."[18]

Peal attended Morris Brown College in Atlanta on an athletic scholarship, where he competed in several sports. After the army, he landed a coaching job at Peabody High School. During a fifteen-year period, he coached football, baseball, basketball, and golf at Peabody and became the head basketball coach at Petersburg when the schools integrated in 1970.[19]

Peal was a taskmaster who expected complete obedience from his players. He didn't tolerate mental mistakes or lack of effort and made sure his players took care of their schoolwork. "Coach Peal was a guy that, you know, he didn't look at us just as a star, he just looked at each of us as players and his sons on the team," remembered Gonzell Phillips.[20] It was difficult for Moses to find or afford clothes his size. Peal arranged for clothes to be donated to his star center and provided Moses and Mary with a little extra money for food.[21]

Coach Peal and his assistant, Pro Hayes, made a strong team. Peal designed practices, determined what type of offensive and defensive systems the team would run, and disciplined and motivated the players. Hayes handled play calling. Peal also added a young coach named Jimmy Williams, who had played for him at Peabody.

Peal demanded that his team play disciplined basketball. No showboating or wild shots were tolerated. The coach was determined for his players to be in excellent physical condition. The Crimson Wave ran and ran and ran. Sometimes players would leave the gym and run the streets of the city. Wyatt Curtis, a member of the 1973–74 team, said he ran more under Coach Peal than he did on his basketball team in the military.[22]

Peal preached that defense was the foundation of a great team. "Anybody could score," he'd say. The key was stopping the opponent from scoring.[23] The Crimson Wave played a 1-3-1 matchup zone most of the time, with Moses on the back line, protecting the basket. With their length and quickness, the players generated a lot of turnovers, allowing them to get out on the fast break.[24]

It was useless for other teams to press Petersburg. Stanley Taylor zoomed through any trap to create easy baskets. In the halfcourt, the Wave ran a motion offense: Pass. Screen. Cut. Look back door. Once comfortably ahead, Peal instituted the four-corners offense, a stall technique popularized by Dean Smith at the University of North Carolina.[25]

The Wave looked to work the ball inside to Moses, but players didn't force-feed him, as was common practice with a big man of his ability. Bill

Littlepage, the longtime coach at Hopewell High School, wondered why Petersburg didn't make Moses more of a focal point of the offense.[26] The truth is, they didn't need to. The best way to get Moses the ball around the basket was off a missed shot. Nobody could keep him off the backboard.

Moses pummeled defenders in the paint and on the glass, as the Crimson Wave steamrolled its opponents during the 1972–73 season. He posted 34 points, 29 rebounds, and 8 blocks in a win over the Manchester Lancers on December 8, 1972. A few nights later, he compiled 26 points and 24 rebounds against John Marshall High School. Teams began to double and triple team him, but it didn't make a difference.

January was more of the same. Moses dropped 35 points and snagged 30 rebounds against Meadowbrook High School. Later in the month, he scored 35 points, snatched 37 rebounds, and blocked 11 shots against Midlothian High School. In a February victory over Midlothian, he scored 30 points and gobbled up 37 rebounds. Midlothian had 21 rebounds as a team. His gaudy statistics were even more impressive considering high school games were only thirty-two minutes long, teams stalled—before the advent of a shot clock—to keep the ball out of Petersburg's hands, and Malone often sat for much, if not all, of the fourth quarters because games had already been decided.

Moses's stellar play began to draw the attention of college coaches. Lefty Driesell, of the University of Maryland, and Norm Sloan, from North Carolina State University, were some of the first to arrive in Petersburg to check out the 6-foot-10 sensation. It was exciting for Moses's teammates, who were unaccustomed to seeing coaches from big-time programs. "We saw Bobby Boyd of Southern California," said Ronald Robinson. "To us that was the moon, all the way on the other side of the country, for a person like me. I'd never been past Washington DC, and this guy's coming from California. That's like to the moon to me."[27]

The coaches were impressed. "He is the best high school player I've seen," said Virginia Commonwealth University (VCU) coach Chuck Noe at the end of Moses's junior season. "He could do more for VCU than Artis Gilmore did for Jacksonville. He could put us in the top ten, and I could put him in pro basketball."[28]

Moses appeared unfazed by the attention. He never bragged about the accolades or mentioned the famous coaches who had come to see him. He didn't demand the ball, instead choosing to contribute in less glamorous ways by controlling the paint on defense and attacking the offensive glass. When the team struggled, which was rare, he placed the blame on himself, rather than on coaches or teammates.[29]

One incident exemplified to Assistant Coach Jimmy Williams what type of teammate Moses was. The boy had an apple after practice, which he could have easily eaten by himself. Instead, he sat down at the bottom of the stoop outside the gym with a knife and cut a piece for everybody on the team.[30]

Malone didn't need to say much; he led through his actions. He never talked back to the coaches and took their instructions to heart. He didn't cut corners during drills at practice. Every time players ran line drills, he finished in the top three, outpacing some of the guards. Malone's commitment to the team, his craft, and winning earned the respect and loyalty of teammates. Even the coaches looked up to him.[31]

More than fifty years later, one sequence stands out to teammate Ronald Robinson. Moses was chasing the other team's ball handler from behind on a fast break, ran him down, and dove to knock the ball away. Robinson said, "This guy is the number one player in the country. He could have messed his elbow up. He could have messed his knee up. And I said to myself, *If he can do that, why can't I do that?*"[32]

The Crimson Wave finished the 1972–73 regular season undefeated, with sights set on a state championship. Petersburg destroyed the defending state champions Hopewell, 95–43, to capture the school's first Central District Tournament championship. Moses had 38 points, one shy of his season high, and 37 rebounds. The following week, Petersburg defeated John Marshall High School in the Central Regional Final, behind 30 points and 15 rebounds from Moses, to advance to the four-team state tournament at the University of Virginia in Charlottesville, about an hour and a half northwest of Petersburg.[33]

The integration of Petersburg High School had gone as well as administrators could have hoped. Racist white students who couldn't accept mixed-race schools transferred. Petersburg students don't remember any racial tension at school. They were exposed to Black and white teachers and administrators and became friendly with classmates of different races, though there were still unwritten rules. Black students wouldn't go to the home of a white classmate, and vice versa.

Sports can break down racial barriers by transforming the us-and-them mentality from a racial context to a geographic one. Petersburg was a sports town, and like any fan base, the residents got behind a winner. "Crimson Wave Country" bumper stickers began to appear on cars throughout town, and proprietors went out of their way to help Moses and some of his cash-strapped teammates with clothing and other needs. Moses and the Crimson Wave generated so much interest that Athletic Director Bob Kilbourne moved the team's games to Virginia State's Daniel Gymnasium to accommodate the crowds. Many Petersburg residents, Black and white, made the trip to Charlottesville for the state tournament. However, it didn't escape Malone that none of the white people who cheered for him offered him a ride home after the games.[34]

Petersburg High School hosted a massive pep rally prior to the basketball team's departure for Charlottesville. The students came outside and cheered as the team bus pulled away. Principal Jimmy Sublett informed the players that they'd be treated to a steak dinner whether they won the tournament or not.[35] The coaches kept the team secluded in their Charlottesville hotel to avoid the distractions of a bigger city and family and friends who made the trip.

Petersburg faced West Springfield High School in the semifinals. The Spartans' big men, Ed Tiernan and Bob Ferris, were 6 feet 4 and 6 feet 5, respectively, and had never competed against a 6-foot-10 center. At practice, Dave Koesters, who was sidelined by injury, contested every West Springfield player's shot with a broom to simulate what it would be like to face Moses.[36]

West Springfield played keep-away with Petersburg, moving the ball around the perimeter to shorten the game and draw Moses away from the basket. They were unsuccessful. Petersburg won, 52–41, to move on to the championship game, where it faced Halifax High School. The Comets tried to confuse the Wave by switching between a zone and man-to-man defense. Calvin Crews, a 6-foot-11 center who would later be drafted by the Atlanta Hawks, was the primary defender on Malone, though the Comets had two or three bodies draped over him at all times. He had just 3 points at the half and finished the game with 12. His teammates picked up the slack. Three other starters scored in double figures, and Petersburg won, 59–51.[37]

The Petersburg Crimson Wave capped off a 25-0 undefeated season with the school's first state championship. Their star center averaged 29.6 points and 20 rebounds. Moses had fulfilled the prophecy that he tucked into the family Bible a few years earlier. He was the best high school player in the country. It was time to place another note in the holy book. This time, Moses stated that he was going to be the first player to jump directly from high school to professional basketball.[38]

4

Five Stars

Howard Garfinkel was a bit eccentric. He dined on onion sandwiches covered in salt, chain-smoked Chesterfield cigarettes, and never drove a car. Garf, as he was known to friends, resembled a lawyer from the neck up, with thick-framed glasses and slicked-back hair, and had a theatrical style, which friends described as Runyonesque.[1] "If Garf's parents had taught him singing and dancing or sent him to acting school, he could have spent his lifetime in the road company of *Guys and Dolls*," said his business partner Will Klein.[2]

Garfinkel, born in New York City in 1929, grew up in an apartment on Park Avenue surrounded by his mother's friends in the entertainment business. Al Jolson sang "Sonny Boy" to him on his fifth birthday. Milton Berle, Sophie Tucker, Henry "Henny" Youngman, and Ted Lewis performed at his Bar Mitzvah. His favorite entertainer was actress-singer Judy Garland.[3]

Garfinkel's father owned a lucrative woolen business and wanted his son to follow in his footsteps, but Howard shunned the textile industry to pursue his passion for basketball. He began coaching "outdoor teams," a precursor to AAU basketball, and made a name for himself as a shrewd talent evaluator who knew every prospect in the five boroughs. In the 1950s New York City was producing more basketball talent than the local colleges could handle, and scouts began funneling players to Atlantic Coast Conference (ACC) schools. Vic Bubas, then an assistant coach at North Carolina State, hired Garf as an unofficial scout.[4]

Garf debuted his personal scouting report, *High School Basketball Illustrated*, or *HSBI*, in 1965. It was the first scouting service of its kind, a comprehensive breakdown of all high school basketball prospects in the New York area. He soon expanded it to cover the territory from West Virginia to Maine. The typewritten reports, which included Garf's unique catchphrases and colorful language, provided a rating for every prospect, from one to five stars. Five stars were reserved for players who were projected to be starters at a top-tier college program. The term *five-star prospect* would become standard in the recruiting industry.[5] Hubie Brown, a Hall of Fame coach who paced the sidelines at every level from high school to the NBA, said, "Howard Garfinkel is still the best evaluator of high school talent that I've ever seen or been around."[6]

Coaches could subscribe to Garf's service for $50. Bob Knight, an upstart coach at Army, didn't have a recruiting budget that would allow him to travel to see kids play. He relied on Garf's reports to know which prospects to pursue. Another one of Garf's early subscribers was John Wooden. The legendary UCLA coach was inspired by a report in *HSBI* to recruit a kid from Power Memorial Academy in Manhattan named Lew Alcindor (later, Kareem Abdul-Jabbar).[7]

In 1966 Garf founded Five-Star Basketball Camp with Long Island University coach Roy Rubin and high school coach Will Klein. Rubin dropped out after a couple of years. Klein took care of the logistics and finances, which allowed Garf to focus on basketball. The mission of the camp was to teach the game and prepare high school kids for the upcoming season at a time when virtually no organized basketball was played between March and November. Great athletes changed sports with the seasons, and with the exceptions of the Rucker Tournament in New York and Baker League in Philadelphia, summer basketball was limited to pickup games.[8]

Five-Star became the template for basketball camps, a destination where prospects tested themselves against elite competition and players and coaches gained exposure to further their careers. The first camp was held at Camp Orin-Sekwa in Niverville, New York. One of the initial instructors was Hubie Brown, then the coach of Fair Lawn High School in New Jersey. The keynote speaker that summer was another future Hall of Famer, Chuck Daly, who was then an assistant coach at Duke University. The following summer, Five-Star moved to its long-term home at Camp Rosemont in Honesdale, Pennsylvania. The head counselor that year was fiery young coach Bob Knight. He instituted teaching stations, which became a staple of the camp, where coaches demonstrated the techniques behind various basketball skills. The players were drafted onto teams for the week and played games in the afternoons.[9]

Garf infused the camp with the theatrical influences of his youth. He woke the athletes up every morning by imitating the sound of a bugle, then blasted Frank Sinatra over the loudspeaker.[10] Five-Star included a featured speaker every afternoon, typically one of the marquee names in college coaching, and Garf introduced each one with a flourish of words befitting a king or queen. "For a college or pro coach to get the opportunity to speak at one of his [Garf] camps was like getting an opportunity to perform at Carnegie Hall," Duke coach Mike Krzyzewski told the *New York Times* in 2013. "If you got that opportunity, you knew you had arrived."[11]

Word spread that Five-Star was the place for players and coaches to be seen. The camp initially attracted players from the New York–New Jersey area, though kids soon began arriving from New England, as far west as Chicago, and down South past the Washington DC area.[12] Grant Hill, who attended high school in Virginia before starring at Duke and in the NBA, was first introduced to Five-Star by a 1984 article in *Sports Illustrated*. "It was like this mythical place where you could go—if you were fortunate enough to go—and then maybe have a chance to play in college," Hill said. "I remember being blown away by the idea of it."[13]

College coaches attended Five-Star in the hope of finding players to take their program to the next level, though they were just as likely to secure a talented young assistant. The coaches earned their basketball PhDs over drinks at the Fireside Inn in town, where many of the brightest minds in the game used salt and pepper shakers to diagram plays late into the night.[14] Some of the many coaches who launched their careers at Five-Star included John Calipari, Rick Pitino, Hubie Brown, Dick Vitale, Mike Fratello, and Brendan Malone.

Fratello, known at the camp as "The Alligator," worked at Five-Star for the first time in 1968. When campers arrived late for breakfast or spoke while a coach was giving instructions, they were sentenced to the "alligator pit," where Fratello pushed them through intense conditioning drills. The young coach was hired as Lou Campanelli's assistant at Madison College (now James Madison University) in 1972. Campanelli instructed Fratello to send an introductory letter to all the high school coaches in the Virginia-DC area. Fratello included a postcard and asked the coaches to jumpstart Madison's recruiting process by listing the top five underclassmen they had seen. He received numerous replies about a phenomenal big man from Petersburg named Moses Malone.

Fratello called Moses's coach and informed him about Five-Star, then told Garf about Malone. Garf made some calls and got back to Fratello, instructing him to offer Moses a scholarship.[15] Each summer the top players in the camp were granted partial scholarships for half the cost of tuition. In return, they worked in the cafeteria. Moses was one of the campers responsible for cleaning up the tables after everyone had eaten. "It was an honor to be on scholarship," Grant Hill said years later. "You were exalted and put on a pedestal if you were invited to be a servant."[16]

Malone was initially reluctant to attend Five-Star, believing the camp had nothing to offer him, but Pro Hayes convinced him that it would be a good opportunity to measure himself against some of the best players in the country.[17] Moses had no way of traveling to Pennsylvania, so Hayes dropped him off at Madison College, and Fratello took him from there. Malone barely said a word the entire car ride.[18]

Tom McCorry had the first pick in the Five-Star draft in August of 1973. An assistant coach at Fairfield University in Connecticut, he'd never heard of Malone. He wasn't alone. Recruiting was largely regional at that time, and in the days before ESPN, social media, and the deification of prepubescent athletes, many of the high school and college coaches at the esteemed camp were unaware of the 6-foot-10 prospect from Petersburg. McCorry recalled that Garf and his right-hand man, Tom Konchalski, "almost broke my arm to make sure that I picked him [Malone]. And I did."[19]

Coaches and players in attendance remember Moses being extremely quiet. "He didn't really look people in the eye at that point," said McCorry. "He wasn't disrespectful in any way, shape, or form. You just knew that he was listening, but making eye contact was not something that he was used to having to do."[20]

Five-Star had expanded to two sessions, one in June, and another in late August. Moses attended the second one. Marc Iavaroni, who would later be a teammate with Moses on the Philadelphia 76ers, attended both sessions, as did Al Dutch, a 6-foot-7 forward from Archbishop Carroll High School in Washington DC. Dutch was selected MVP of the first session and would be named a *Parade* magazine All-American. "He was kicking everybody's ass," recalled Iavaroni, and in the second session "Moses destroyed Al Dutch."[21]

"I had never seen a player at 6 foot 10 who could run from basket to basket as quick as he could," Hubie Brown remembered. "His athleticism was off the charts."[22] George Raveling, the coach at Washington State University, marveled at how quickly Malone elevated for rebounds and blocked shots. Will Klein overheard a conversation between Raveling and his former boss Lefty Driesell of the University of Maryland. "They had just seen Moses Malone play in a game, and they don't see me," relayed Klein. "And they're walking down a hill and Raveling is saying, 'I can't believe what I just saw. Every time a shot goes up, all I hear is *whoosh, whoosh.*' That's Moses blocking the shot out to half court," said Klein.[23]

One play stands out to McCorry. Malone's team was facing a squad that featured a highly touted center named Tommy Scates, who played for John Thompson at St. Anthony High School and then followed him to Georgetown University. Scates was 6 feet 11 and 250 pounds. "Big, big, big monster of a guy," recalled McCorry. "So, one time Moses went up for a dunk, and Scates tried to block the shot. And Moses dunked the ball and Scates's hand and everything through the rim," said McCorry. "I mean it was just— You know, I mean nobody got hurt. But it was just unbelievable the strength he had."[24]

Dick Vitale, a keynote speaker at the session, rolled up to the camp in a red Cadillac convertible with "Dick Vitale" and "University of Detroit" scripted on the side of the car. What jumped out at him was Moses's work ethic. "Anyway, it was raining cats and dogs in Honesdale one day, and everybody was trying to get something to eat, and here's this kid—all alone—throwing the ball against the backboard," Vitale recalled. "He's grabbing rebounds. He flips the ball and grabs it again. And he's doing a tap drill twenty times with the right hand, twenty times with the left hand. Nobody is there supervising him. He's all by himself. . . . He went after every rebound like it was his last meal."[25]

Garf was equally impressed by Malone's attitude. "The thing I really liked about him [Malone] was the individual instruction part of the camp. The individual instruction is at the end of the day and it's optional," Garf said in a 1983 interview. He continued:

A kid goes to Station B and he works the fundamentals. Of the 108 kids, only 30 or 40 go to the individual instruction, but Malone was there more than he wasn't. I won't say he was there all the time because he wasn't. But he was there half the time, which was remarkable. It was remarkable because what the hell was anyone going to teach him? But Moses has a sixth sense of the right thing to do. It's a leadership thing. He was a leader, and he was leading. Patrick Ewing went to that individual instruction segment once in two years, and Ewing didn't have a move then. He's only got one or two now. He should have gone. Moses did, and he didn't have to; he went out of respect for the coach who was teaching.[26]

Malone's team went undefeated (11-0), demolishing all competition along the way. When Garf handed out awards at the end of the week, he referred to them as "the only undefeated, untied, unscored-upon team in the history of the camp." Hubie Brown reflected on Moses's memorable showing twenty-two years later as a speaker at Five-Star in the summer of 1995: "And all you guys who are *Parade* magazine All-Americans. He didn't give a shit who they were 'cause nobody knew him. He came in here and kicked *everybody's* ass—and did it without even talking."[27]

The Five-Star experience had a profound impact on Moses. He thought his team didn't have much talent when he arrived, and it meant a great deal to him to excel against top prospects from New York and New Jersey. "When I left camp, Garf rated me one of the best," Moses recalled. "He didn't give me five stars or a five-plus, he gave me more than a five-plus and he was one of the top guys in the world at doing that. I did not know I was that good."[28]

In subsequent years, many of the greatest players in basketball history showcased their skills at Five-Star, including Michael Jordan, Patrick Ewing, Isiah Thomas, Dominique Wilkins, Chris Mullin, Grant Hill, LeBron James, Chris Paul, Carmelo Anthony, Kevin Durant, and Stephen Curry. Garf maintained that "Moses Malone was the only player who was ever too good for the camp."[29]

Five-Star exposed Moses to a larger audience, though his most remarkable feat that summer occurred weeks earlier at the All Pro Basketball Camp run by NBA All-Star Dave Bing and long-time college coach Howie Landa. Situated in the idyllic woodlands of Pocono Pines, Pennsylvania, the camp included four basketball courts, nine cabins, a cafeteria, a canteen, and a charming old barn.[30] Campy Russell, who attended several years as a camper and counselor and would go on to a distinguished NBA career, referred to his time there as a "life-changing experience," where he was exposed to people from different races and backgrounds while receiving excellent basketball instruction. Maurice Lucas, Ralph Simpson, Terry Furlow, and John Brisker are some of the other campers and counselors who went on to play pro ball.[31]

During the weekend, campers went into town to do laundry and catch a movie or grab a bite to eat. Moses joined some of them, including Furlow and Benny White, two guards who had just finished their freshman year at Michigan State, at the cafe. Furlow ordered apple pie à la mode for dessert. Moses silently pointed to the waitress, then to Furlow's pie and nodded his head. The waitress brought Moses a piece of pie, and he gobbled it up. She returned and asked if anybody wanted anything else. Moses replied in his guttural voice, "Give me another piece of that pie." Everybody at the table cracked up. "It was the first time I heard him talk," recalled White. "He had been there all week."[32]

Back at the camp, Moses crushed campers and counselors in games of one-on-one, including Furlow, who would lead the Big Ten in scoring before being selected twelfth by the 76ers in the 1976 draft. But he was just the appetizer. Each summer, Bing challenged some of the best players in camp to a game of one on one. No high school kid could compete with one of the top guards in the NBA—until Moses. Shockingly, Malone beat Bing in a game of one-on-one to 20.

"Moses blocked all of David's shots and beat him in front of a crowd of people," said Dave Pritchett, a Maryland assistant coach and a camp regular. "Bing was mad, made the kid come back and physically beat him up, but word spread about what Moses was capable of." It took all of Bing's strength and guile to edge out Malone by 2 points in the rematch.[33] "I just couldn't believe how good that guy was at that age," Bing recalled.[34] Moses was seven inches taller than the Pistons guard, but Bing led the NBA in scoring a few years earlier and was in the prime of his Hall of

Fame career. He was named to the All-NBA Second Team the following season. Moses still had another year of high school.

The word was out. The biggest high school prospect in years was a 6-foot-10 kid from Petersburg, Virginia. Regional colleges recruited Malone during his sophomore and junior years. After his performances in the summer of 1973, coaches from around the country descended upon Petersburg in droves.

5

Lefty and the Milkman

Lefty Driesell shared the frustration of all coaches who recruited Moses. The young man didn't look them in the eye and delivered monosyllabic replies to their attempts at engagement. If a coach approached him to chat, Moses would say a few words and continue walking. He abruptly stood up and walked out in the middle of a meeting with North Carolina State assistant coach Eddie Biedenbach for no apparent reason. Mary Malone simply said, "Well, that's Moses."[1]

"He's so quiet," said Driesell, "and the first time I talked with him I tried to draw him out by asking him where he got so good. There wasn't anybody around Petersburg that could make him that good, I told him." Moses said, "I play in the state pen, man," referring to the Virginia State Penitentiary in Richmond, where he competed against the inmates. Driesell continued:

"'You mean they've got some good players in prison?'

'Yeah, lots of good ones, aggressive.'

'Anybody your size?'

'One guy about 6–8. They call him Milkman.'

'Milkman? Why do they call him Milkman?'

'Cause he murdered a milkman, man.'"[2]

Milkman was former Hopewell star Mike James, a.k.a. Spiderman, whom Moses competed against as a freshman. Lefty, always on the lookout for talent, reached out to Virginia governor Mills Godwin to inquire about the possibility of James being released. The coach said he'd provide the inmate with a scholarship to attend college, and of course, play basketball. Word came back that "the Milkman was never getting out."[3]

Lefty Driesell was born and raised in Norfolk, Virginia. His stellar play at Granby High School earned him a basketball scholarship to Duke University. After graduating from Duke, Lefty took an office job with the Ford Motor Company but soon jumped at the opportunity to return to basketball as the junior varsity coach at his former high school. To offset the reduction in income, Driesell sold *World Book* encyclopedias door-to-door.

He later attributed his zeal as a basketball recruiter to his experience as an encyclopedia salesman. "The guy who got me involved with that told me, 'If you knock on 50 doors, you might not sell anything. But the 51st door, the guy is gonna grab you and tell you he'd been waitin' for the chance to buy a World Book all his life.' I just kept knockin' on doors until I found people who wanted to buy what I was sellin,'" Driesell told *Basketball Digest*.[4]

Lefty was promoted to varsity coach and a few years later accepted the head coaching job at powerhouse Newport News High School, where his team won 57-consecutive games, still a Virginia state record. Then he received an opportunity to put his skills to the test at the collegiate level as head coach of Davidson College. A small liberal arts school in North Carolina, Davidson had a student population of about nine hundred when Lefty took over the program in 1960. The Wildcats hadn't had a winning record since the 1940s. The people at Davidson thought he was "smoking pot," as he put it, when he declared that he was going to "put Davidson in the top ten."[5]

The coach backed up his words. The Wildcats finished in the AP top ten four times in his nine seasons at the school. The man who could spin a tale as well as a basketball had established himself as one of the premier recruiters in the nation. Lefty had a $500 recruiting budget when he arrived at Davidson and saved money during recruiting trips by sleeping on a mattress in the back of an old, green Chevrolet station wagon owned by the athletic department.[6] His greatest asset was his ability to connect with recruits' parents.

Driesell's long-time assistant coach Joe Harrington shared a story about Driesell's first big recruit at Davidson, Fred Hetzel, a 6-foot-8-inch forward who went on to be the first pick in the 1965 NBA draft. "He [Driesell] was on a home visit with the family, and he's sitting across the way from Mr. and Mrs. Hetzel. And he's sitting on the couch or whatever. And there's a ficus tree over his right shoulder, and it starts to move a little bit. And coach looked up there and it was a snake. And coach took the snake and wrapped it around his arm and let it play on his shoulder and everything. And Mrs. Hetzel said, 'Well, the last coach in here said, "We stomp on those things where I'm from."' So as the story goes, later on, when he finally signed with Davidson, which was unbelievable that he did that, Mrs. Hetzel said, 'I knew that that man would take care of my son. Anybody that would love my pet snake, I knew would take care of my son.'"[7]

After leading Davidson to a 27-3 record and a trip to the regional final in the NCAA Tournament in 1969, Lefty was offered the University of Maryland coaching job by athletic director Jim Kehoe. Initially, Lefty wasn't interested. He had a great job at Davidson. But Kehoe persisted and appealed to Driesell's ego by stating, "We'll have Vince Lombardi in the fall (coach of the Washington Redskins), Ted Williams in the spring (manager of the Washington Senators) and you in the winter." Lefty took the job.[8]

Maryland was a mediocre program that had never won the ACC. Once again, Lefty turned heads at his introductory press conference when he declared that Maryland "has the potential to be the UCLA of the East Coast or I wouldn't be here."[9] UCLA was in the middle of a historic run of ten national championships under John Wooden.

Lefty brought excitement to the Maryland program. The pep band played "Hail to the Chief" as he walked onto the court at Cole Field House while flashing his trademark victory sign with the index and middle fingers in a *V* shape on both hands.[10] He developed innovative approaches to recruiting, such as placing advertisements in an athlete's local newspaper and posting billboards or passing out flyers in the student's hometown.[11] In his third season at College Park, Lefty created what came to be known as Midnight Madness. The NCAA dictated that teams could not practice until October 15, 1971, so Lefty put his players through a one mile run at 12:03 a.m. on October 15. Two years later, the event evolved into an open practice attended by thousands of fans and later became a tradition for programs around the country.[12]

Driesell inherited a Terrapin squad that had a losing record the previous three seasons. His third year in College Park, Maryland finished 27-5. He lured top recruits to the school, including Tom McMillen, considered by many to be the number one prospect in the high school class of 1970. Len Elmore was another highly touted member of Maryland's 1970 recruiting class, and two years later, Lefty secured a splendid point guard named John Lucas.

In 1973 Driesell aggressively pursued a local high school star named Adrian Dantley. "That man could charm the birds right out of the trees," Dantley's mother, Virginia, said of Lefty, though her son chose to attend Notre Dame. To soothe his sorrow, Lefty went on a fishing trip in Bethany Beach, Delaware. He and a couple of friends were on a boat when he looked up and saw townhouses on fire. He rushed to the scene to warn the residents. Driesell heard children screaming from inside a house but couldn't open the door. He finally kicked it down and scooped up several children, two at a time. He saved ten children that day and was given the NCAA's first Valor Award.[13]

The coach had yet to land a generational talent—like Lew Alcindor or Bill Walton at UCLA—who could lead the Terrapins to national championships. Moses Malone was that kind of player. Driesell had a formidable group of assistants working with him on the recruitment of Malone. Hall of Famer George Raveling was on the Maryland staff until 1972. Lefty was also joined on the bench by former Maryland hoops standouts Joe Harrington and Howard White.

The coach's biggest weapon in the ruthless college recruiting wars was Dave Pritchett, known as "Pitstop" in coaching circles for his obsessive pursuit of high school prospects. Billy Hahn, who played for Pritchett and Driesell at Maryland and later served as Pritchett's assistant coach at Davidson, called Pritchett "an absolute mad, mad, mad dog on the road, a guy that never went off the road, was constantly recruiting."[14] Pritchett once boasted that his personal record was "seven rent-a-cars in one day."[15]

Harrington was the first member of the Maryland staff to see Moses in action at a summer league after his freshman year. The coach was shocked at how quick Moses was around the basket and impressed by his strength and tenacity. He returned to College Park and told Driesell, "He's the best I've ever seen." Driesell responded, "Joe, you're young. You don't know what you're doing."[16]

Pritchett also recalled the first time he watched Moses play. "One of those eerie moments," he told the *Washington Post* in 1981. "I can remember the game, but I can't remember the other team scoring a point. It was on an outdoor court, this awesome 6-10 eraser against a bunch of 5-10s,

Moses going 94 feet to reject shots and then sticking it in at the other end. And it wasn't like he was just standing under the basket waiting for everybody. He'd move out, 15 feet or so, and when somebody would drive from the strong side, he'd move over and swipe the shot away. I'd never seen such intensity. I went back to the office and quietly shut the door," Pritchett continued. "Recruiting is sort of like having an affair; you don't want some things to leave the room. And I told coach: 'There's a God in heaven and he's been great to us. One hour and 15 minutes down the road [in Petersburg, Virginia] is the greatest player I've seen in 12 years.'"[17]

Lefty made the trip to Petersburg early in Moses's sophomore season. He recalled Malone scoring 45 or 50 points that night. "And they never passed him the ball," said Driesell. "He got all of them off of a rebound. It was unbelievable."[18] Harrington was waiting for Driesell upon his return to College Park. "Well, what do you think, coach?" Harrington asked.

"I'll tell you what I think," Lefty replied. "If Moses would guarantee me 10 percent of all the money he will make as a pro, I'll quit coaching right now and just work with him."[19]

From that point on, Lefty's staff pursued the phenom from Petersburg with a fervor reminiscent of The Police song "Every Breath You Take." Howard White had been a big-time prospect himself when he committed to Maryland in 1969. Known simply as "H" (the letter appeared on the back of his jersey at Maryland instead of his last name), White was drafted to the NBA in 1973, but a knee injury derailed his career. He was young and Black and took the lead in wooing Moses.

White immediately hit it off with Mary Malone. The first time he went to the Malone home, Moses wasn't there, and Mary invited him in. The two fell asleep on Mary's couch watching soap operas while waiting for Moses to come home. "I was from Virginia," White said. "That probably helped. I was from Hampton. I had been the product of a single mother, growing up in that and just understanding them. . . . Probably the biggest thing is understanding them as people, versus a commodity, versus somebody that might change a program, versus a basketball player."[20] Lefty, the parent-whisperer, made Mary feel comfortable as well.

Pro Hayes assisted the Malones with the recruiting process. He accompanied Moses to meetings with college coaches and helped him sift through the various offers. Hayes believed Moses would benefit from staying close to his support system. Hayes, like Mary, made no secret of his preference for Maryland. He referred to Lefty as "my main man" and went out of his way to make the Maryland coaches feel welcome in Petersburg.[21]

Hayes invited Harrington to his house for a catfish dinner one night. "I'll never forget it," recalled Harrington. "I'm sitting there, and he said, 'I gotta get some grease. I gotta make some corn fritters first.' And he had this can of grease on the back of the stove, and it was just reused grease. It took about an hour to fix up this catfish, and he made corn fritters. He said, 'I'm gonna look over here in the freezer.' And he looked in the freezer and there was something in there that looked like a cat. I said, 'What's that?' He said, 'That's a muskrat. I'd have to unthaw it to cook it, but here's a catfish. We'll cook this.' I ate that catfish and told Pro, 'Best I ever had.'"[22]

Lefty and his staff intensified their pursuit during Moses's senior year. Despite College Park being only about a two-and-a-half-hour drive from Petersburg, White, Pritchett, and Driesell racked up a $20,000 bill (the equivalent of about $140,000 in 2024) at the Holiday Inn in Petersburg.[23] Pritchett estimated that each of the Maryland coaches visited Moses's hometown at least fifteen times that year. They talked to Malone's friends, family, classmates, teachers, local merchants, and anyone else they could find.[24]

The coaches enlisted the assistance of John Lucas, who had a sensational sophomore season for the Terrapins. "Luc," as his teammates called him, had heard a great deal about Moses. He went to see him play at the Capital Classic in Landover, Maryland, during Moses's senior year and left determined to convince the big man to join him in College Park. Lucas and Malone would agree to meet at the Malone house at a specific time, then Moses wouldn't be there when Luc showed up. The point guard soon realized he could always find Moses on the basketball court. Sometimes he joined Malone and his friends in pickup games.[25] Two other Terrapins, Mo Howard and Owen Brown, made a trip to Malone's hometown as well.[26]

By that time, the Maryland contingent had plenty of company in Petersburg. Countless coaches made pilgrimages to southeast Virginia to witness the prophet who could lead their program to the promised land. Malone received scholarship offers from hundreds of schools. The Petersburg post office sent out a Christmas message in 1973 that said, "Greetings from Petersburg, home of Moses Malone."[27]

Coaches began calling and visiting the Malone home at all hours. Clint Bufford, who grew up two houses down from Moses, remembers the commotion it caused in the neighborhood. "Oh, that was Lefty Driesell, that was Oral Roberts, that was this person, that was that person."[28] Moses's close friend James Mitchell told sportswriter Ray Didinger, "At first it was like a game, all these big coaches coming around. Norm Sloan. Lefty Driesell. Dick Vitale. But then it got out of hand. Every day there were eight, maybe ten of them at the house."[29]

Years later, Malone reflected on that period to George White of the *Houston Chronicle*: "Every time I left my house I saw those guys. Some of them just moved into the hotels for the entire basketball season. They lived there three or four months." Members of the media also called and showed up at the Malone home at all hours.[30] Moses attempted to evade his pursuers, but at 6-foot-10 it wasn't easy for the most famous person in Petersburg to hide. "I would try to sneak home at three in the morning, and they would be waiting in my front yard," Moses told George White. "They would call my house all hours of the night and day. They finally got my girlfriend's number and started calling me when I went there. It was unbelievable."

Moses ran when he saw recruiters, and if he couldn't escape, he simply kept his mouth shut. He pretended to sleep during the car ride from Petersburg to the University of Maryland for his campus visit so he didn't have to talk to Lefty.[31] Sometimes he lay down on the floor of his house with the lights off so coaches wouldn't know he was home, and he developed a secret knock for friends to use on his door to signal whether a recruiter was around. He began hiding at the homes of his girlfriend, Cathy Stith, and friends Panther and Pair, though inevitably the coaches tracked him down at those places as well. Pair and Moses drove around for hours to avoid recruiters. When they finally returned to the neighborhood, they'd park the car at Pair's father's house a street over, then walk through Pair's backyard and in the back door of his house. Sometimes the two friends lay on Pair's floor for hours with no lights on, just talking.[32]

Malone was so coveted that coaches felt compelled to recruit him just for the optics. Guy Lewis of the University of Houston told another coach that he knew he had no chance of signing Malone. "But if I don't show up here for a few days and give it a try," Lewis said, "my alumni will kill me. I at least have to pretend that I'm trying."[33]

College coaches' job security rests on their ability to attract top ballplayers to their schools. A generational prospect who can lead a team to the final four or a national title can alter the trajectory of a program. Such achievements elevate a school's brand, which attracts more applicants, other top-tier prospects, and an influx of money, leading to raises, promotions, and job security for coaches and administrators. If coaches fail to bring in elite talent, they're fired. Such pressure causes many to bend or break NCAA rules to land coveted high school kids. Boosters associated with the program have their own motives for stepping outside the legal bounds of recruiting.

Coaches arrived in Petersburg with various enticements for Moses and those around him. "There were schools that offered him everything," Pro Hayes told the *Albuquerque Journal*. "Cash and anything else you can think of." Hayes said some schools offered him a coaching job if he delivered Malone.[34] Coach Peal singled out the University of Minnesota for guaranteeing him a job if Moses went to school there.[35] A VCU coach offered Pair money to steer Moses to the school, and according to Panther, Lefty and Dick Vitale suggested he could have a scholarship if he convinced Moses to attend their respective schools.[36]

Moses's estranged father even joined the recruiting circus. The University of Houston cajoled the elder Malone to attempt to convince his son to attend school in the Lone Star State. Moses arrived at Pair's house distraught one afternoon after his father visited him.[37] Mary told Lefty she was furious that her ex-husband had called her house. "I slammed down the phone so hard I might've broken it," she said.[38]

The most egregious enticement came from Oral Roberts, the nationally renowned Christian evangelist, who made the trip to Petersburg on behalf of his eponymous university. Mary was a frail woman who had recently been hospitalized for a bleeding ulcer. *Sports Illustrated* reported that Roberts promised to heal her ulcer if Moses attended Oral Roberts University.[39]

Rumors of impropriety led to speculation that whoever landed Moses would be penalized for NCAA infractions. ACC commissioner Bob James called the Malone case "the worst recruiting mess I've ever seen."[40] Most programs were not deterred. One Maryland backer rationalized that Malone's impact on the court would outweigh any potential punishment: "I'd take a year's probation to get a Moses Malone—or a David Thompson. Sure, getting Thompson could cost State a year's suspension; it also won them a national championship. It's worth it."[41]

6

The Decision

Moses and Hal Miles organized the dice games at Petersburg High School in their senior year. During breaks between classes or at lunchtime, students gathered on the landing outside the school to shoot dice. It was low stakes, for quarters. Malone and Miles took a cut if it was a low crap (2 or 3) or high crap (12). Some teachers and administrators perceived Moses to be stupid. The boy had poor grades and rarely spoke in class. When he did, it was with his head down. He was inarticulate and difficult to understand. Miles knew better. To control a dice game, you needed street cred and mathematical ability. "You had to be sharp," said Miles.[1]

Moses simply had no interest in school. Cindy Ruffa, a classmate who was assigned by her teacher, Ms. Moyer, to tutor Moses in math, was frustrated by his unwillingness to engage with the material.[2] He didn't stay in Ms. Moyer's class long. Petersburg High's athletic director, Bob Kilbourne, informed her he was moving Moses to a class that would be easier for him to pass. Lefty believed it was a matter of goals with Moses. "I firmly believe that if Mo had put it in his Bible to be a B student, then he would have become one," said the Maryland coach.[3]

Marie Maniego took a special interest in Moses. She was his senior year English teacher and worked with him on his speech during a free period. Ms. Maniego objected to the way teachers treated Malone. "He is definitely not dumb," she said. "He has good reasoning ability, but none of his teachers have given him a chance to perform. When he first got to high school, he was shy and wouldn't say anything. So, they treated him like some kind of animal, and as long as he sat in class and kept quiet they would pass him," she said. "Now the damage is done."[4]

Kilbourne walked a fine line with Malone. The NCAA required students to graduate with a C average to be eligible to play college ball. Moses's average was just below a C heading into his senior year.[5] Kilbourne was criticized for steering Moses away from academic challenges, though he believed that was preferable to standing by while Moses failed classes and lost the ability to play college basketball, a life-altering opportunity.

The basketball court remained Malone's refuge, and he and his teammates were focused on another state championship. Coach Peal's squad was not as talented or deep as the previous year. Starters Walker and Fultz graduated, as did key reserve Ronald Robinson. Midway through Moses's senior season, Michael Howard was ruled ineligible. The losses placed a greater burden on Malone. Teams deployed collapsible zones against Petersburg to deny him the ball. So, Moses grabbed it off the backboard.

He opened the season with 40 points and 23 rebounds in a win over John Marshall. In mid-December, he outscored the entire Manchester team, 44-42, and pulled down 23 boards.[6] The next month, he amassed 52 points while outscoring and outrebounding the entire Dinwiddie team.[7] A week after that, Moses posted 37 points and 20 rebounds against Prince George High School. On one possession, a Prince George player elevated for a jump shot, saw Moses's hand in front of him, and threw the ball to the floor in disgust.[8]

Once again, Petersburg cruised through the regular season undefeated. Malone scored 46 points and grabbed 42 rebounds as the Wave dismantled Manchester in the opening round of the Central District Tournament.[9] He followed that up with 34 points against Colonial Heights to win the tournament.[10] The Wave returned to Charlottesville for the state championship, where it disposed of Halifax in the semifinals, setting up a showdown with the West Springfield High School Spartans. Petersburg and West Springfield were both 24-0.

The game was tight throughout, with fifteen lead changes, and Petersburg trailed at the end of three quarters for the first time all season.[11] Moses took control in the fourth. He tapped in a missed shot with 5:56 remaining to give his team a three-point advantage, then sprinted down court to take a pass from Tony Threatt for a basket twenty seconds later that increased the lead to five. He scored again to provide Petersburg its biggest lead, 50–44, with 1:45 remaining.[12] West Springfield cut it to 50–48 with seconds left. They inbounded the ball to Dave Koesters, who was immediately trapped by a few Petersburg players, including Malone. Moses stole the ball and held it victoriously above his head as the final buzzer sounded.[13]

The Crimson Wave concluded a magical two-year run with a 50-0 record and back-to-back state championships. Moses's statistics vary a bit by source, though he averaged about 36 points, 25 rebounds, and between 10 and 12 blocked shots per game during his senior season. He was named a *Parade* magazine All American for the second year in a row.

Petersburg hosted Moses Malone Day. Team members were picked up in a limousine and taken to the event, where Moses was given a key to the city. Lefty and Vitale spoke, and the school retired Malone's No. 24 jersey.[14] The man of honor deflected attention from himself. The celebration took place the day before his birthday. Moses walked across the stage and told the woman prepared to lead the audience in a rendition of "Happy Birthday" not to. When she asked why, he replied, "Because I don't want to." He stood emotionless as the crowd gave him a standing ovation and took the microphone only to declare that students had a ten-minute break before going back to class.

"That's what just blows my mind about Mo," said Stanley Taylor. "All this stuff is happening, and he is the same guy he always has been—hasn't changed a bit." Moses claimed there was a conscious effort behind his cool demeanor. "When I was young, I used to listen to my mother and to what she told me," he told a reporter, "and she told me not to let things go to my head."[15]

Next up for Moses were All-Star Games: the Seamco Classic in upstate New York, the Dapper Dan Roundball Classic in Pittsburgh, and the inaugural Capital Classic (later renamed the McDonald's All-American Game), to name a few. The Dapper Dan was founded by future sneaker executive Sonny Vaccaro in 1965 and had become the premiere high school All-Star Game in the country. Garf was brought in for player introductions and introduced his former camper by quoting the gospel according to Moses: "Thou shall not pass. Thou shall not shoot. Thou shall not enter the lane. Honor thy left hand as well as thy right. Thou shall have no other supers before me."[16] The game featured U.S. All-Stars against Pennsylvania All-Stars. Moses dunked the ball with two seconds remaining to give the

U.S. team the win, 77–76. He scored 31 points and grabbed 20 rebounds. Years later, Vaccaro called Moses the most valuable player in the history of the game.[17]

A few days later, a reporter at the Capital Classic suggested to Moses that his high school must be doing a lot for him. Moses replied,

> To tell you the truth, Petersburg isn't really doing anything for me or the other guys on the team. We did get new uniforms last year, but we didn't get warm-up suits, which the football team got. We've won fifty-straight games and two state championships, yet the baseball team is treated better, and I don't know when they last won a game. People don't think I know about these things, but the basketball team brought in about $40,000 this past year. We had nothing but sellouts, and the year before was $30,000. But we have a Black coach and Black players, and even at the banquet all I got was a certificate, no most valuable player award or anything.[18]

Malone's high school experience was a valuable lesson about the business of basketball. Going forward, he'd fight for what he was worth and maintain caution toward the people around him, particularly those in a position to exploit him. That included the college coaches drooling over him at All-Star Games. He understood that the money he could generate for their institutions was worth way more than the scholarship he'd receive in return.

Malone hadn't selected a college by the spring of his senior year. Maryland remained the frontrunner, though it faced stiff competition. VCU was one of the first schools to pursue Moses. Its biggest advantage was a campus in nearby Richmond. VCU coach Chuck Noe was a brilliant tactician who invented the four-corners offense. He had two assistant coaches, Charlie Moses and Mike Pollio. Charlie was assigned to Malone and developed a deep friendship with Moses and Mary. Moses's girlfriend, Cathy Stith, graduated from Petersburg High School a year before him and was attending VCU. He visited her in Richmond and hung out at Charlie Moses's Paragon Pharmacy.

VCU tried to entice Malone by signing his distant cousin Morris Fultz a year earlier. Fultz was a solid high school player, though VCU recruited him zealously because of his relation to Malone. "Let's face it, it was a legal thing to do, but . . . ," Pollio said as his voice trailed off.

Noe grew concerned about rumors of impropriety in the recruitment of Malone and feared an investigation. That spring, he wrote a letter to Moses withdrawing from consideration. "I delivered that letter," said Pollio. "I cried all the way from Richmond to Petersburg, which is thirty miles, twenty-five miles, not very far. . . . I cried all the way because I knew if we got him my career was made. I hated to be selfish about it, but if you recruit Moses to VCU . . . We knew how great he was."[19]

NC State was another program monitoring Malone. All-American forward David Thompson traveled to Petersburg to meet with him. The school was simultaneously pursuing Tom Barker, a big man out of Texas who had been named junior college player of the year. In May, Barker informed assistant coach Eddie Biedenbach that he'd sign with NC State if it agreed not to pursue Malone. It was late in the recruiting season. Moses hadn't made up his mind, and State desperately needed a big man to replace Tom Burleson. Sloan agreed to Barker's demand.[20]

Then there was Vitale, the exuberant coach of the University of Detroit. His assistant coaches Jim Boyce and Smokey Gaines made frequent visits to Petersburg, with Gaines taking the lead. "One night, we went over to Moses' house, and there was a pack of wild dogs around," Gaines said. "There must have been twenty-five of them, all jumping up, snapping at the car. Vitale was scared to death."

Moses's home and neighborhood made an impression on Gaines and other recruiters. "I've seen a lot of poverty traveling through Alabama and Mississippi, but Moses' situation was the worst," Gaines said. "It was a tough neighborhood," he added. "Guys hanging on the corner, drinking all night. You put a kid there with no father, no brothers, no sisters, he's going to be tested to the max. And Moses was, every day."[21]

Vitale said decades later that Malone was one of the four greatest high school players he'd ever seen, along with Magic Johnson, Kobe Byrant, and LeBron James.[22] However, when Moses hadn't committed by late May, the coach devoted his final scholarship to guard John Long.

Despite his desperate attempts to escape the attention, Moses relished the opportunities created by the recruiting bonanza. "A lot of that was pretty awful at the time, but for a guy who had a relatively quiet life, it was also exciting," he revealed a few years later. "I found I could handle the pressure and I actually relaxed and enjoyed much of it."[23] Moses visited twenty-four schools, which opened his eyes to a world beyond Petersburg. "I went everywhere," he told George White of the *Houston Chronicle*. "I went around the West Coast, Hawaii, even Mexico City to some college down there. I really like Hawaii. I think if it had been closer to home I would have gone there."[24]

He met university presidents and politicians. Many schools set him up on dates during campus visits. When he returned home, the girls called long distance (a costly endeavor in 1974). "They'd pretend to be in love with me," Moses said. "What kind of stuff is that?"[25] The University of Minnesota arranged for the school's dance line to perform for him in their bathing suits by the pool at the hotel where he was staying while Moses watched from a chaise lounge.[26] Some of the recruiters who broadened Malone's horizons became lifelong friends, including Lefty, Gaines, Howard White, and Charlie Moses.

By June, Malone appeared to narrow his choices to Maryland, the University of New Mexico, and Clemson University. Norm Ellenberger, known as "Stormin' Norman" in Albuquerque, had just finished his second season as coach of the New Mexico Lobos and was searching for a superstar to catapult his program. His assistant coach John Whisenant moved into the Howard Johnson hotel in Petersburg after the Lobos' season ended in March and lived there for the next three months at $11 per day.[27]

Whisenant's laid back approach was a welcome alternative for Malone. "Moses would come by and talk—about girls, basketball, cars—anything just to get away from everyone," said Whisenant. Malone and Whisenant watched Henry Aaron hit his record-breaking 715th home run together in the coach's hotel room on April 8, 1974.[28] Sometimes Moses brought his friend Nathan "Panther" Dickerson with him. "They would sit there and sing," Whisenant told Mark Whicker of the *Los Angeles Daily News*. "Nathan was a great singer, and Moses would do backup. They sang Motown songs. Sometimes I hear songs on the radio and I think of those two." They took Whisenant to a club called the Mouse Trap. The coach was the only white person in the joint and marveled at how far he'd come from his hometown of Gore, Oklahoma.[29]

Moses told Whisenant that he wanted to be a Lobo, but they faced a major obstacle: Mary Malone. Moses's mother had an affinity for Driesell and was adamant about her only child staying close to home. She told Whisenant that she wouldn't sign a letter of intent for Moses to attend New Mexico.[30]

Meanwhile, Clemson made a late charge for her son. Skip Wise of Dunbar High School in Baltimore was considered the top guard prospect in the country. He and Moses bonded at the Seamco Classic in May, and Wise, who had committed to Clemson, sold Moses on the idea of joining forces.[31] Clemson was coached by Tates Locke, a disciplinarian whose first head coaching job was at West Point, where he developed a close relationship with his assistant coach, Bob Knight. Clemson hired Locke in 1970 to ignite their dormant program and compete with the major ACC schools in the region. The coach soon discovered the magnitude of the task and concluded it was impossible—unless he cheated.[32]

Locke later documented a series of NCAA violations committed by him and others at Clemson in his book *Caught in the Net*. It began with him working with an academic advisor to fudge high school players' transcripts to make them academically eligible and escalated to substantial payments to players and their families. Locke claimed he wasn't personally involved with the payments. A slush fund was set up by three or four Clemson alumni. "Their original intent was to supplement this secret account by the sale of Tiger Paw rags, a gimmick similar to the Pittsburgh Steelers' Terrible Towel," wrote Locke. "Because several of the boosters had connections with local textile plants, the rags could be produced quite economically, about 15 cents apiece," he continued. "Then the rags were sold for $2 each with a dollar going back into the slush fund to repay monies being loaned to athletes. In this way, the money was untraceable. It was cash."[33]

Benjamin C. "B. C." Inabinet, the owner of an industrial maintenance company in Columbia, South Carolina, was the most influential Clemson booster. He was an imposing figure at 6 feet 8 and 365 pounds and was a gifted salesman who met with every major prospect on Clemson's radar. Locke knew what Inabinet and the other alumni were up to. "Our players had a monthly spending allowance and received a number of gifts from various sources," Locke wrote. "Items like radios, stereos, and items of that nature. I don't know who got what. In some cases, the appliances were put in their parents' homes. Sometimes I'm not so sure it wasn't the mothers of the players who were doing the asking for these gifts."[34]

During the 1972–73 season, Locke actively sought the assistance of boosters for the first time, indicating he needed "a program" for Tree Rollins, a towering center out of Georgia. The program worked, and Rollins enrolled at Clemson. He later played eighteen seasons in the NBA. Years after leaving Clemson, he said, "If someone asked me to put a figure on what I got from B.C. and the rest of the alums over the course of my career at Clemson, which began in 1973–74 and was completed in 1976–77, I guess the sum totaled around $60,000 [the equivalent of about $332,000 in 2024]. I'd say that figure was very close cause I was getting about $14,000 a year. That's counting the money being paid for my Monte Carlo, the clothing allowances, gas money and pocket money."[35] Clemson wasn't the only school that offered Rollins money. It wasn't even the highest bidder. Such was the state of big-time college basketball.[36]

Clemson had a small Black enrollment in the early 1970s. It was challenging for Locke to present a welcoming environment for Black recruits who visited the campus, so he created a phony Black fraternity. He took over a Quonset hut on campus and arranged for Black high school kids from the surrounding communities to be there when a Black recruit was in town. He even brought in bands and staged dances for the "fraternity members."[37]

Skip Wise informed Locke that Malone was interested in attending Clemson, and the coach took it from there. Moses liked the idea of playing power forward, with Rollins at center, and Clemson would have had a stacked lineup with Malone, Rollins, Wise, and two other top recruits in Stan Rome and Colon Abraham.[38] Moses visited the school on the evening of June 6 and stayed there until midafternoon on June 9. He spent time alone with Inabinet. Locke and his assistant coach Charlie Harrison followed Malone home on the 9th and checked into the Holiday Inn in Petersburg. According to Locke, Moses told him that night that he was going to sign with Clemson. Then he asked the coach to hide him until after graduation. The pressure from coaches and the media had become overwhelming.

Locke provided Mary's brother Charlie Hudgins money to put Moses up in a "fleabag" hotel. "We hid Mo away for two or three days," wrote Locke. "Got him some beer and stuff to eat. I think he brought along a woman, but I never saw the girl. Charlie Harrison told me he saw one. That's how I know."[39] Then the most sought-after player in the country vanished. Nobody could find Malone for days. Coaches staked out his house and contacted friends and family. There would be rumors of a Moses sighting, and all the coaches would go running.

The Maryland coaches were unaware that Locke and Harrison didn't know Malone's whereabouts. One night, Harrison went out to buy sandwiches and beer. He noticed someone following him. It was Maryland coach Dave Pritchett. Harrison returned to the hotel and informed Locke. The two decided to go for a ride—a long ride. Locke and Harrison drove up and down every street in Petersburg for four hours, stopping only for beer and a bathroom break. Pitstop tailed them the entire way.[40]

The press speculated that Moses would announce his decision on the day of his graduation, June 14. That date came and went. The Maryland and Clemson coaches waited impatiently at the Holiday Inn while Whisenant was holed up across the street at Howard Johnson. On June 15 Mary told Lefty that Moses was ready to sign with Maryland, but when Lefty arrived at the Malone home, Moses said he wanted to visit a couple of more schools.[41]

Mary was spotted driving a new burgundy Chrysler Imperial, which rumor had it was a gift from Maryland. Lefty had arranged for the Malones to lease the car with their own money, with the understanding that Maryland would help Moses secure a construction job to pay for it. He cleared the arrangement with ACC commissioner Bob James. Moses was seen driving a different car that was believed to belong to the University of New Mexico.

On June 17 Moses told Lefty he was ready to sign and would call him the next day. He didn't call. Howard White reached him on the 19th, and Malone agreed to sign the following morning.[42] Lefty was scheduled to meet Moses at his home at 9:00 a.m. on the 20th. Pritchett insisted that they sleep in the car outside the Malone house to make sure no other coaches tried to talk to Moses. Lefty didn't think that was necessary, but

Pritchett refused to drive back to their hotel, and they spent the night in a car on St. Matthew Street.

"Finally, about 7:00 [a.m.] Pritchett woke me up," Lefty recalled. "There's somebody going in his house!" Pritchett yelled. The coaches rushed inside. Chuck Noe was there with a VCU alum. The coach apparently reconsidered his decision to abandon the chase. Mary told Lefty to go up to Moses's room. The coach found Moses lying in bed and presented him with a letter of intent to attend the University of Maryland. Moses signed the document, rolled over, and went back to sleep.[43] That concluded what Whisenant referred to as "the most unusual situation ever in college recruiting."[44]

Lefty was ecstatic. "We are very hopeful to be the UCLA of the East with Moses," he said. Fifty years later, he still had Moses's signed letter of intent framed on the wall of his apartment in Virginia Beach.[45] When asked why, Lefty said, "Because I worked damn hard to get that signature."[46]

Locke was disgusted by the whole process. "During those 11 days in Petersburg, I can't tell you how much I felt like a fool," he wrote. "I remember Harrison telling me, 'Tates, this thing stunk. I'm making up my mind I'm never going to do it again. If this is what it takes to win the national championship, I don't want it. This is not what basketball is all about. Or recruiting.' I couldn't agree more. If I had to do it over again, I would have left Petersburg the first day."[47]

Whisenant took a different tone. "I really hate to think there's any good in coming in second," he said. "But we probably got the most complete coverage and exposure presswise for the development of our program than at any other one specific time in Lobo basketball history." The Lobo staff spent $10,000 of the basketball program's $24,900 annual recruiting budget on Malone. Whisenant believed it was worth every penny.[48]

The NCAA immediately opened an investigation into Moses's recruitment. The day after he signed with Maryland, two investigators arrived in Petersburg. They met with Moses, Mary, Pair, Hayes, Peal, and Kilbourne.[49] Mary told the *Richmond Times-Dispatch* that somebody associated with Clemson gave her brother Charlie $1,000 to buy Moses a car. The deal fell through when Charlie couldn't secure financing. He refuted his sister's claim. Mary also stated that Whisenant lent Moses a car. She called the coach and told him to take it back and leave town.[50]

In December 1974 New Mexico coaches Ellenberger and Whisenant were censured by the Western Athletic Conference for recruiting violations, including lending an automobile to Moses.[51] Tates Locke resigned before he could be fired in 1975 amid an avalanche of accusations spanning his five years at Clemson. The NCAA found him responsible for offering to buy Mary a house and pay her utilities while Moses was enrolled at Clemson.[52] Maryland walked away unscathed. It won the recruiting war for Moses. Little did the university know, a greater battle lay ahead.

7
Stop Jivin' Me, Coach

Bucky Buckwalter and Jim Collier parked their car behind Moses's house and waited. They were trying to avoid being detected by Lefty and his assistants who were staking out their top prospect. Buckwalter eventually exited the car and began crawling through the grass on the side of the Malone home when he was attacked by a dog. It was late August 1974, and the forty-year-old had recently been named director of player personnel for the American Basketball Association's (ABA) Utah Stars. Collier was the team's new owner. The Stars drafted Moses in April, and Buckwalter, Collier, and General Manager Arnie Ferrin had come to Petersburg to sign him.

Buckwalter wanted to make an impression on the Malones, so he laid out $5,000 in $100 bills on the orange crate that served as their dining room table. He said it was spending money for Moses and his buddies, just a taste of the life he could expect if he signed with the Stars. That was an entire year's salary for Mary. Then Buckwalter told Moses he could do better than the Crysler Imperial parked in front of his house, and Buckwalter pulled out a picture of a Lincoln Mark IV. Moses looked out the window for a while, then asked Buckwalter if he could install a television in the Lincoln. Buckwalter said yes. He knew he had him.[1]

In the league's early years, a few young men played in the NBA without college experience. Tony Kappen, a guard out of Forest Hills High School in Queens, New York, was the first, signing with the Boston Celtics of the Basketball Association of America (BAA) in 1946. (The BAA merged with the National Basketball League to form the NBA in 1949.) He was twenty-seven years old and had played in other professional leagues for ten years. That same season, the Celtics signed another Queens kid, Connie Simmons, who hadn't played college ball. Simmons was twenty-one and may have played in other leagues before joining the BAA.[2] Joe Graboski signed with the Chicago Stags straight out of high school in 1948.[3]

The NBA instituted a rule in the 1950s prohibiting a player from joining the league until four years after his class graduated high school. There was an exception stating that a player could be drafted if he didn't enter college and had been out of high school for a full year. In 1962, the Detroit Pistons drafted a local kid from Eastern High School named Reggie Harding.[4] The 7-footer led Eastern to its third consecutive city championship in his senior season, 1961.[5] His grades weren't high enough to play college ball, so he enrolled in a college preparatory school in Nashville, Tennessee for the 1961–62 school year. Other NBA owners argued that the preparatory school rendered him ineligible to play in the NBA in 1962. The league agreed and told the Pistons they could keep his rights if they drafted him again the next year, which they did.[6] Harding played for the Holland Oilers of the Midwest Professional Basketball League before joining the Pistons in January 1964.[7]

Reggie was a thug and heroin addict who didn't last long in the league. He was arrested several times for offenses ranging from assault and battery to armed robbery.[8] After a stint in jail, he signed with the ABA's Indiana Pacers. During his tenure in Indiana, he put a gun to teammate Jim Rayl's head in their hotel room and threatened to shoot general manager Mike Storen on live television.[9] The NBA eliminated the exception to the four-year rule.

Then came Spencer Haywood. Born in 1949 in Silver City, Mississippi, to a family of sharecroppers, Haywood grew up in abject poverty. His mother feared that white people in their town would hurt or imprison her son to prevent him from succeeding and sent him to live with his brother Leroy in Chicago when he was fourteen. Leroy saw how talented Spencer was and secured a tryout with Will Robinson, the coach of Pershing High School in Detroit.[10] Haywood made the team, relocated to Detroit, and led Pershing to the state championship.

He spent one year at Trinidad State Junior College, then represented his country in the 1968 Olympics in Mexico City, where he was the leading scorer for an American squad that won the gold medal.[11] After the Olympics, he transferred to the University of Detroit, where he averaged 32 points and 22 rebounds for his sophomore season, though he quickly grew disillusioned with the school when the athletic director reneged on a promise to hire Robinson as the team's coach. Haywood was also frustrated that his mother and siblings were still picking cotton in Mississippi for $2 a day. He wanted to make money.[12]

The NBA held tight to its four-year rule, but another option was available to Haywood: the ABA. The league was formed in 1967 by owners hoping to force a merger with the NBA, just as the American Football League (AFL) did with the NFL. To succeed, they needed talent, and fast. The league was barely surviving without a television deal. Teams relocated or folded on a regular basis. The owners turned to the college ranks.

The Denver Rockets selected Haywood in the 1969 ABA draft, calling him a "hardship exception" because of his family's financial situation. Haywood averaged 30 points and 19.5 rebounds in his rookie season and was named ABA Rookie of the Year and MVP. Then he discovered he'd been deceived again. The five-year, $1.9 million contract he signed with the Rockets was misleading. A large portion of the money was in the form of deferred payments, which were far from guaranteed in the shaky ABA. Some of the money was put into mutual funds that wouldn't vest until Haywood turned fifty.[13]

He hired attorney Al Ross, who reached out to NBA teams. Sam Schulman, owner of the Seattle SuperSonics, agreed to honor the remainder of Haywood's contract with the Rockets in real dollars, no deferred payments.[14] The NBA blocked the signing as a violation of the four-year rule, and with Schulman's support, Haywood sued the league for violating the Sherman Anti-Trust Act. The case went to the Supreme Court, which ruled that the NBA couldn't prohibit Haywood from earning a living. The two sides settled on the introduction of a hardship rule. An underclassman could enter the NBA draft if he proved that it would be a financial hardship for him or his family if he was to stay in school. The league was liberal in its interpretation.[15]

Haywood's journey to the ABA and landmark case opened the floodgates for underclassmen to join the professional ranks. The NBA held a special hardship draft in 1971. Julius Erving, George Gervin, George McGinnis, and Phil Chenier were some of the players to leave school early for pro ball. A player jumping from high school to the pros was the next logical step.

The Stars didn't intend to make a splash at the 1974 ABA draft. They hadn't even discussed the possibility of selecting a high school kid. The team had been losing money, and owner Bill Daniels was trying to sell. Team president Vince Boryla believed it didn't matter whom they drafted because there was no money to sign him anyway.[16] The draft was held at Essex House in New York City on April 17.

Boryla spent nine seasons with the New York Knicks, first as a player, then a coach. He was friendly with the other ABA general managers, some of whom had played in the NBA. Al Bianchi, coach and GM of the Virginia Squires, had seen Moses play in high school. He told Boryla and the others, "You know the best damn ballplayer in this draft is a guy in high school." Boryla didn't know who he was talking about. The Stars' president figured if Malone was really that good, he'd eventually sign with the NBA, but it was worth taking a flyer on him in the third round. Maybe they could trade the high school kid for cash. With the twenty-second pick in the 1974 ABA draft, the Utah Stars selected Moses Malone.[17]

Moses had no idea he'd be drafted. He was on his campus visit at the University of Maryland at the time. Some friends told him the news, and he said they were crazy. Then he heard about it on the radio.[18] Coach Peal was shocked. "I think he should go to college," he said. "You can't jump right form high school to pro basketball." Peal believed his star center needed to fill out before competing against grown men.[19]

"We think he might be in the caliber of Julius Erving or George McGinnis, both of whom left college early and became outstanding pros in our league," Ferrin said.[20] The Stars' GM questioned whether Moses could get into or stay in college due to his academic struggles. He said the Stars wouldn't push Moses to sign with them but merely present him with an alternative.[21]

The Stars had no money, their players were unhappy, and the owner was trying to sell the team. They informed Moses that they'd get back to him after the ownership change, though given the state of the team and the possibility of the league merging with the NBA or folding, there was no reason to believe anything would come of it. Moses went to College Park for the summer, where he worked a construction job in the mornings. During his free time, he played ball on an Urban Coalition team, in a tournament at Melvin's Crabhouse, and in pickup games in Maryland and DC.[22]

Meanwhile, Bill Daniels sold the Stars to a group of Salt Lake City businessmen led by James "Jim" Collier.[23] The new owners faced contract disputes with two of the team's stars, Jimmy Jones and Zelmo Beaty, both of whom ultimately jumped to the NBA for the 1974–75 season. Beaty had been their starting center, and neither of the big men they drafted in the first two rounds joined the team. Desperate for size and a star to boost ticket sales, Collier turned to Malone.

Buckwalter, Collier, and Ferrin flew to Petersburg on August 22. They had until September 1 to sign Malone; otherwise, they'd lose his rights under ABA rules. Buckwalter sold Moses on the benefits of turning pro, most notably, four more years of earning power. Malone sat quietly and listened. He didn't ask questions or provide responses. The big man just mumbled, "Mmmm" in a neutral pitch. Bucky didn't know if Moses approved or disapproved of what he was saying.[24]

Buckwalter also focused on convincing Mary that it was in her son's best interest to skip college. He found Mrs. Malone to be feisty and very protective of her son. She wanted Moses to attend Maryland. When Buckwalter suggested buying her a new house and securing her a better job, Mary opened to the idea of Moses going pro.[25] Buckwalter had no moral issue with convincing Moses to skip college. He spent many years on the recruiting trail and was familiar with the promises, legal and illegal, that coaches and boosters made to high school kids, some of which weren't kept. He knew that many athletes didn't receive a quality education in college, and it was evident from the Malone home that the two needed the money.[26]

On Friday, August 24, Buckwalter picked up Moses and Mary, drove them to the Holiday Inn where he was staying, and offered Moses a contract. At that point, they agreed they should inform Lefty about their discussions. Buckwalter wanted to do right by the Maryland coach.[27] The next day, Buckwalter drove to Driesell's home in College Park with the contract. Lefty looked it over and called Donald Dell, a former professional tennis player who turned partner at the law firm of Dell, Craighill, Fentress, and Benton. The firm represented tennis players, and Dell had established a relationship with UNC coach Dean Smith, who recommended his players to the firm. Dell also did some work for Maryland star Tom McMillen.[28]

He and his partner Lee Fentress read the contract, then met with Moses, Mary, Lefty, and John Lucas. Dell noticed Moses looking at the ground and having a side conversation with his mother while the lawyer discussed the contract. Dell wanted to grab his attention. "Moses, have you ever heard of slavery?" he asked. Moses's eyes opened wide. The attorney explained that although the contract was for eighteen years, it was only guaranteed for two, then the Stars had the right to renew it on an annual basis at the same terms. Moses stood up and said he was going to attend Maryland.

Dell assured him the Stars would come back with another offer and encouraged Moses to call him with any questions. Dell and Fentress couldn't formally represent Malone because he'd lose college eligibility, so they offered to serve as unpaid advisors.[29] The next day, Buckwalter laid out the $5,000 in cash on the Malones' table and began negotiating. Moses called Dell for advice—eleven times. Dell told him not to sign anything.

Lucas called a meeting with his Maryland teammates. The players were given $15 a month for laundry and agreed to offer Moses their share to stay at Maryland. It was wishful thinking. That was a pittance compared to the millions Moses and the Stars were discussing. On the morning of August 28, Lucas woke Moses up for the first day of classes. Moses told him he was going pro.[30]

Moses and Mary drove to Washington to meet with Dell and Fentress again, at which time Moses informed the lawyers that he was going pro and wanted them to represent him. Dell felt obligated to include Lefty in the meeting. Moses and Lefty met alone in Dell's office. Lefty said they'd win the ACC and compete for a national championship if he stayed. He talked about the importance of a college education and argued that Moses would be able to command more money after college. Moses told him about the note he put in the Bible and that he was worried God would punish him if he broke his promise to turn pro after high school. Lefty suggested God wouldn't mind if he waited a year.[31] Sensing he was losing his star recruit, the coach implored Moses to consider attending Maryland for one season, at which point he'd have bargaining power by declaring for the NBA as a hardship case. Moses listened for a while, then forcefully stated, "Stop jivin' me, coach." The conversation was over.

Fentress considered how overwhelming it must have been for the nineteen-year-old. Big-time college and professional teams were vying for his services, and he didn't know whom to trust or have a father to help him through the process.[32] Buckwalter realized the young man was a lot sharper than he appeared. More than twenty years later, he and Moses were on the same NBA goodwill trip to China and went out for a drink. Bucky was shocked to hear Moses repeat to him verbatim the things he'd said when he was trying to convince him to sign with the Stars years earlier.[33]

Dell, Fentress, and the Stars agreed on a deal. Then Moses's lawyers realized he had to be twenty-one to sign a contract in Washington DC, so the group drove to the Ramada Inn in Rosslyn, Virginia, at 10:30 p.m., for the nineteen-year-old to sign.[34] There were varying reports as to the terms of the deal, with some speculating it was worth as much as $3 million. The actual number was more in the range of $200,000 to $250,000 per year for five years and included money for college, a house and monthly allowance for Mary, and other incentive-based compensation.[35]

On August 29 Fentress, Mary, Moses, and neighbor Leroy Cole flew with the Stars executives to New York for a press conference at the Americana Hotel. Moses arrived in sweatpants and basketball sneakers. The Stars provided him with a sport jacket and bowtie, then took him shoe shopping at Florsheim in Times Square.[36] It made for a funny anecdote, but Mary took offense to the notion that she couldn't afford shoes. "I always kept shoes on his feet and clothes on his back," she said proudly.[37]

Moses spoke at the press conference about his idol Spencer Haywood and the promise he made in his Bible. Then the media peppered him with questions. In a sign of things to come, he was evasive. Fentress deemed all questions pertaining to money as "personal." When asked his middle name, Moses replied, "They call me Sweet Moses." (His middle name was Eugene.) When a reporter inquired as to his date of birth, he said, "See my lawyer."[38]

Michael Goldberg, the general counsel for the ABA, was in attendance. It was the first time he'd seen Moses and thought he looked like a "very large pencil, tall and thin." The boy was quiet and shy. Goldberg thought to himself, *My goodness, we're taking a player like this? He looks like he belongs in school and that his mother should be bringing him in the morning.*[39]

Lefty was devastated. "The night I lost Moses, I went home and slept like a baby," he told the Rotary Club of Annapolis a few weeks later. "I woke up every hour and cried."[40] Most of his public comments weren't so good-humored. He lashed out at the ABA, calling it a "bush league, a beach ball league."[41] Coaches at other colleges expressed outrage over the Malone signing as well, fearing that they too would lose talented recruits to professional teams. Jim Kehoe, the Maryland athletic director, claimed the Stars "came by the back door secretly with subterfuge and deceit to prevail upon a high school graduate in this way." Tellingly, he moved on to the money, complaining that the university had sold out every game based on Malone's commitment.[42] Kehoe went so far as to pursue a congressional inquiry into professional sports teams signing high school athletes. He blasted what he called "the growing arrogance and insensitivity of pro sports owners, who are motivated by pure selfishness and greed and have no regard for the long-range interests of athletics or the individuals involved."[43]

There was blatant hypocrisy in Kehoe's comments. The college coaches pursuing Malone were so intrusive that Moses felt compelled to lie on the floor of his house with the lights off. At least in the pros young men were paid what they were worth, unshackled from the label *student-athlete*, a legal construct first developed by the NCAA to avoid paying workers compensation to the family of a player who was killed on the football field.[44] By designating athletes amateurs, the NCAA kept the millions of dollars flowing through college sports in the hands of universities and coaches. Athletes generated the revenue but weren't allowed to receive a salary or profit off their name, image, or likeness.

It was a sham. Football and basketball players at big-time college programs weren't regular students. Being a college athlete was essentially a full-time job. They often had their own dorms, cafeterias, and less demanding academic schedule. Many were receiving money under the table. As Larry Merchant of the *New York Post* noted, "Wherever he went, Moses Malone would have been, by any honest definition, a professional."[45]

Not all coaches objected to Moses's decision. Digger Phelps of Notre Dame and Lou Carnesecca of St. John's said they couldn't blame the kid for taking the money. Norm Sloan wondered, "What's so bad about a player becoming a guaranteed millionaire at 19? Why should he have to wait until he's 24?"[46]

It wasn't just coaches who were critical of the Stars signing Malone. "How low will the pros go in their quest for talent?" scoffed Rob Sieb of *Basketball Weekly*. "If a college degree is superfluous, then might not a high school diploma also be considered unnecessary?"[47] Sieb failed to consider that Moses was unique. You could count on one hand the number of players who had been considered ready for pro ball out of high school in the preceding twenty years, and only two more were given the opportunity over the next twenty.

Coaches and members of the media preached about the sanctity of a college education, as if Malone wouldn't have been pushed through the system at Maryland. For many, if not most athletes, college is the best path forward, though it is not for everybody. Baseball and tennis players had been choosing pro sports instead of college for years. There appeared to be a more paternalistic view of the system that exploited the labor of primarily Black basketball players.

African American columnist Carl Rowan opined, "The overriding factor is that in playing for the Stars, Malone will not gain the education, the self-assurance, the ability to cope in all situations—things he needs far more desperately than a pocket full of money."[48] That's easy to say when you don't have a hole to the outside world in the wall of your bedroom. After Moses signed his contract, he purchased his mother a new house in nearby Ettrick. The old one was condemned, deemed unlivable. Moses was more prepared to play pro ball than to take college courses and needed the money more than an education. His contract with the Stars also set aside money for him to earn a degree.

There were basketball-related concerns about Moses's jump to the pros. The professional game was much more physical and complex than high school ball. Celtics coach Tommy Heinsohn stated, "It's utterly ridiculous to pay this kind of money to a kid like this. He may be great but there's no way a 19-year-old kid is going to step into pro basketball and be great right off the bat. I've seen all of them—Chamberlain, Jabbar—all of them—and I don't think any of them could have played right out of high school."[49] It was also fair to wonder whether Moses had the emotional maturity to be a professional. It helped that at nineteen he was a year older than most high school graduates.

Even some close to Malone questioned the wisdom of his decision. “I would have wanted him to get a couple of years of education,” said Pro Hayes. “If he could get a million dollars for a high school education, what could he get after two years of college?” Kilbourne assumed Moses wouldn't play much early on and worried about his confidence.[50] It didn't take long for Moses to prove his doubters wrong.

8

A Star Is Born

George Mikan was the first NBA star, a 6-foot-11-inch behemoth who led the Minneapolis Lakers to five BAA or NBA championships in the late 1940s and early 1950s. The ABA tabbed him as its first commissioner, believing he would provide instant credibility and NBA connections that could help with a merger. Mikan was nearsighted and wore coke-bottle glasses. He could barely see the NBA's orange ball on grainy black and white television sets and enthusiastically adopted a suggestion by one of the league's founders, Connie Seredin, that the ABA's ball should be red, white, and blue.[1]

That ball came to symbolize the fledgling league, for better or worse. It was popular among children, though NBA people believed "that red, white and blue ball belongs on the nose of a seal."[2] The league had eleven teams in its inaugural season, with names like the Minnesota Muskies and Dallas Chaparrals, and a ragtag bunch of owners who scraped together $50,000 or $100,000 in the hope of earning a payday through a merger.[3] The ABA lacked a television contract, and attendance was sparse.

Teams tried everything to put fans in the seats. The Miami Floridians hired ball girls to prance around in bikinis. The Pacers had Victor the Wrestling Bear perform at halftime and a cow-milking contest during intermission of another game. Some teams, like the Virginia Squires, split their home games between numerous cities. Franchises were constantly on the brink of folding and regularly changed owners, names, and locations. Players worried their checks would bounce and rushed to the bank to cash them.

The league accumulated talent by opening its doors to those cast aside by the NBA: Black players who were victims of the NBA's unofficial quota system; New Yorkers Roger Brown, Connie Hawkins, and Doug Moe, who had been banned from the senior league for tenuous relationships with gamblers; and underclassmen like Haywood, Erving, and Gervin.[4] The upstart league also convinced NBA stars Rick Barry, Billy Cuningham, and Zelmo Beaty, as well as coaches and officials, to jump leagues. Freddie Lewis, who played in the NBA before the ABA, believed the ABA was initially like a Minor League, but by the time his Pacers won their second ABA championship in 1972, there wasn't much difference in quality between the two leagues.[5]

The Anaheim Amigos were charter members. After one season, they were sold and renamed the Los Angeles Stars. In 1969–70, they advanced to the ABA Finals, losing to the Pacers. Still, the team failed to draw. Only 971 fans showed up for a playoff game against Dallas, and that included a giveaway of 500 free tickets. In 1970 a cable television entrepreneur named Bill Daniels bought the team and moved it to Salt Lake City, Utah.[6]

The largely Mormon community embraced the Utah Stars immediately. People in Salt Lake had developed an appreciation for quality basketball by watching BYU and the University of Utah, which won a national championship in 1944 and reached the Final Four twice in the 1960s. Salt Lake radio stations played a catchy jingle welcoming the team: "Here come the Stars, Here come the stars, Here come the Stars. Pro basketball is here at last, Here come the Stars."[7]

The Stars signed All-Star Zelmo Beaty away from the Atlanta Hawks, and he led them to the 1971 championship. Utah averaged 6,246 fans that season at its home arena, the Salt Palace, and 11,811 in the playoffs.[8] With a core of Beaty, Willie Wise, Jimmy Jones, and Ron Boone, the team won the Western Division in each of the next three seasons, the last of which, in 1974, it advanced to the ABA Finals. Despite their success, the Stars lost money. They averaged between six thousand and seven thousand fans per game in 1973–74, a high mark for the ABA, but below their breakeven point of nine thousand.[9]

The team Moses joined in the fall of 1974 was completely different from the one that reached the finals months earlier. Daniels sold the Stars to Collier's group. (The sale eventually fell through when the group couldn't make payments.) Beaty and Jones jumped to the NBA, and Wise demanded a trade.[10] Joe Mullaney quit as coach in August, when told that the team couldn't meet the terms of his contract. He was replaced by Buckwalter.

The Stars opened training camp on September 20 at North Rich High School in Laketown, Utah. The veterans didn't know what to make of young Moses. He was the first of his kind, and nobody had seen him play.[11] "It took maybe about ten minutes" for Malone to adjust to the speed and physicality of the professional game, according to athletic trainer Bill Bean.[12] He ran the floor faster than most guards and leaped off the court once, twice, even three times in a row with shocking quickness.[13]

The veteran big men, some of whom outweighed Moses by forty or fifty pounds, tried to push him around. "They know he's young and a lot of guys have really laid it on him, trying to intimidate him. Elbows, knees, grabbing, shoving, the whole bag. And he's given it right back," Buckwalter told Pat Putnam of *Sports Illustrated*. "That kid doesn't back up an inch. I knew what was going to happen, so I told our guys to go after him right from the first day of practice. We had to find out. They used to kid him by calling him 'the rookie.' Then one day after a rough workout he walked into the locker room and told them, 'You guys can keep on calling me a rookie, but I'm the toughest damn rookie you ever saw.'"[14] Soon they began calling him "Sweet Moses" instead. "Coming out of high school, I had an attitude. I wasn't afraid," Malone said years later. "I loved the contact, which is the way I learned on the playground."[15]

It would have been understandable for the veterans to resent the high school kid with the huge contract who was trying to take their jobs. Randy Denton and Jim Eakins were competing with Moses for minutes. He earned their respect with his work ethic.[16] The kid was coachable and receptive to advice from veterans.[17] Perhaps most important, he helped them win.

The Stars played their first preseason game before 7,314 fans in Richmond, Virginia, against the Virginia Squires. The Squires won easily, though Moses shined with 14 points and 13 rebounds in twenty-nine minutes off the bench.[18] A few nights later, he garnered attention with 22 points, 14 rebounds, 5 blocked shots, and 6 steals against the Denver Nuggets.[19]

Bob Ryan of the *Boston Globe* was at the Salt Palace to see Moses play a preseason game when Larry Brown, coach of the Nuggets, told him, "Moses Malone is the greatest offensive rebounder I have ever seen in my life." Ryan was incredulous. The kid hadn't even played a regular-season game.[20] Moses averaged 15.5 points and 12.8 rebounds on 53.6 percent shooting while coming off the bench over eight preseason games.

When Moses signed with the Stars, GM Arnie Ferrin explained they were going to bring him along slowly.[21] The plan changed. The Stars needed a force down low after Beaty's departure, and Malone was much farther along than expected. When Wise left the team right before the start of the regular season, the heralded rookie was thrust into the starting lineup on opening night against the defending-champion Nets.

Moses jumped center against Billy Paultz to start the game, then moved to forward. Buckwalter believed that was the best position for him until he put on more weight. He scored the first two baskets of the game, the first on a running layup and the second on a tip-in of teammate Al Smith's miss, and held his own against Larry Kenon and Julius Erving, two of the top forwards in the league. Malone posted 19 points, 11 rebounds, and 2 blocks before leaving the game with 3:45 remaining with a sprained ankle.[22]

New Jersey won, 105–89, though Malone was the story after the game. Nets coach Kevin Loughery said, "He [Malone] showed me the quickness of Bill Russell." Moses followed up that performance with 20 points against the Squires the following night. There were bumps in the road. Another highly touted rookie, Marvin Barnes of the Spirits of St. Louis, held him to just 4 points in the third game of the season.[23] He was torched by the league's leading scorer, George McGinnis, and had trouble getting off his shot over Kentucky's Artis Gilmore. But the kid didn't stop coming. He put up 28 points and 24 rebounds against the San Diego Conquistadors on November 9, then 21 and 19 against the Pacers. By mid-December, he was averaging 18 points and 13 rebounds per game on 60 percent shooting.

Malone's game was raw. He couldn't shoot and scored almost all his points on fast breaks and offensive rebounds. He dribbled too much and was turnover prone. As always, he made his mark on the boards. Moses had feet like a ballerina, preternatural instincts for where the ball would come off the rim, and an endless motor. Bigger players tried to push him around, to no avail. He seemed to enjoy the contact, even thrive off it.

Teammates were impressed with how quickly he digested a complex playbook, and Buckwalter marveled at his understanding of defensive schemes, something rookies with four years of college experience typically struggled with.[24] However, it was Malone's physical attributes that drew the most attention. Del Harris, who became an assistant coach with the Stars in Moses's second season, recalled one incident that demonstrated Moses's athleticism. "We had a player who said he could run up, jump, and touch his head on the rim. He did it, but Moses wasn't impressed. He grunted, walked under the basket and, standing still, jumped up and touched his head on the rim, which is pretty amazing when you think about it."[25]

The rookie continued to pile up huge numbers: 23 points and 25 rebounds in a win over the Spurs in December, 33 and 25 a few nights later against the Pacers. The following week, he scored 36 points and snatched 25 boards in a loss to the Nuggets.

"I just have to keep saying to myself that he's only 19," said Buckwalter.[26] Dan Pattison of the *Deseret News* predicted, "Malone is going to have his name inscribed with the greats—Kareem Abdul-Jabbar, Dave Cowens, Julius Erving, John Havlicek before he's through. Maybe before this season is over."[27] Doug Moe and Bill Sharman joined the list of coaches to crown him the greatest offensive rebounder they'd ever seen.[28]

The Stars attempted to capitalize on the youngster. They hung "Moses Will Lead Us" billboards around Salt Lake City[29] and held a Teen Night in November in honor of Malone. Paying customers could bring a date for free, and all teens paid half price. As if that wasn't enough enticement, the *Deseret News* informed fans that "right after the Stars whip the Kentucky Colonels there'll be a sock hop featuring the KSRP Dance Machine. This'll be a hoot. Get it on and be there Saturday night!"[30]

Moses's transition to pro ball wasn't as smooth off the court. Within weeks of his arrival in Utah, Tom Barberi of KOA radio dubbed him "Mumbles Malone."[31] It was a cruel moniker for a nineteen-year-old with a speech impediment, but the name stuck. Moses was hurt and withdrew from the media.

Malone was difficult to understand. In addition to a slight stutter, he had an extremely deep voice; spoke with a Southern accent in a unique, rapid-fire cadence; and failed to annunciate his words. It didn't help that he looked down when he spoke. One day, Moses was talking in the locker room, and Jim Eakins asked Roger Brown what he was saying.

"Why are you asking me?" questioned Brown.

Eakins replied, "Well, you're Black; don't you understand him?"

"Heck no," Brown said.[32]

Yet there were teammates like Gerald Govan who had no trouble understanding Moses, and in what would become a theme throughout his career, some believed he intentionally garbled his words to discourage reporters from talking to him. Steve Rudman covered the Stars for the *Salt Lake Tribune*. Searching for a way to connect with Moses, he asked the team photographer for photographs of Malone and showed them to the rookie. Moses asked if he could keep them. Rudman said they were his if he sat down for an interview.

They talked for three hours. "There was no such thing as mumbles," recalled Rudman. "He was perfectly clear in all of his speech. He made sense. He was a bright, intelligent kid. He answered every question that I asked him, and he was very friendly. And every time I saw him after that he was the same way."[33] Not all reporters brought photographs, and Moses typically wasn't so accommodating.

As the first modern player to jump from high school to the pros, Malone was in high demand. Govan, who'd been in the ABA since the league's inception, was amazed by the number of reporters in the Stars' locker room after the team's first game, including females, something he'd never seen before.[34] Moses answered questions in as few words as possible.

A reporter asked him how he felt after his first game. "I feel about the same as when I was in high school. There's no change," he answered.

"What's the difference between high school and pro ball?" asked another reporter.

"The difference? People get old; in high school they are young."

"How about the pressure of playing your first game in New York? Do you get up more for a game here?"

"A game's a game. You got five people in the crowd that can play the game. It's not where you play; you play to win."

The press wasn't sure how to react. Working the media can be a game, and they didn't know if Moses was playing.[35]

The rookie began wearing headphones in the locker room to ward off reporters.[36] When a CBS news crew showed up to film him for a segment on Walter Cronkite's *CBS Evening News*, he put his warmup on inside out so they couldn't see his name. After attempting to interview him, Rick Hummel of the *St. Louis Post-Dispatch* concluded, "Malone was either painfully shy, painfully rude or both."[37]

Veterans explained to Moses that talking to the media was part of the job. Harvey Kirkpatrick, the team's head of public relations, tried to persuade him that the media could help his image and career, with little success.[38] Malone was a private person. "If a person is going to keep cool," he told Rudman, "he has to keep things to himself. The person who talks all the time always thinks he's the coolest. If you are going to be cool about what you're doing, you've got to keep it all to yourself."[39] His silence led members of the media to conclude that he wasn't intelligent. Kirkpatrick, the team's PR man, agreed.[40] They pointed to his high school grades, lack of education, and poor verbal skills as evidence.

Moses was homesick and weary from the constant travel.[41] He lived in Triarch Travelodge, a hotel about six blocks from the Salt Palace, and ate many of his meals in an economy steakhouse.[42] Most of his teammates "were old enough to be my daddy," as he put it, and had families. He spent a lot of time in his hotel room, watching TV and listening to his stereo.[43] He missed family and friends and hated the cold weather.[44]

Salt Lake City was more than 99 percent white. "I think the first few weeks I was there I saw one African American," recalled Wali Jones.[45] Salt Lake residents went out of their way to make the Stars feel welcome. Businessmen invited players to their homes for dinner,[46] and Moses was accustomed to being around white people from high school.

It was a lack of comfort and connection that was challenging for Moses and the other Black players. Wise described the culture shock:

> Where are all the Black people? Where's the ghetto? Where are the boys hanging out on the corner? Where do you go? Of course, we were beyond this, but where do you go when you just want to hoop with your boys? It was gone. And where are the ones that really understand how you're talking and how you're speaking? And understand where you're coming from? And where are those who can validate your experience of growing up in the '50s and '60s as a Black person? It was no fault of anyone there. So, for us, you know, and so you can't

expect them to adjust. So, the adjustment was incumbent upon us as African Americans, which we did to a certain degree.[47]

In his Stars locker, Malone kept the Maryland Terrapins jersey he received when he signed with the school, though he never regretted his decision to turn pro.[48] The money was life-changing. When he signed with the Stars, he went to the Safeway where his mother worked and informed management that Mary was retired. In addition to a new home, he purchased her a Chrysler Imperial and sent her a monthly stipend.[49] He ordered himself that Lincoln Mark IV.[50] Yet he never forgot what it was like to be poor. The Stars' athletic trainer handed out envelopes to the players with a $25 per diem for meals when they were on the road. Moses sought out the nearest McDonald's or KFC and saved as much of that money as possible.[51]

Veteran teammates looked out for Malone, starting with Boone, Govan, and Jones. Jones and Govan lived in the same hotel as Moses. Jones broke down games with him and brought Moses along when he ran clinics on Native American reservations. He taught Malone to set goals and the importance of being on time for practices, games, and flights, a lesson Moses adhered to for the rest of his life. Malone told Jones his first goal was to lead the ABA and all professional basketball in rebounding.[52]

Boone invited Moses to his home, where his wife cooked them dinner. The veteran demonstrated how to prepare for games and eat right.[53] "Ron Boone was like a father to me," Moses told *Slam* magazine years later. "He saw I needed guidance and he gave it to me, helped me mature as a person."[54] Govan was Malone's roommate on the road and sat next to him on the team bus. He explained the ins and outs of the league and protected him on the court when opponents tried to bully him.[55]

For the most part, Moses appeared mature beyond his years. There was no discernible difference between him and a twenty-two-year-old rookie. His teammates respected him and enjoyed his company. He was friendly, fearless, and hardworking, and he added youthful exuberance to a veteran locker room. Buckwalter thought there was a sweetness to Moses.[56] The rookie stayed on the court after games to shoot around with kids.[57]

Naturally, there were times when Moses showed his age. He didn't know basic social customs like how to tip at a restaurant. When he received his first paycheck, he went shopping at a toy store in Salt Lake for Christmas presents for family and friends. He ended up playing with and breaking most of them before the holidays and had to go back to buy more.[58]

Moses was selected to the All-Star team in his rookie season and scored 6 points with 10 rebounds in twenty minutes of action.[59] Two weeks later, Buckwalter was fired and replaced by Tom Nissalke. The Stars were 24-32 at the time.[60] Bucky made a habit of leaving his team's afternoon shootarounds to grab a few drinks at a restaurant and nightclub called Winery, a block from the Salt Palace. Daniels deemed that unacceptable and let him go.[61]

Nissalke was a gregarious fellow who showed up to games at 4:30 to hobnob with reporters. He'd made the rounds in college and pro ball, including gigs as the head coach of the ABA's Chaparrals and Spurs. Nissalke was enamored with Moses's talent and took a special interest in the young man, working with him one-on-one after practice, while trying to get to know him off the court.[62] He didn't coddle the rookie. Sometimes during timeouts, he'd stop addressing the team and demand that Moses lift his head and look him in the eye while he was talking.[63]

Moses finished the year strong, including a season-high 37 points in a win over the Spirits. He was second on the team in scoring with 18.8 points per game, on 57 percent shooting (third in the league), and averaged 14.6 rebounds (fourth in the league and first in offensive rebounds with 455) and 1.5 blocked shots. He played in 83 of 84 games. Moses was named to the ABA's All Rookie Team and finished third in Rookie of the Year voting behind Marvin Barnes and Bobby Jones, both of whom spent four years in college.

The Stars went 14-14 under Nissalke, for a final record of 38-46, good enough for a playoff spot. They faced the Nuggets in the first round. Moses posted 25 points and 19 rebounds in his first playoff game, and 30 points and an astounding 33 rebounds in his third. The Stars were eliminated in six games, during which Malone averaged 22.7 points and 17.5 rebounds. "Moses was awesome, devastating. I saw greatness in him," Nissalke recalled.[64] Malone had just scratched the surface of his potential.

9

Bad News and the Spirits

"Foot broken." Moses pulled himself from an exhibition game during training camp in the fall of 1975. The athletic trainer examined his right foot and couldn't find anything wrong with it. "Foot broken," Moses repeated, and refused to go back in the game. Sure enough, a doctor found a fracture in his foot.[1]

The Stars held a minicamp for free agents in Ponce, Puerto Rico, in late July.[2] Moses attended and tweaked his foot during an exhibition game. Training camp started on September 21, and a few days later the Stars played an exhibition game at a local high school. Randy Denton was running down the court and accidentally stepped on Moses's injured foot, breaking a bone. His right foot was placed in a cast but failed to heal completely and Malone underwent bone-graft surgery in late October.[3]

The Stars lost Govan to the Squires and Wali Jones to the NBA. They added role players in sharpshooter John Roche, rookie Steve Green, and forward Goo Kennedy. Nissalke's squad struggled out of the gate without Malone, beginning the season 4-12. Then the chaos of the ABA caught up with them.

Bill Daniels was an amateur boxer in his youth and served as a fighter pilot in the navy during World War II and the Korean War. He was a sociable entrepreneur who made his money in the cable industry before purchasing the Stars in 1970.[4] Despite the Stars' success, Daniels lost $3.1 million on the team.[5] He suffered additional losses backing heavyweight boxer Ron Lyle and IndyCar racers. The final straw was a huge sum of personal money Daniels poured into a failed gubernatorial run in Colorado.[6] By late 1975 he was out of money and living in a Howard Johnson hotel next to the Salt Palace where he paid for his stay with Stars tickets.[7]

Daniels had been trying to sell the team since January 1974 and was intent on finding buyers who would keep the Stars in Salt Lake City.[8]

They had a loyal fan base, but without a television deal or significant corporate backing, it was difficult to find a buyer. One deal fell through, then another with the Collier group. Daniels had an agreement to sell the team to Snell and Lyle Johnson, two local businessmen, in June 1975, but that deal crumbled as well.[9]

The Baltimore Claws folded after three exhibition games in 1975, and the San Diego Sails followed in November. By mid-November, there were rumors that the Stars might not be able to make payroll. Later that month, Daniels met with the owners of the Spirits of St. Louis, another struggling franchise, about the possibility of combining the two teams and playing out the season in Salt Lake City. The merger was contingent on Daniels raising $600,000 from local businesses, which he was unable to do.[10]

The Stars had a game scheduled for December 2. Daniels showed up at the morning shootaround and told athletic trainer Bill Bean to call the players into the locker room. His eyes were bloodshot. "Obviously he'd been throwing down some sauce," recalled Bean.[11] Daniels was heartbroken. He loved the team and had done everything he could to save it. With tears in his eyes and a bottle of whisky in hand, he got right to the point. "Fellas, this is the saddest day of my life. I can't pay you," he said. "We're closing the doors."[12]

The players started cleaning out their lockers. Steve Green, a rookie out of Indiana University, bolted for the bank to cash his last check.[13] Bean opened the storage locker for the players to take what they wanted. Moses and Goo Kennedy grabbed a shopping cart and loaded it with whatever they could find—jerseys, T-shirts, towels, basketballs.[14] Nissalke and Del Harris were driving away from the arena when they spotted Moses hobbling down the street with a cast on his right foot, pushing the cart full of merchandise toward his hotel.[15]

League officials, including Donald Schupak, part owner of the Spirits, arranged for Moses, Boone, Green, and Denton to be sold to the Spirits. The Stars were the third ABA team to fold that season, and the Spirits and Squires were in danger of going under as well. The long-discussed ABA-NBA merger appeared to be imminent, and league officials hoped to improve the Spirits' attendance and likelihood of joining the NBA with the addition of the Stars' four most desirable players. The remainder of the Utah Stars were placed on waivers and could be claimed by any team.[16]

Moses was indignant about being shipped to St. Louis. "I'm a Utah Star, man," he told reporters.[17] His agent, Lee Fentress, contested the sale on legal grounds, arguing that Moses's contract was nontransferable.[18] Moses went home to Petersburg. The cast was removed from his foot, and he began shooting around and using the whirlpool at his old high school.[19]

Meanwhile, Fentress explored Malone's options. He met with Simon Gourdine, the deputy commissioner of the NBA, and informed him of his belief that Moses's sale to the Spirits breached the terms of his contract and was therefore invalid. He inquired as to whether there was a mechanism in place for Moses to join the NBA.[20] No team had drafted his rights. The Pistons had attempted to select him in the fourth round of the 1975 draft but were prohibited by the league because Moses had not applied for a hardship exception.[21]

Gourdine explained that a couple of weeks earlier the NBA informed teams that they were considering a special draft for specific ABA players. The ABA was in trouble. Three teams had folded and there was speculation that more, perhaps even the entire league, would follow. There were a handful of players like Malone who had left school before their college class graduated but never applied for a hardship exception to the NBA. The league wanted to ensure that those players could join immediately if they became available. Fentress encouraged Gourdine to schedule a draft, and the deputy commissioner obliged.[22]

The NBA held a special draft on December 30. The New Orleans Jazz chose Malone as the first pick and surrendered their next available first-round pick in the NBA draft, which was in 1977, for his rights. Moses was one of five players selected, along with Mark Olberding of the Spurs, Mel Bennett of the Squires, Charlie Jordan of the Pacers, and Skip Wise, who had been cut by San Antonio and was not part of a team at the time.[23]

The Jazz were excited about the possibility of pairing Moses with flashy guard Pete Maravich. However, their rights to Malone were contingent upon him not being contractually obligated to an ABA team. ABA commissioner Dave DeBusschere condemned the special draft, calling the NBA "vultures," and Spirits management assured the Jazz that they had a valid contract with Moses.[24] New Orleans took them at their word and vowed not to sign Malone unless the Spirits folded.[25] Other ABA teams contacted Spirits general manager Harry Weltman to see if he was interested in trading Moses, which he was not.[26]

Fentress worked out the contractual issues with St. Louis, and Moses began practicing with the team on January 8, 1976. The Spirits were the third iteration of one of the original ABA teams, the Houston Mavericks, which moved to North Carolina in 1969 to become the Carolina Cougars. Ozzie and Daniel Silna purchased the team in 1974 and relocated it to St. Louis as the Spirits. The team was essentially an expansion franchise in 1974–75, carrying over just three players from the Cougars, but made the playoffs despite only 32 wins. Then the Spirits knocked off the defending champion Nets in a shocking first-round upset.[27]

With the addition of Moses and his three Stars teammates, the Spirits had as much talent as any team in either league. Malone joined a frontcourt that included Marvin Barnes, Caldwell Jones, and M. L. Carr. At guard, the Spirits featured Ron Boone, Freddie Lewis, Don Chaney, and Mike D'Antoni. Rod Thorn was the coach, and Bob Costas, a young broadcaster fresh out of Syracuse University, called the games on radio.

Barnes was the most talented player on the Spirits. "I've been around a long time," said reserve guard Barry Parkhill, "and when Marvin Barnes wanted to play, he was one of the greatest players I've ever laid eyes on."[28] The 6-foot-8-inch forward was selected second overall in the 1974 NBA draft out of Providence College but opted to play in the ABA, where he averaged 24 points, 15.6 rebounds, and nearly 2 blocks per game on his way to being named Rookie of the Year. He even outplayed the great Julius Erving at times in the Spirits' playoff upset of the Nets.

Marvin was kind-hearted with a colorful personality. There's a famous story about the time he refused to board a team flight scheduled to leave Louisville at 8:00 a.m. eastern time and arrive in St. Louis at 7:56 a.m. central time. "I ain't getting on no time machine," he said, and rented a car.[29] Unfortunately, Marvin loved the streets more than the game. He started using drugs and hanging out with drug dealers during his second season. He told teammates he wanted to be a gangster.[30] Legal trouble followed, and he began arriving late or completely missing team flights, practices, and games. The press called him "Bad News Barnes."

Thorn tried to hold the club together, but it's difficult for a unit to function when its most important player is unreliable. Plus, for all their talent, the Spirits' roster was poorly constructed. The team had a lot of players who needed the ball and not enough facilitators, role players, or minutes to go around. St. Louis was 19-21 when Moses suited up for the first time against the Colonels on January 15. He scored 19 points in twenty minutes off the bench, which was impressive considering he had only participated in a few practices after missing several months of action with a broken foot. He scored 24 points and grabbed 15 rebounds in a rematch with the Colonels five nights later.

Moses wasn't the same player during his tenure in St. Louis. He was fifteen to twenty pounds overweight after the injury and rusty from months of inaction.[31] He played alongside a back-to-the-basket center in Caldwell Jones, forcing him to face up and put the ball on the floor, which wasn't his strength. He looked lost offensively and committed a ghastly number of turnovers, as many as 13 in one game.[32]

Malone was generally coachable but could be stubborn and had a unique way of making it known when he wasn't pleased. Thorn had the Spirits run through their plays during practice one day early in Moses's tenure. There were about five plays, with variations on each of them. Moses was working with the second unit and kept screwing up the plays. Thorn informed the team that they would continue practicing until they did them correctly. Moses continued to make mistakes. Thorn realized that he was messing up on purpose and wasn't going to stop. This went on for about thirty minutes. The coach had to figure out a way to end the exercise while saving face. He looked at his watch and said he had to leave for a meeting with the general manager. "It wasn't anything malicious at all," recalled Thorn. "It was just that 'I don't want to do this. This guy's stupid enough to keep making us do this. Okay, we'll see where this goes.'"[33]

Thorn had difficulty understanding Malone when he spoke, but the coach discovered during his short time with Moses that a sharp mind was behind the youngster's detached demeanor. During a team flight from St. Louis to Virginia, Moses muttered something to Thorn that the coach couldn't make out. A few minutes later, it dawned on Thorn. "Did you say 'Princeton?'" he asked Moses. Malone nodded and laughed. He had pointed out that the plane was flying over Thorn's hometown of Princeton, West Virginia. Thorn had no idea how Malone knew where he was from.[34]

The Spirits fired Thorn on January 30. The team had underperformed at 20-27, and management disapproved of his handling of Barnes. He was replaced by Joe Mullaney. Before Mullaney's first game, he discussed the game plan in the locker room. While he was addressing the team, Moses stood up and walked away. Mullaney said, "Hey, Moses, what the hell? Where you going?"

Moses provided a one-word response: "Pee."

"I think Joe Mullaney was thinking, *Oh my god, I've been coaching 150 years, and no one's ever done anything close*," recalled Steve Green. Malone's teammates laughed. They knew he wasn't trying to show the coach up. He just had his own way of doing things and was a man of few words.[35] Spirits guard Don Chaney remembered Malone as "a young guy, very naive. He was looked upon almost as a renegade—different, wild and strange." On another occasion, Malone was sucking on a Coke bottle [making whistling sounds] during one of Mullaney's pregame talks. Mullaney said, "I can't take it anymore" and walked out.[36]

The coach moved Moses and Freddie Lewis to the bench. It was a difficult transition for both men. Lewis was a four-time All-Star who won three championships and a playoff MVP award with the Pacers. Yet it was the second-year player, Malone, who repeatedly told Lewis to keep his head up. "Things would work out," he said.[37] Two factions were on the dysfunctional Spirits, one led by Bad News Barnes and another consisting of those devoted to their craft, like Lewis and Caldwell Jones. Moses gravitated toward the latter, growing particularly close with Jones, which Thorn believed demonstrated a great deal about his instincts and character.[38]

Moses's play was inconsistent for the remainder of the season. Mullaney began starting him against bigger lineups and going with M. L. Carr as the starting forward alongside Barnes versus smaller teams. Malone worked himself back into shape and posted some 20-point, double-digit-rebound games but never really found his groove. He averaged 14.3 points and 9.6 rebounds in twenty-seven minutes over forty-three games with the Spirits.

Despite their immense talent, the Spirits finished 35-49 and failed to make the playoffs. It was essentially a lost year for Moses and the franchise. "That three months felt like three years, you know," said Boone.[39] The city of St. Louis failed to support the team. At a game against San Antonio, the announced attendance was 808 people at St. Louis Arena, which had a capacity of eighteen thousand. Broadcasters Bob Costas and Terry Stembridge counted the crowd for themselves and came up with a little over five hundred people. The Spirits averaged about three thousand fans per game.[40]

The Silna brothers explored relocating the team to Memphis, Tennessee; Hollywood, Florida; and Hartford, Connecticut, before announcing in late March that they'd reached an agreement to move to Salt Lake City for the 1976–77 season. The team would be renamed the Utah Rockies.[41] The Spirits' owners believed they had a better chance of joining the NBA with the team in Utah. "If you move into a Salt Lake City and 3,000 or 5,000 season tickets are sold, I can't imagine the NBA not wanting to bring in a team to play a team with Ron Boone or a Caldwell Jones or a Moses Malone or a Marvin Barnes," reasoned Donald Schupak, a Spirits minority owner.[42]

Schupak was incorrect. The NBA agreed to absorb four ABA teams, but the Spirits were not one of them. Moses would play for a new team in a different league for the 1976–77 season. It was just the beginning of his peripatetic journey through professional basketball.

10

Wandering Moses

Oscar Robertson scored 30 points while leading Crispus Attucks High School to the first Indiana state championship by an all-Black team, in March 1956. He and his teammates cut down the nets at Butler Fieldhouse, attended a small awards ceremony, then climbed onto the top of a red fire truck. It was tradition in the Hoosier state for the champions to take a victory lap around the squares in downtown Indianapolis.

The fire truck followed Mayor Clark's limousine and police motorcycles. Several buses and cars joined the caravan, honking their horns and cheering. The motorcade made a lap around the fountains and statues of Civil War veterans at Monument Circle, then headed up Indiana Avenue and north on West Street. Robertson noticed something was wrong. They had veered off the parade route that led downtown through the heart of the city. Instead, the buses and cars headed toward the Black neighborhoods where people poured into the streets to celebrate. Robertson later discovered that city officials were concerned the players would start riots downtown.

Oscar's teammates were euphoric celebrating with their family and friends. They remember the night fondly. Not Oscar—dejected, he left the celebration to return to his father's home. That night has gnawed at him to this day.[1]

Robertson went on to become one of the most outstanding basketball players to ever step on a court, though his greatest legacy played out in a courtroom. "The Big O" was born in segregated Tennessee and raised in Ku Klux Klan–infested Indianapolis. He was called the N-word and had things thrown at him when his University of Cincinnati team played in North Carolina, and he was forced to find separate accommodations when the team traveled to Houston for an exhibition game. Robertson objected to a system in which NBA teams drafted kids out of college and owned their rights for the duration of their careers through the option clause.[2]

The NBA and ABA initially agreed to a merger in May 1970. The ABA had an antitrust lawsuit pending against the NBA, and the senior league, which was struggling financially, saw a merger as a way of avoiding the cost of litigation while raking in $1.25 million per year for ten years from each ABA team to join the league. The merger was ratified in 1971.[3]

The ABA gave players bargaining power and freedom of movement. If the leagues merged with the current draft and option clause in place, there would not be a free market for their services. The players association, with its president, Oscar Robertson, as the lead plaintiff, filed an antitrust lawsuit against the NBA to block the merger, abolish the draft, and eliminate the option clause, in a case known as *Robertson v. National Basketball Association*.[4]

The *New York Times* announced Robertson's retirement on August 28, 1974, the day Moses signed with the Stars, though the case bearing his name continued.[5] The NBA believed it had a losing position. It was a violation of the country's antitrust laws to bind a player for life through a draft system with essentially no collective bargaining.[6] The federal judge overseeing the case, Robert L. Carter of the Southern District of New York, strongly urged the two sides to reach a settlement in early 1976.[7] The NBA coveted ABA stars like Julius Erving, David Thompson, and Artis Gilmore, as well as the end to the bidding wars and lawsuits with the ABA. The ABA owners, who had been hoping to merge since the league's inception, were now desperate for a deal, with three teams folding and more on the verge.

Dave DeBusschere, who'd been hired in May 1975 as the seventh ABA commissioner, began intensive negotiations with NBA commissioner Larry O'Brien. The two men and their attorneys ironed out an agreement during NBA All-Star weekend in 1976, which was signed and filed with Judge Carter on April 12, 1976.[8] The terms included a to-be-determined number of ABA teams joining the NBA and a plan for free agency. The free-agency process would be rolled out gradually. For the first five years, any team that signed a free agent would have to compensate the player's old team with assets determined by the league. After five years, players could enter restricted free agency, with teams maintaining a right to match any contract offered to their player by another team. Finally, after ten years, there would be a pathway for players to become unrestricted free agents.[9]

The ABA folded the Virginia Squires in May 1976 after the team missed a league-mandated deadline to produce back salaries for their players and payments to the league.[10] Just six ABA teams remained. In late April, DeBusschere presented the NBA with three alternative plans for a merger: One plan had the San Antonio Spurs, Denver Nuggets, Indiana Pacers, and New York Nets joining the NBA. Another plan included those four teams plus the Spirits of St. Louis, and a third option involved all six teams, the last of which being the Kentucky Colonels.[11]

Many NBA executives felt animosity toward the ABA. "I was an NBA loyalist and wanted to bury them," said Milwaukee Bucks general manager Wayne Embry. "I hated the ball, everything. We thought they were making a mockery of the game."[12] The NBA knew the ABA was desperate and was able to dictate the terms of the deal.

Executives and attorneys from both leagues met at the Cape Cod Room at Dunfey Family's Hyannis Resort in Hyannis, Massachusetts, in mid-June to finalize the terms.[13] The NBA accepted the four-team plan, with the Spurs, Nuggets, Nets, and Pacers joining the league, and was unwilling to call it a merger or recognize ABA statistics. The four would be treated like expansion teams and be required to pay a $3.2 million fee to join. The Nets were forced to pay an additional $4.8 million to the New York Knicks as compensation for invading their territory. The deal was finalized on June 17.[14]

The Colonels were given $3 million to fold their franchise, but the Spirits owners held out for more. Daniel and Ozzie Silna negotiated their own deal with the help of Donald Schupak. They would be paid for every Spirits player drafted by NBA teams, which amounted to $2.2 million. Additionally, they'd receive one-seventh share of the "visual media rights" of each of the four ABA teams, *in perpetuity*, that entered the NBA. Cable television was in its infancy, and no one could have imagined how enormous that payout would be. The Silnas had received a reported $300 million as of 2014 when they negotiated an end to the agreement for an additional $500 million.[15]

As part of the deal between the two leagues, the New Orleans Jazz relinquished its rights to Moses from the December draft. That didn't stop Jazz minority owner Shelly Beychok from trying to sign Moses before the dispersal draft, which drew a written rebuke from Deputy Commissioner Gourdine.[16] Such shenanigans were indicative of the NBA in the 1970s, a small-time operation fighting for credibility while staving off insolvency.

The NBA agreed to honor all ABA contracts, and the four ABA teams joined with their rosters intact. The Spirits and Colonels entered what was called a dispersal draft, in which teams could select them for a fee determined by the league on an individual basis. Artis Gilmore, a 7-foot-2-inch center who had won a championship with the Colonels, was valued the highest at $1.1 million, followed by Marvin Barnes at $500,000, Moses at $350,000, Maurice Lucas at $300,000 and Ron Boone at $250,000.[17]

The Chicago Bulls selected Gilmore first. Bucky Buckwalter was working as a scout for the Trail Blazers and pushed them to choose Malone, which they did with the fifth pick. The Blazers also selected Maurice Lucas with the second pick, which they had acquired form the Atlanta Hawks the day before the draft.[18]

Berlyn Hodges served many roles for the Trail Blazers since their inception in 1970 and was working in ticket sales when they acquired Malone. He picked up Moses from the airport in Portland and drove the young center forty-five miles to Salem, where the team held training camp at Willamette University. Hodges turned on the car radio, and the two men heard a radio personality announce that Malone wouldn't be in Portland long. The Trail Blazers were going to trade him.

Hodges knew the report was true and frantically changed the station. He tried to fill the awkward silence by asking Malone if he had any hobbies. Moses mumbled something that sounded like "swimming pools." Hodges asked, "Your hobby is building swimming pools?" "No," Malone replied, "swimming and pool. Man, playing pool." They drove the rest of the way in silence.[19]

Jack Ramsay was the new coach of the Blazers and was intrigued about adding Malone to the roster. He was immediately informed by owner Larry Weinberg that they selected Moses for the purpose of trading him.[20] The Blazers had a crowded frontcourt with Bill Walton and Maurice Lucas slated to start at center and power forward and a serviceable backup at both positions in Lloyd Neal. Management was unwilling to pay Malone's draft fee and significant salary for a bench player.

Ramsay was also skeptical as to whether Moses could play in his system. The coach wanted to run a "play action offense" based on reading and reacting rather than set plays. He sought highly skilled, intelligent players who could contribute immediately.[21] Moses was a poor passer, couldn't shoot, and had received relatively minimal coaching. It would take time for him to develop.

Malone was naturally quiet, and the knowledge that he wasn't wanted in Portland caused him to withdraw further. He'd sit on the trainer's table to be taped before practice, point to his feet, and say to the athletic trainer, Ron Culp, "Feet." Once during a scrimmage, he said, "Wrist" to Culp, though Culp thought he said, "Rest."

The trainer yelled to Ramsay, "Moses wants to come out and take a rest."

"No," said Malone, pointing to his wrist, "not *rest*, *wrist*."[22]

Moses failed to impress Ramsay during the team's six-day training camp. He wasn't familiar with the offense and was tentative with the ball. The coach played him just one minute in the Blazers' first preseason game against the Los Angeles Lakers and four minutes in the second game against the Seattle SuperSonics. Lloyd Neal underwent knee surgery after the Seattle game, resulting in a slight uptick in Moses's playing time to sixteen, sixteen, ten, and eleven minutes over the next four games. Ramsay didn't give him a chance.[23]

Lucas knew Moses could play from their battles in the ABA. As for the rest of guys, "his game and talent preceded him," said Walton.[24] Johnny Davis was a rookie on the team and recalls Walton and Malone going at one another day after day in practice. They had two very different styles but were both dominant in their own way. Lucas was a fierce competitor, and he and Malone talked trash to each other throughout practice. Lloyd Neal liked to mix it up down low as well. Davis played ten years in the NBA and coached in the league for twenty-five more. Those were the most intense practices he's ever seen.

Moses grew more comfortable with his teammates, and they enjoyed his presence. He played practical jokes on the guys. Davis went to get his ankles taped before practice one day and couldn't find his shoes when he returned to his locker. He looked all over. Then he noticed Moses staring at him, and the big fellow erupted in laughter.[25]

Lucas immediately established himself as the leader of the team and the ringleader in the locker room. Walton and Malone both stuttered, and he teased them mercilessly about their trouble speaking. "The whole rest of the team would just be howling with laughter," said Walton. "And tears of fun would be streaming down our cheeks."[26]

The Trail Blazers tried to trade Moses over the summer and during training camp. However, unless an NBA executive's team had played an interleague exhibition against the Stars or Spirits, the executive likely hadn't seen the Petersburg product play, and there was a stigma against ABA guys. General manager Harry Glickman offered the Celtics Malone and Sidney Wicks for All-Star guard Jo Jo White, but Red Auerbach turned him down.[27] Denver inquired about Malone before trading for veteran Paul Silas instead.[28] Portland reached out to Knicks general manager Eddie Donovan to gauge his interest in Moses. Donovan asked, "Is he better than Gianelli?" referring to John Gianelli, the team's journeyman center.[29]

The Buffalo Braves finally stepped forward with an offer of a first-round pick for Malone, but they wanted to see him play first.[30] Portland told Braves executives to attend the team's last preseason game on October 16, against Seattle. Moses entered the game at the start of the second quarter with Portland leading 32–27. He scored 11 points in his first five minutes and ended up with 15 points and 10 rebounds in the second quarter alone. The Blazers outscored the Sonics 35–14 during that stretch for a 70–41 halftime lead. Moses finished with 24 points on 11 of 14 shooting and 12 rebounds in twenty-six minutes.[31]

Blazers president Larry Weinberg and his wife Barbi were in attendance. Midway through the second quarter Barbi said, "Larry, you can't trade Moses."[32] Walton had been pushing Ramsay to keep Malone, and the coach admitted after the game that he needed to reevaluate his position on Moses. At a team meeting a couple of days later, Ramsay and others voted to keep him, though Glickman interrupted to tell them that Moses had already been traded to Buffalo.[33] The Braves surrendered a first-round draft pick and $232,000 (the remaining two payments of the dispersal-draft fee).

Ramsay informed the team of the trade at practice later that day. "What did you get for him?" Walton asked.

"We got a first," Ramsay answered.

"You didn't trade him away," Walton said, "you gave him away."[34]

Portland won the NBA championship that season and started the 1977–78 campaign 50-10 before Walton was sidelined with chronic foot problems. He missed the entire following season, his last with Portland, while Moses was named the league's Most Valuable Player. "I believe if we had kept Moses, we would have won multiple championships even with Bill Walton hurt," said guard Lionel Hollins.[35] "They should have kept Moses and traded me," Walton said in 2006.[36]

Malone joined a talented squad in Buffalo that included three-time scoring champion Bob McAdoo, a heralded rookie out of Notre Dame named Adrian Dantley, and speedster Randy Smith. But it was a franchise in flux. Owner Paul Snyder had threatened to move the team to Toronto or Florida if it couldn't sell five thousand season tickets, and McAdoo requested a trade heading into the final year of his contract when management wouldn't meet his financial demands. Snyder sold half of the team to John Y. Brown, the former owner of the Kentucky Colonels.[37]

Moses allowed the Braves to move McAdoo to power forward and served as insurance in case he left. The Braves' new coach was Tates Locke, the former Clemson coach who had recruited Moses and was fired for violations, in part involving Malone. Tates acted as if he didn't hold a grudge, but Moses felt otherwise.[38] Locke played him a total of six minutes in the first two games, and that was with McAdoo missing the first one.

It was bizarre for the Braves to give up a first-round pick and significant cash for Malone and then not play him. There were rumors that people within the organization believed he wasn't intelligent and didn't want to invest in his development. The Braves reworked Moses's contract when they acquired him, then, according to Snyder, Fentress demanded an additional clause guaranteeing that Moses would play at least twenty-four minutes per game. Fentress denied that and began working the phones in search of a new destination for Malone.[39]

Claude Terry was a veteran guard who had also recently joined the Braves. He and his wife were staying at a two-bedroom efficiency in Buffalo until they were able to move into their rental. When the team acquired

Moses, they set him up two doors down from the Terrys. Claude spent four seasons with the Denver Nuggets, so he was familiar with Moses from the ABA. One day, he returned home from shopping with his wife and saw Malone sitting on the curb with his bags packed. Terry asked what was going on.

Moses replied, "I was just traded."

Terry was in disbelief, as Malone had just arrived a week earlier. He asked what happened. Moses explained that it had something to do with his contract. He appeared to be unfazed by the turn of events.

Players didn't get involved with team affairs at that time, particularly a journeyman like Terry. He had never contacted a general manger before but felt compelled to call Braves GM Bob MacKinnon to find out what happened. MacKinnon gave a vague answer.

Terry told him, "I watched this kid in the ABA, and you possibly could have traded the best offensive rebounder in the history of basketball."[40]

The Braves traded McAdoo six weeks later, and Locke was fired midway through the season. "If we had kept that one club together, maybe we could have won the championship," MacKinnon said years later. "We had Moses Malone, Bob McAdoo, [John] Shumate and [Adrian] Dantley, all on one club. To let that slip through our hands was very poor."[41]

Tom Nissalke had recently taken over the reins of the Houston Rockets and had been pushing GM Ray Patterson to trade for his former player. Patterson had seen Moses play a few times and wasn't that impressed, though he engaged in discussions with Portland based on Nissalke's strong recommendation. He was offended when Portland asked for the entire $232,000 up front, and Patterson backed out. Moses's agents, Donald Dell and Lee Fentress, also represented John Lucas, whom the Rockets selected first overall in the 1976 draft. They developed a strong relationship with Patterson during contract negotiations, and Fentress contacted the general manager to inform him that Moses was available again. This time Nissalke pushed harder. "Ray said, 'If you're that impressed with him, we'll roll the dice,'" he recalled.

Snyder had been ambivalent about acquiring Malone. Brown, who knew Moses from the ABA, was the driving force behind the deal. The Rockets offered to reimburse Buffalo for the $232,000 they sent to Portland and throw in two first-round picks for Moses. Brown was overseas at the time, and Snyder jumped at the opportunity to turn the pick they sent out for Malone into two a week later. "If Brown had been there, the trade never would have happened," said Fentress.[42]

In less than a year, Moses had been shunted between five teams (six, if you count the New Orleans Jazz) across two leagues. He was on the trade block for months without generating much interest, and executives voiced doubts about his skills and intelligence. It was a lot to handle for a young man two years removed from high school.

"When he started to consider the pros, I was concerned for him," Moses's high school coach Pro Hayes told Frank Deford of *Sports Illustrated*. "I was afraid that if he was defeated then, he could be destroyed. And so much more has happened than we ever feared—his team folding, then the league, being traded all around, so much—and he's still Moses. The same Moses. He's not Billy Showboat. No, sir. You see, Moses had a lot more faith in himself than we did."[43]

11
A Launch Pad

Ray Patterson was a child of the Depression, the product of a single-parent home, who relied on wit and guile to survive a childhood in rough neighborhoods throughout the Midwest. He was a raconteur who knew how to relate to people. In the fall of 1976 Patterson was on the receiving end of a tall tale about a 7-foot-2 center who could score like Wilt Chamberlain and rebound like Bill Russell. Nissalke laid it on thick when trying to convince his GM to acquire Malone.[1]

Patterson risked his job in trading for the third-year center. The Rockets were cash-strapped, and the GM sacrificed cheap labor in the form of first-round draft picks for Moses and his hefty salary. Patterson met Moses in Houston and immediately realized the center wasn't 7 feet 2 but more like 6 feet 10. Then the two men shook hands, and Ray went pale. Moses's hands were tiny for a big man, dwarfed by the size of the 6-foot-3 Patterson's. This was the guy he had bet his job and the future of the franchise on?[2]

The Moses trade wasn't the first time Patterson put his neck on the line for the Rockets. The team had been in financial trouble since moving to Houston in 1971 and came within days of selling its best players to save the franchise. Ray brought staff members with him from the Milwaukee Bucks when he joined the Rockets in 1972 and felt a responsibility to them, in addition to the organization. On one dire occasion, he took out a second mortgage on his home to meet payroll. "My mother wasn't too happy about that," recalled his son Steve.[3]

The club joined the NBA in 1967 as the San Diego Rockets. San Diego was using the slogan "a city in motion" to promote its emergence as a first-class city. The name Rockets fit the theme and was even better suited for Houston, home of the Space Center, where they relocated in 1971. A group of Houston businessmen led by Wayne Duddleston, Billy Goldberg, and Mickey Herskowitz hoped to build on the excitement generated by the Game of the Century in 1968 between the University of Houston and UCLA that drew fifty-three thousand spectators at the Astrodome.[4] The hero of that game, Elvin Hayes, played for the Rockets and was expected to put fans in the seats.

Unfortunately, Houston didn't have an arena to host professional basketball. During their first season in Space City, the Rockets played "home" games in Waco, El Paso, and San Antonio, in addition to three Houston locations: Astrohall, Hofheinz Pavilion, and the Astrodome. A mere 759 people attended their first game in Waco, and the Rockets used fake crowd noise for the radio broadcast.[5]

Texas was football country. Bud Adams, the owner of the NFL's Houston Oilers, told Patterson and anybody else who would listen that basketball would never make it in Houston.[6] The team scheduled an appearance for the players at a mall to generate interest. Nobody talked to them. After two hours, a little old lady approached and said, "Oh my God, I love you guys, I love you." They signed autographs for her and posed for a picture. Then the woman asked, "How do you guys fit into those spaceships?" She thought they were astronauts.[7]

The Rockets brought in Patterson and traded Hayes after that first season. In their second year in Houston (1972–73), they reduced their home courts to Hofheinz Pavilion and HemisFair Arena in San Antonio. "The good news was that we drew large crowds to HemisFair Arena," recalled Rudy Tomjanovich. "The bad news was that those crowds generally cheered for the other team."[8] In 1973–74, they played before less than 3,000 spectators at home games eleven times, and only 2,160 showed up at Hofheinz for the home opener in 1974–75.[9]

The Rockets went through a series of owners and were placed in receivership after one of them, Irv Kaplan, filed for bankruptcy in 1975.[10] The franchise's fortunes began to turn that year when they moved into a permanent home in a new arena called The Summit. Then they were thrown a lifeline by the NBA-ABA "merger" when each NBA team received $700,000 in cash from the ABA teams joining the league. That was enough to keep the Rockets afloat and convince the holding company to add Malone.[11]

Patterson believed the franchise would have folded or moved had it been located in any other city. Houston was a boom town in the '70s, with people making millions overnight on oil. Development was rapid, and real estate prices soared. Optimism and a sense of adventure were in the air.[12] Moses joined a franchise that had experienced as much turnover as he had, though he shared the hope and resilience of his new city. The two would grow together.

Houston was a welcoming environment for Malone. The Rockets paid a significant price to acquire him and were invested in his future. In Nissalke and assistant Del Harris, he had coaches who cared about him and believed in his abilities. He and John Lucas, whom the Rockets drafted months earlier, moved into the same apartment complex and became close friends.[13] Nissalke also brought in Goo Kennedy, Malone's buddy from the Stars.[14]

Moses had support off the court as well. His aunt Naomi and cousin Diane moved from Petersburg to Houston during his early teen years. Moses stayed with them in the Fifth Ward neighborhood the summer before his junior year of high school and contemplated relocating to Houston to play for powerhouse Wheatley High School.[15] Naomi served as a surrogate mother for him, and Diane was the sister he never had.

Moses joined a Rockets team that had never posted a winning record, though suddenly the future looked bright in Houston. The NBA of the 1960s and '70s was dominated by big men. Oscar Robertson in 1964 was the only noncenter to win the MVP award between 1960 and 1980. The other key component to a successful team was a point guard who could run the offense. Over a few months, the Rockets acquired dynamic prospects at both positions in Malone and Lucas.

Lucas was a pass-first point guard who ignited the offense by delivering timely passes to the team's shooters. He also brought enthusiasm to the locker room, pumping up guys before games and pulling Moses out of his shell.[16] Calvin Murphy was an explosive scorer despite his diminutive 5-foot-9 frame. Malone would later call him the greatest shooter he ever played with.[17] He was joined in the backcourt by another sharpshooter in Mike Newlin, and All-Star Rudy Tomjanovich had excellent range for a forward.

Malone's new teammates were curious about the twenty-one-year-old with the big Afro. They noticed his unusually small hands and wondered if he would play forward or center. He remained a mystery for much of his first season in Houston, slow to let down his guard after being discarded by Portland and Buffalo.[18]

It was easy to forget that Malone was only twenty-one and just two years removed from high school. Developmentally, he was the equivalent of a junior in college. His game was still raw, and he lacked fundamentals. He didn't position his feet wide enough apart to create a solid base when battling for position, routinely dribbled after grabbing an offensive rebound rather than going right back up with the ball, and released layups from his hip instead of above his head.[19]

The one thing the Rockets agreed on was that the man could jump. "There are bigger players in the league and ones who can jump higher," said Murphy, but no one elevated quicker, he concluded. Most players squat before leaping. Moses barely flexed his knees, which enabled him to come down and go back up again faster than anybody else.[20]

Nissalke focused primarily on the guards and Harris the big men, though the head coach often worked one-on-one with Malone after practice. In one drill, he threw the ball at the basket, and Moses had to grab the rebound and dunk it 20 times in a row without stopping. Sweat poured from his face as Nissalke told him to do the drill again, pointing out that he had to learn to push through fatigue late in games.[21]

It took a few months for Nissalke to figure out how to best utilize Moses. He initially brought Malone off the bench as a backup to center Kevin Kunnert. After a couple weeks, he began starting Moses and Kunnert together against big lineups, with Moses guarding power forwards. In early December, Moses took over the center position, and Kunnert moved to the bench.

Initially, Malone was ineffective offensively. His confidence appeared shaken after being shuffled around two leagues. He held the ball down low where guards could swipe at it and dribbled too much. He also shot poorly from the free-throw line. It was his defense that impressed the coaches early in the season. He had 7 blocked shots, including one in the closing seconds to win the game against Philadelphia on December 29.

Hoping for more stability at center, Nissalke reinserted Kunnert into the lineup and moved Moses back to power forward in January. The move jump-started Malone's game. No longer required to bang with the opponent's biggest player, he was free to roam on defense and block shots. Power forwards struggled to keep him off the backboards.

Despite the youngster's up-and-down play, Nissalke consistently praised him to the press. "I think Moses has got the potential to be another Bill Russell," the coach said in December. "He's probably the fastest guy on our squad. Calvin Murphy is the quickest, but in a 100-yard dash it would be Moses."[22]

Malone gradually rediscovered the form that made him an All-Star in his rookie season. His shooting percentage skyrocketed in March and April, and he began pummeling teams on the glass, repeatedly topping the 20-rebound mark. In early March he outscored and outrebounded the great Kareem Abdul-Jabbar in a Rockets win over the Lakers.[23] A few nights later, Moses contributed 19 points and 21 rebounds against the Nets. "That's as good a domination of a game as I've seen this year," said Nets coach Kevin Loughery.[24]

The Rockets found their groove over the final two months of the season, winning nine-consecutive games in March. They finished atop the Central Division with a record of 49-33. "They're the success story of the league," said 76ers general manager Pat Williams. "Six months ago, they had no ownership, there was worry that the league would have to assume operation of the franchise. All of a sudden, it all just completely turned around."[25] Nissalke was named Coach of the Year.

Moses averaged 13.5 points and 13.4 rebounds (third in the league behind Abdul-Jabbar and Walton) and ranked seventh in blocked shots, while playing just thirty minutes per game. He also set an NBA record for offensive rebounds with 437, shattering Paul Silas's record of 365.[26]

The Rockets received a bye in the first round of the playoffs and faced a Washington Bullets squad featuring Wes Unseld and Elvin Hayes in the second round. Houston lost Game One, then evened the series behind 31 points and 26 rebounds (15 offensive) from Malone. Washington won Game Three, followed by three consecutive Houston wins to close out the series. Malone averaged 19.5 points and 16.7 rebounds against Washington, prompting Bullets coach Dick Motta to say he "is going to be a dominant force in this league."[27]

The Rockets faced a stacked 76ers team in the Eastern Conference Finals in a contrast of styles. The 76ers pushed the ball up the court and relied on the speed and scoring ability of forwards Julius Erving and George McGinnis, whereas the Rockets played at a slower pace, utilizing Malone's and Kunnert's size. One Philly sportswriter compared the matchup to a cheetah versus a water buffalo.[28]

Philly pulled out a hard-fought six-game series. The final game hinged on a dubious charge call against Lucas in the final seconds of a two-point game. The Rockets believed they were robbed of an opportunity to win the championship. Philly lost to Portland in the Finals. Houston won three of four games against Portland that season and would have had home-court advantage in the series.[29]

Moses's offense was inconsistent against the 76ers, though his performance in the Bullets series was enough to establish him as a budding star. "In that Washington series, we truly began to see the form that would eventually turn Malone into an MVP," wrote Tomjanovich in his autobiography. "Moses had shown flashes throughout the regular season, but now he was, at times, dominating the likes of Elvin Hayes and Wes Unseld. The maturity Moses gained in that first year with the Rockets was amazing. We all had the feeling this was indeed a Moses who could take us to the promised land."[30]

Moses returned to Petersburg for the summer as he had after his first two professional seasons. He stayed at his mother's house and met up with Gholson and his boys from the Heights. They played ball at Lee Park with his high school teammates and some younger guys. Petersburg native Mark West, who later played in the NBA, was five years younger than Moses and in awe of him. He couldn't believe that one of the best players in the NBA showed up at his park and played with him and his friends. "He's just playing for the love of the game and the love of the neighborhood and his hometown," recalled West.[31] Moses stopped by the courts at Farmer Street and Mackenzie Street as well, where he taught young kids the fundamentals of the game.[32]

It was evident to anybody who encountered him how much he loved basketball. If he was in town during the season, he'd attend a Hopewell or Petersburg game with Gholson or drive up to Richmond to catch a VCU game.[33] He followed the local high school and college teams in Houston too.[34] During the season, when teammates went home to rest after a long practice, Moses stuck around the gym to play one-on-one with Newlin, or H-O-R-S-E with a rookie.[35] It was that extraordinary love of the game that convinced teammates Moses would achieve greatness.

Big Mo, as they called him, took on a leadership role in his second season in Houston. Robert Reid was one of the rookies to participate in summer league. Moses showed up to get in some extra work and encouraged Reid from the start. The rookie was a longshot to make the team, though he impressed Nissalke enough to earn an invitation to veteran's camp. Malone's locker was across from Reid's, and he regularly exhorted the rookie on. "Reid, just work hard," he'd say. "Just work hard. I like your game. Big Mo likes your game. Just work hard." It was a tremendous boost for the youngster.[36]

Phil Bond, Houston's third-round pick, was also inspired by Malone. The rookie had never seen a player compete with such intensity. "You almost had the confidence to shoot because if you missed there was a real good chance he was gonna get the offensive rebound," he said. The Rockets took some of their players to the Dominican Republic before the start of the season. Bond was standing on the sideline during practice when Moses grabbed him from behind and started wrestling him. The gesture made him feel welcome. When the players drove around the island, Moses stuck his head out of the car and hollered at women. Bond was struck by the contrast between the two sides of Moses: the focused professional and the juvenile clown.[37]

The Rockets had lofty expectations for the 1977–78 season after advancing to the conference finals. They returned the same nucleus, with Reid, a pleasant surprise out of St. Mary's University, joining the rotation. Houston began the season 6-12, including nine losses in ten games in late November. Nissalke moved Kunnert to the bench and introduced new plays designed to create more scoring opportunities.[38] The Rockets responded with three wins in four games.

Then the team flew to L.A. to play the Lakers on December 9. Early in the third quarter, Kunnert and Lakers forward Kermit Washington engaged in a scuffle in the backcourt. Rudy Tomjanovich was filling the lane on the fast break when he heard whistles blow and turned around to see Abdul-Jabbar grabbing Kunnert from behind while Washington continued to swing at him. Rudy ran toward the action. Washington saw him out of the corner of his eye, reared back and punched him in the face.[39]

Tomjanovich crumbled to the floor in a pool of his own blood. C. J. Kupec, a backup forward on the Rockets, saw yellow stuff oozing from Rudy's head, which turned out to be spinal fluid.[40] The punch shattered bones in his face and nearly killed him. Tomjanovich's teammates were horrified. He was respected in the locker room as the longest-tenured Rocket, along with Murphy. The injury hung like a pall over the rest of their season.

Moses produced some sensational performances, including 39 points and 26 rebounds (16 offensive) in a November 16 loss to the Braves. "They ought to find a new league for Moses," said Braves coach Cotton Fitzsimmons. "They ought to take him out of the NBA and find him someplace to play where the rest of the people are immortals like he is. There's no one in this league who can play with him. I just haven't seen anything quite like what he did tonight."[41] Malone failed to string together those types of performances and turned in some disappointing results, particularly on the road, where he appeared to be uncharacteristically unfocused at times. Despite the team's struggles and his inconsistent play, Moses was selected to his first NBA All-Star Game.

Big Mo began experiencing soreness in his right foot in mid-February. He sat out a game against the Pistons on February 22. The swelling went down, and he returned to the lineup against the Nets on the 24th. Late in the first half, he turned to Murphy on the bench and said, "Murph, I broke my foot."

Murphy responded, "What do you mean your foot's broken? You have like 13 rebounds."[42]

Moses finished with 28 points and 24 rebounds. Sure enough, he'd been playing with a stress fracture in his right foot and was out for the rest of the season. Moses lived by the old-school mentality that one should show up for work every day, regardless of the circumstances. Throughout his career he played through broken bones, badly sprained ankles, the flu, and other ailments.

He was the sixth Rocket to break a bone that season. Houston went into a tailspin and finished 28-54. Moses averaged 19.4 points and 15.0 rebounds (second only to Truck Robinson) and led the league in total offensive rebounds even though he missed twenty-three games. After four years of professional experience, which he referred to as his "college years," Malone was on the threshold of stardom.

12

Chairman of the Boards

Shortly after Moses's first season with the Rockets, he found himself sitting next to a beautiful woman named Marilyn Hartfield on a flight to Houston. The two started talking, and Moses asked her out on a date. Marilyn, an eighth-grade science teacher at Furr High School in Houston, said, "I'll tell you what. My favorite student is flunking my class. If you talk to him and get him to get his grades up, I'll go on a date with you." That student's name was Floy Johnson.

Moses agreed and told Marilyn to have Floy meet him at Fonde Recreation Center, where he worked out in the offseason. The fourteen-year-old showed up early and waited for Moses on the first row of bleachers. Moses walked in and asked, "Are you Floy Johnson?" The two talked. Moses had his date with Marilyn, though nothing came of it. Instead, he gained a sidekick.

Moses invited Floy to hang out at his house on numerous occasions. When the boy turned sixteen, he began joining Moses at the clubs. They hit on women together, leading to some wild nights. Floy did favors for Moses, like driving him to the airport and cleaning out his garage, and became a regular in the Rockets locker room. People started calling him "Lil Mo." Some of Moses's teammates and friends resented having a high school kid around, but Moses didn't care. Floy was his boy.

Floy's friendship with Moses opened doors for him. Floy drove Darryl Dawkins to the club one night and entertained the 76ers center until Moses arrived. Years later, he was invited to one of Michael Jordan's exclusive card games after Jordan and Malone's teams faced off. In 1985 Moses introduced him to Heisman Trophy winner Mike Rozier. Rozier suggested that Floy should become a sports promoter, given his connections. He went on to have a successful career with the support of Rozier and Malone.

In high school, Floy befriended a boy a few years older named Leonard Mitchell from Booker T. Washington High School. "Big Mitch" played basketball and football at the University of Houston before spending six seasons in the NFL. He also hooped at Fonde Rec Center with Moses during the summer. When Floy was in tenth grade, he hung out with Mitchell at the U of H dorm called The Towers. Moses began spending a lot of time there as well.

He was in the dorm lobby during the fall semester of 1978 with his friend Stretch Campbell when a beautiful Alpha Kappa Alpha sorority sister named Alfreda Gill caught his eye. Moses struck up a conversation with her and got her number. Stretch and Moses usually spoke daily, though several days passed without Stretch hearing from his friend. When Moses finally called, he said he'd been shacked up with Alfreda.[1] It was Moses's sense of humor that initially attracted her to him.[2] Before long, she was driving around campus in Moses's black Porsche 928.[3]

Alfreda was one of seven siblings from a middle-class family in Dickinson, Texas. Her father, Louis Gill, served on the city council for many years and eventually became mayor pro tem.[4] Mr. Gill grew up on a ranch and kept cows, chickens, and horses on his property when Alfreda was a child. Moses liked to tell the story about the first time he went to Alfreda's house. He was sitting on the green couch in the den when he looked out the window and saw one of Mr. Gill's prized bulls staring at him.

Alfreda's cousin Kirk Williams visited the Gill home while on break from college during December 1978. He was surprised to see Alfreda ironing and folding an extremely long pair of pants. They belonged to Moses, who attended the family gathering. The Gills treated him like one of their own, and as the only child of a single mother, he enjoyed being part of a big family.[5] Alfreda gave birth to their first child, Moses Malone Jr., on December 12, 1979.

Houston had become home. Moses moved into a townhouse in the southwest part of the city and filled it with plants and artwork. There was a painting of him in his high school uniform that had been presented to him on Moses Malone Day. The centerpiece of the living room captured the essence of Moses, simple on the surface but with hidden complexity. It was a large painting of a woman's naked backside, though when examined closely it revealed the profile of Abraham Lincoln.[6]

After four years of professional experience, Malone was primed for greatness. He'd refined his game, eliminating the excessive dribbling and wasted movements. He also added an eight-to-ten-foot jumper and a hook shot to his repertoire.

Basketball players in the 1970s didn't do much weight training. It was believed that too much mass would negatively impact flexibility and accuracy. Moses found a trainer at a small gym in the basement of an office building whom he worked out with four days a week. He didn't tell anybody about it.[7] He bulked up to 235 pounds by the start of the 1978–79 season, ready to withstand the pounding that comes with playing center in the NBA.[8] Kevin Kunnert had signed with the Celtics, so Malone would be receiving more time in the pivot.

Offensive rebounding continued to be the skill that separated him from his peers. Before the three-point shot took over the game, half-court basketball was contained in a tight space around the basket. Players shot close to the rim, leading to short rebounds. Offensive players were boxed out by the defense and had to battle through a scrum of hulking bodies to gain position to secure the ball.

Opponents were in awe of how the ball seemed to gravitate toward Moses's hands, as if attracted by a magnet. It was all by design. Malone saw the court like an engineer sees a grid, dividing it into quadrants while assessing angles.[9] Long before the use of analytics and spatial technology, he compiled a mental database on shooting trends and his teammates' tendencies.

He explained his thought process to George White of the *Houston Chronicle* in January 1979:

> Most shooters at this level are going to hit the rim. Most of the good shooters will hit the top of the rim and go in. But you've got to study the guys to learn how they shoot to know where the ball likely will go if they miss. Most of the really good shooters will miss long, especially the ones with those soft arching floaters that sort of glide up there. You've got to know if a player shoots a flat shot or shoots with an arch. Naturally you know the guys on your team better so you ought to have an advantage right there on offensive rebounding. For example, I know that Rudy T shoots a flat shot that will probably bounce back,

> and Murph shoots with an arch, so I play the ball to come off the rim a little differently depending on who's shooting.[10]

Carroll Dawson, a Rockets assistant coach, couldn't comprehend how a player with small hands who wasn't among the highest leapers in the league—his weight gain decreased his vertical leap a bit—continuously pulled down so many rebounds. He studied the big man, and what jumped out at him were Malone's feet. "He was like a boxer," said Dawson. "His feet kept moving when the ball went up. Big guys would just stand there and when the ball got over them, they would jump again. Moses's feet were constantly moving until he had the ball." Dawson began teaching his players to keep their feet moving when they pursued rebounds.[11]

The instant a shot was released, Moses began calculating the probabilities and moving into place while following the trajectory of the ball. Then he fought for the best position possible. One technique he employed was to come from the baseline under the basket and use his backside to push defenders out of position. Once the shot ricocheted off the basket, Moses elevated quicker than his opponents and often contorted his body at unusual angles. Sometimes it appeared as if he was moving sideways in the air while slithering through tight spaces.

Though he had small hands for his size and struggled to hold onto the ball at times below his waist, he had no trouble snatching it out of the air with his arms above his head. "Moses' hands are like flypaper when he gets up there for a rebound," said Mike Newlin. "It's almost like a frog's tongue nailing an insect. Even though his body is twisted and contorted, he gets those arms out quicker than any man I have ever seen."[12] In the event that he wasn't able to snag the ball, he'd tip it to himself in the air or off the glass, come down and go back up again, two, three, four times, if necessary, until he could grab it. His added strength enabled him to fend off centers and hold his position.

Some of his peers speculated that he missed shots on purpose to pad his rebound stats. He offered conflicting answers to that question over the years. Most, if not all, of the time, he threw the ball off the backboard to gain better position and make it easier for him to score once he grabbed it again. If he did in fact occasionally miss on purpose, it's remarkable that he was able to do so successfully against elite competition.

Ultimately, most basketball insiders agreed that for all of Moses's skill, intelligence, athleticism, and quickness, the quality that made him the greatest offensive rebounder ever was his desire. He simply wanted the ball more than anybody else and attacked the glass with a hunger that those who grew up with a full refrigerator couldn't understand. "Anybody can shoot a jump shot," he told Frank Deford of *Sports Illustrated*. He took pride in outworking the competition for the ball.[13]

"I've coached two great offensive rebounders in my pro career—Paul Silas and John Drew," said Kansas City coach Cotton Fitzsimmons. "Silas was a great tipper and Drew was a great catcher. They both wanted the ball. But neither of them wanted it as badly as Moses does. That's where you start when you discuss Moses Malone—his overwhelming desire." Silas and Drew were forwards, as are many of the great offensive rebounders. They tend to be more agile than the lumbering centers and can rebound across a wider radius. Most centers wait for the ball to come to them. Moses went and got it.

"The one reason he is the greatest is because he will go after 150 rebounds a game," said Del Harris. "His percentage isn't any better than a lot of players. But he gets 20 out of those 150. Other rebounders go after 20 and get five or six. Moses pursues a minimum of 100 a game. He doesn't forfeit any rebound unless it's just a totally hopeless situation."[14]

Malone's tenacity on the glass was so overwhelming that opponents resorted to animal metaphors to describe it. "You feel like you're trying to box out an octopus," Caldwell Jones of the 76ers said.[15] Otto Moore, an opposing center who befriended Moses later in life, told Malone that he reminded him of a wolf. "Once a wolf get on the hunt, they don't stop until they get the prey," Moore said. "You're like a wolf, once the game start you're relentless."[16] When asked about his rebounding prowess, Moses simply said, "I goes to the rack."[17]

Moses never seemed to tire, no matter how many bodies were thrown at him or how physical the game. And he relished the contact. "When I'm moving no one can block me out consistently," Malone said. "And when there's a lot of contact and bumping around, I just get stronger. There's some guys who can block me out for two or three quarters, but I'm just waiting for that big quarter to come. I'm patient."[18]

Players and coaches referred to him as the "James Brown of basketball," the hardest-working man in the game, and he sweat like it. Moses worked himself into a froth sitting at his locker before heading out for warmups.[19] There would be a huge puddle on the floor after he worked out on an exercise bike, and ball boys ran out with multiple towels to wipe up the foul line every time he shot a free throw. During breaks in the action, a ball boy brought a tray of water into the huddle. Moses would drink the whole thing himself, five or ten cups at a time.[20]

The 20-and-10 scoring and rebounding nights turned into 30-and-20 games during the 1978–79 season. Moses was working so hard that Elvin Hayes of the Bullets predicted he'd burn out by January. He only grew stronger. The Rockets played Abdul-Jabbar and the Lakers on January 19. The day before, Moses hung around after practice for an extended run of one-on-one. Then he accumulated 34 points and 25 rebounds in fifty minutes against Abdul-Jabbar in an overtime win.[21]

Dick Vitale left the University of Detroit to become coach of the Detroit Pistons in 1978. His star player was Bob Lanier, a Hall of Famer known for his toughness. Before a game against Malone and the Rockets, Lanier pulled Vitale aside and said, "Dick, get some backups ready because this guy [Malone] wears you out." The coach was shocked to hear that from a fierce competitor like Lanier. Vitale and Moses had a chance to catch up briefly before the game. "Remember Mary, my mother?" Malone asked Vitale. "She was working in those houses as a maid helping everybody in those big homes." Vitale nodded. Malone said, "Dick, she's not working there anymore. She lives there."[22]

On February 9 Malone grabbed 37 rebounds against the Jazz, 19 of them offensive. "This league hasn't seen a performance like that since Wilt," said Murphy in the locker room after the game.[23] Nine days later, Malone scored a then career-high 45 points in a loss to the Nets.

Prior to that season, Moses had been relatively unknown for a player of his stature. He missed out on a national profile that comes from playing college basketball and spent two seasons in the underpublicized ABA. The Rockets were still a relatively new team without much national or local exposure playing in a football city.

Moses's style of play didn't lend itself to highlight reels. His performances weren't punctuated by rim-rattling dunks or fancy passes. He was like a waterfall, a constant flow of energy with no beginning or end, quarter after quarter, game after game. There were no breaks in his effort to contrast with his relentless pursuit of the ball, resulting in each offensive rebound and score blending together in the minds of those watching.

After the Jazz game in which he snared 37 rebounds, Newlin said, "He does it so quietly you don't even notice." New teammate Rick Barry concurred: "I wasn't even aware of what he was accomplishing. You just get so accustomed to see Moses do this kind of stuff. I knew he was getting almost every missed shot, but it seems like he ALWAYS does that."[24]

Moses didn't draw attention to himself. He stepped on the court with a warrior mentality, always on high alert, ready to pounce, and unwilling to allow anything to break his concentration. Big Mo walked slightly hunched over and paced around the court like a bear prowling his turf. The determined expression on his face rarely changed. He didn't make elaborate hand gestures or release a primal scream after a basket, and his limited trash-talking consisted of brief utterances under his breath. His opponents usually didn't understand what he said, anyway.[25]

Reporters and fans couldn't help but notice as Moses compiled staggering numbers during the 1978–79 season. He was voted a starter in the All-Star Game by both the players and fans and was featured on the cover of *Sports Illustrated* in February with the title "Chairman of the Boards." *The Sporting News* also featured a cover story on him that month.

Malone's breakout season wasn't accompanied by the team success management had envisioned. The Rockets pursued free agent Rick Barry in the summer of 1978. The forward had been one of the best players in the game, a brilliant passer who could score from anywhere on the court. Patterson also believed Barry would put fans in the seats after the Rockets' attendance plummeted during the disappointing 1977–78 season.[26] Barry was insulted by the contract the Warriors offered him and thought he could win a championship in Houston.[27] League rules mandated that the Rockets provide the Warriors compensation for Barry, who had averaged 23.1 points per game the previous season. The teams attempted to reach a settlement. Warriors general manager Scotty Stirling requested Moses and John Lucas. The Rockets were thinking more along the lines of draft picks and cash. Barry was a surefire Hall of Famer but at thirty-four years old was on the downside of his career. After six weeks of negotiations, the two sides were at a stalemate, and commissioner O'Brien asked them to submit written recommendations.[28]

Nissalke was devastated when O'Brien awarded the Warriors Lucas. The coach believed it wasn't fair to equate a thirty-four-year-old with a budding twenty-four-year-old. Barry had been excited to play with Lucas and claimed he wouldn't have signed with Houston if he knew the point guard wouldn't be there.[29] The Rockets were still excited about pairing Moses and Barry.

Houston missed Lucas's creativity; although it began the season 5-1, it then lost eleven of the next sixteen to fall below .500. Barry's legs were starting to go, and he was forced to play as more of a distributor than a scorer. He believes that was the most talented team he ever played for and blamed poor coaching for its lack of success.[30]

There were periods when it looked like the Rockets were coming together, but they proved to be unsustainable. Houston finished the season 47-35, a game behind San Antonio in the Central Division, then lost the first two games of a best-of-three playoff series with Atlanta. "I honestly believe that if we had been able to keep him [Lucas], we would have had a good chance at the league championship," said Nissalke.[31]

Moses was named the NBA's Most Valuable Player. He led the league in minutes played at 3,390 (41.2 per game), finished fourth in scoring at 24.8 points per game, and posted a league-leading 17.6 rebounds per game. He grabbed 587 offensive rebounds (a record that still stands today), 250 more than the second-place finisher.

It was arguably the greatest rebounding season in NBA history to that point. Chamberlain and Russell regularly averaged over 20 per game, with Wilt setting the mark at 27.2 in 1960–61. But teams played at a faster pace and shot a lower percentage during Chamberlain and Russell's careers, leading to many more rebound opportunities. Russell's Celtics regularly averaged well over 70 per game. Wilt's Philadelphia Warriors averaged 75.2 rebounds per game in 1960–61. His record 27.2 accounted for 36.2 percent of the team's total. When Moses secured 17.6 per game in 1978–79, it accounted for 38.4 percent of the Rockets' 45.9 rebounds.[32] Big Mo was truly the Chairman of the Boards.

13

Four Guys from Petersburg

The Rockets' public-address announcer introduced the players before their home opener for the 1979–80 season. He concluded with, "And now, the NBA's Most Valuable Player, Moses Malone." The crowd erupted. Moses posted 44 points and 29 rebounds in a win over the Pacers. After the game, he quietly asked the public-address announcer to introduce him as just Moses Malone, without the superlatives.[1]

Big Mo had signed a contract extension a few months earlier, which according to his agent, Lee Fentress, made him the "highest paid player in team sports." Estimates ranged from $800,000 to $1 million per year. George Maloof, a businessman from Albuquerque, New Mexico, bought the Rockets in May 1979, and he and Fentress hammered out a two-year extension that would keep Moses in Houston through the 1981–82 season. Fentress believed it was prudent to keep Malone's options open for another big payday by signing a short-term deal.[2]

"The money doesn't change anything," said Malone. "It just changes what you can get."[3] His humility baffled those around him. "There isn't a guy on the team who is easier to work with," said Rockets trainer Dick Vandervoort, who was also tasked with arranging team hotels, flights, and buses. "You would never know he's a superstar. He never misses a bus, he never misses a plane, he's always on time for practice. He endures the rough travel like the lowest rookie on the team, and you never hear a beep from him."[4]

Paul Mokeski, a rookie that season, couldn't believe that the reigning MVP treated him, a lowly second-round draft pick, as an equal. Moses took the time to teach Mokeski life skills such as how to check into a hotel or tip a porter at the airport. The rookie learned from Moses that you should never act as if you're better than anybody, a lesson he instilled in his children and the players he later coached.[5]

The jokes flowed freely when Moses was comfortable with those around him. There was a childish side to him that derived great pleasure from juvenile locker room pranks. He'd tell a rookie that he left his bag on the bus and ask the player to retrieve it for him. There wouldn't be a bag on the bus.[6] He'd hide teammates' shoes or jerseys and delight in their fruitless searches.[7] During a trip to Portland, he used the trainer's tape to mummify the hotel room doors of some teammates, resulting in them nearly missing the bus in the morning.

One summer, Moses and some of his buddies played a charity game at Boston Garden. In the locker room, he told the guys that Mel Hughlett would lead them onto the court. Mel had some family in the crowd and swelled with pride. The team gathered at the end of the tunnel near the entrance to the court, put their hands in the middle, and chanted, "One, two, three, huh!" Hughlett ran onto the court. Then he turned around and saw that nobody had followed him. Moses held everyone back.[8]

Other times Malone's humor was more biting. He was quick with one-liners—"little darts," Newlin called them. Calvin Murphy was one of his favorite targets. Upon hearing that the Rockets would be hosting a Calvin Murphy Night in March 1978, Moses asked, "What are they going to do, bury Murph at halfcourt?"[9] Maloof bought a twenty-foot-high fake rocket that emitted fog and was covered in lights. He wanted the players to run through it during introductions. "I think you oughta put Murphy in it and shoot him to the moon," Moses quipped. The big fella was frustrated with Murphy's shot selection, and that was his humorous way of getting his point across.[10] When Mo won the MVP award, he thanked Murphy and Tomjanovich for missing so many shots so that he could put them back in.[11]

Reggie Theus, who played with Moses later in his career, thought Big Mo had "the most fucked up laugh," along with Bill Russell. Russell had a high-pitched cackle. Theus referred to Moses's laugh as an "under-the-breath cackle."[12] To some it sounded like a hearty rumble emanating from his chest. Moses often started cracking up in the middle of his jokes. He was difficult to understand to begin with, and it was almost impossible to pick up the punch line while he was laughing. Teammates were amused by his laughter even if they didn't comprehend the joke.[13]

As soon as an outsider, especially a reporter, entered the room, Moses immediately flipped to his quiet and evasive persona. He referred to the beat writers who covered the Rockets for the *Houston Chronicle* and *Houston Post* as "Chronicle" and "Post" instead of by name and often replied to questions with "no comment" or by essentially rephrasing the question.[14] If asked, "Do you think your offensive rebounds helped turn around the game in the fourth quarter," he'd answer, "Yeah, I think my offensive rebounds helped turn around the game in the fourth quarter."[15]

Maloof's first move as owner was to replace Nissalke with Del Harris. He offered Nissalke the general manager position, but Nissalke left to become the first coach of the Utah Jazz. Patterson stayed on as GM. Harris was prematurely gray and had a professorial air about him. He was a cerebral coach prone to delivering lengthy monologues at practice. He'd been working with the big men in Houston for years, and Malone was comfortable with him.

The Rockets added Tom Henderson and rookie Allen Leavell at point guard. They also signed Major Jones, a forward who'd played in other professional leagues since graduating college in 1976. Major was one of eight siblings from the Jones family of McGehee, Arkansas. Six of them, including Major, played basketball at Albany State University, and three of Major's brothers, Wilbert, Caldwell, and Charles, also made it to the NBA.

Major knew Moses through Caldwell, and they played ball together during the summers at Fonde. Now teammates, they became best friends. Major's family adopted Moses as an honorary brother. Moses attended Jones family gatherings, where he referred to himself as "Moses Malone Jones." Major and Moses called each other's mothers "momma," and Moses traveled for the funerals of Major's parents and siblings. If somebody asked Moses, "Aren't you Moses Malone," he usually said, "No, I'm Major Jones" or "My name is Mike Williams." If he was with Jones, he'd point to him and say, "That's Moses Malone."[16]

Harris infused creativity into the Rockets' attack. He even introduced a play where a guard threw the ball off the backboard so Moses could grab it and put it in.[17] But the coach's options were limited. Houston traded Newlin to the Nets prior to the season, and Barry and Tomjanovich were showing their age. The team had trouble scoring and hovered around .500.

Moses made the 1980 All-Star Game, where his Eastern Conference squad pulled out a hard-fought win. The Rockets' center had been relatively quiet throughout regulation, then dominated Kareem in overtime. He finished with 20 points and 12 rebounds. It was evident as he iced his ankle after the game that he didn't treat it as an exhibition. "No game is fun," he told reporters. "Basketball at this level can't be fun when you're on the court with guys who are professionals. You don't have time to have fun. If someone pays money to see you, you are at work. I wish I could play in a game sometime that was fun, but that's not the way I play. Today I wanted to win. I was serious, and so was everybody else."[18]

Travel in the NBA in the 1970s and '80s was exhausting. Teams flew commercially, so players carried their own bags and waited at the gate like everybody else. If they had back-to-back games, they'd take the first flight out at six or seven the morning after the first game. Each team had stretches when they played three-consecutive nights.

Displeased with the team's performance in the final games of a long road trip, Harris called for practice as soon as they landed in Houston. Mokeski had been watching Moses play over forty minutes per game against the likes of Abdul-Jabbar and Lanier and decided to take it easy on him. He went about three-quarter speed. Midway through practice, Moses yelled at him. "Don't ever take it easy on me in practice. Nobody in the game takes it easy on me. And you can't take it easy in practice, cause you're preparing me to play these other guys." Even in his tired state, Big Mo wanted to be pushed.[19]

The following season, the Rockets endured a brutal stretch of four games in five days, including Friday night, Saturday night, and Sunday afternoon, in three different cities. Malone started off with a 41-point, 14-rebound effort against Chicago on Wednesday night. Friday night he scored 38 points with 12 rebounds in a loss at Phoenix. On Saturday, he tallied 26 points and 14 rebounds in a one-point loss at home to New York. Then he dragged his exhausted body on another flight to Denver, where the Rockets were transported directly to the arena for an afternoon game. Moses played forty-four minutes at high altitude, connected on 14 of 18 shots for 37 points, and pulled down 19 rebounds in the Rockets win. "I don't know when I've seen such a gutty performance under conditions like that," said Harris. For Moses, it was just another day of work.

"There is never an excuse for not being ready to play," Malone said. "If they wake you up at 4 in the morning to go play a game, you ought to be ready to go to work."[20]

Moses averaged 25.8 points and 14.5 rebounds for the '79–'80 season and was named to the Second Team All-NBA, behind Kareem, who won his sixth MVP award. The Rockets finished 41-41. They defeated the Spurs in a best-of-three first-round series, then were swept by the Celtics in the second round.

Houston moved to the Western Conference for the 1980–81 season and began the year with several home losses to bad teams. They lacked a dynamic playmaker on the perimeter who could shoot and drive to the basket. Without a wingman to share the load, Moses was "attracting more attention than Dolly Parton at a nudist camp," according to the *Houston Chronicle's* George White.[21]

Harris attempted to alleviate the burden on Malone by pairing him with 6-foot-11 center Billy Paultz, whom the Rockets acquired the previous season. Known as "The Whopper," Paultz was a three-time ABA All-Star who won a championship with the New York Nets. Harris began experimenting with the twin towers lineup in November against bigger teams and inserted Paultz into the starting lineup permanently on February 19.

The move paid immediate dividends for Malone. "It really takes a lot of pressure off me," Moses said. He continued:

> Billy is so physical; the other team just can't push me around like they do when he's not in there. And when he's playing the center, I'm matched up against a forward. I feel like I can overpower every forward in this league. When you're out there at forward, they can't risk putting two and three men on you. When you're right under the basket at center though, it's very easy for the other team to double and triple team you. It's awfully difficult when you're fighting through three guys trying to get to the basket.[22]

Houston lost its first game with the Malone-Paultz tandem to fall to 28-33. Then the Rockets rattled off five-consecutive wins, followed by five-straight losses, then three-straight wins and three more losses. On

March 20 they were 36-41, one game behind the Kings for the final playoff spot. They won four of their last five and snuck into the playoffs as the sixth seed, with a 40-42 record. Moses averaged a league-high 14.8 rebounds and finished second in scoring with 27.8 points per game.

Houston faced the defending-champion Lakers in a first-round best-of-three miniseries. The Lakers were heavily favored, but Moses was the equalizer. "Kareem hated to see him [Moses] because he would kill him on the offense and defense," said Rocket guard Tom Henderson. "He would beat him up all night, so he knew he had to work against Moses, cause Moses was so physical."[23]

The Lakers preferred to run, so Houston slowed the game down and took a large percentage of its shots in the last five seconds of the shot clock. The Rockets stunned Kareem, Magic, and company by stealing Game One in Los Angeles behind 38 points and 23 rebounds from Malone. The Lakers overcame a 33-point, 15-rebound effort by Malone in Game Two to even the series and send it back to L.A. for a decisive Game Three.

Mike Dunleavy knocked down a fifteen-foot jumper to put the Rockets up 1 with fifteen seconds remaining in Game Three. Magic drove the length of the floor on the ensuing possession and attempted a scoop shot near the basket that fell short. Houston pulled off the shocking upset. Malone averaged 31.3 points and 17.1 rebounds in the three games compared to Abdul-Jabbar's 26.7 points and 16.7 and played all forty-eight minutes in each of the last two games after sitting just two minutes in Game One.

The Rockets' next opponent was the San Antonio Spurs, a 52-win team led by George Gervin and a physical front line known as "the Bruise Brothers." Houston won Game One in San Antonio, followed by a Spurs win in Game Two. At practice between Games Two and Three, Moses walked onto the court at the Summit with boxing gloves tied around his neck, ready for a fight, and delivered a vintage performance in Game Three.[24] Big Mo played all forty-eight minutes and pounded the Bruise Brothers into submission with 41 points and 15 rebounds. The Spurs won two of the next three games, setting up a Game Seven in San Antonio. Harris inserted Murphy, who had been coming off the bench since November, into the starting lineup, and Murph responded with 42 points to punch the Rockets' ticket to the Western Conference Finals.

Next up was the Kings, which also finished 40-42. Before the series, Moses walked around the airport gate with his chest thrust forward inviting teammates to ask about his shirt. It was a white pullover with a big *M* on it and the word *Maryland* underneath. "The 'M' doesn't mean Maryland. It stands for 'money,'" Malone said. "I'm wearing it to remind me that each win means more money."[25]

The Rockets disposed of the Kings, 4-1. Moses contributed 36 points and 11 rebounds in the clincher, prompting Robert Reid to reflect on his greatness. "Someday, it's going to be an honor to sit down and tell my grandkids what it was like to play basketball with Moses Malone," said Reid. "You hear guys talk about how it was to play alongside Wilt, Russell, Mikan. We on the Houston Rockets are playing alongside a guy who might one day be recognized as greater than all of them."[26]

The 40-42 Rockets were headed to the NBA Finals. "Anyone caught a month ago believing they would have gained the final round would have been placed in a straitjacket without a hearing," wrote Ed Fowler of the *Houston Chronicle*. "And yet here they are smelling the roses."[27] They faced a Celtics squad that boasted a frontcourt of Larry Bird, Robert Parish, and Cedric Maxwell, with Kevin McHale coming off the bench. The starting guards were Chris Ford and future Hall of Famer Tiny Archibald. The Celtics had won their last thirteen matchups with the Rockets, including a four-game sweep in the playoffs the previous season.

Game One was tight throughout. Uncharacteristically, the Rockets were beaten on the offensive boards. Bird had 7 himself, including a spectacular one in the fourth quarter. He fired a shot from about 20 feet on the right side of the floor. Immediately realizing it was off, he sprinted toward the baseline, grabbed the rebound, switched it to his left hand while in the air, and made a beautiful scoop shot before falling out of bounds. Celtics general manager Red Auerbach called it the greatest play he'd ever seen.[28] Another Bird offensive rebound and putback with eighteen seconds left sealed the game.

Game Two felt like a must-win for the Rockets, and tempers ran high during a timeout. Harris issued instructions and concluded by saying, "And Mo, you have to get on the boards, man!" Moses interpreted that as Harris questioning his effort and fired back, "Fuck you, coach!" Harris kept his cool and offered the perfect retort to diffuse the situation. "Mo, we can talk about our sex life after the game, but right now I need you to get some rebounds!"[29] Big Mo played all forty-eight minutes, and his 31 points and 15 rebounds lifted the Rockets to victory, 92–90.

Boston thrashed Houston in Game Three. Then Houston evened the series in Game Four behind 24 points and 22 rebounds from Malone, who once again played all forty-eight minutes. Between Games Four and Five, Moses expressed his opinion that the Celtics weren't that good, adding, "I could get four guys off the street from back home in Petersburg and beat them."[30] The quote was out of character for Malone, who rarely exposed his feelings publicly. His teammates weren't pleased.[31] "Why poke the bear?" asked Tom Henderson years later.[32] But they supported the man who carried them to the Finals. "Hey, we ain't from Petersburg, but we're gonna ride with him," recalled Major Jones.[33]

Reid explained his interpretation of Malone's comment. "What happened to him [Malone] is what happened to all of us," said Reid. "We are all so sick of being ridiculed every time we pick up a newspaper and every time we turn on the TV. The people in the East have been unbelievable. We have been called a farce and a disgrace and all kind of trash. We've been treated like outcasts and given the same kind of respect you would give a man who broke into your house. The stuff that's been written and said about us, I think it has been disgraceful."

Reid added, "Moses is a very proud man, one of the proudest men I know. I know how proud he is of the basketball team and things we have accomplished, things which no one wants to give us credit for. You know, you can push a man and push a man until he finally breaks. That's what happened to Moses."[34] Malone was also physically and emotionally exhausted from banging with a cadre of bruising bodies over four playoff series.

The *Boston Globe* ran the quote in giant type, and Celtics coach Bill Fitch personally pasted a copy in the locker of every Boston player.[35] The Celtics took out their anger on the court, crashing the Rockets down to Earth, 109–80, in Game Five. They wrapped up the series in six.

Moses averaged 22.3 points and 15.7 rebounds against Boston but shot just 40 percent. Harris and Malone believed Houston was outworked, though there was a significant talent gap between the two teams, and Moses received little help from his teammates.[36] Still it was a remarkable achievement for the Rockets to make the Finals after a losing season. No team has done it since. They also set a record with eight playoff road victories.

A few days later, the Celtics attended a celebration at Boston's City Hall Plaza. Bird spotted a sign in the crowd that said, "MOSES EATS SHIT." He told the fans, "You're right, Moses does eat shit."[37]

14

King of Fonde

Hakeem Olajuwon walked into the office of Ganiyu Otenigbade, the high school basketball coach at Muslim Teachers College, in late 1979 and announced his desire to play basketball. He was months shy of his seventeenth birthday. Like most boys in Lagos, Nigeria, Olajuwon grew up playing soccer, though he'd recently moved on to handball. The basketball coaches watched him excel on the handball court and told him basketball was the sport for him. It's a big man's game, and Hakeem was 6 feet, 8 inches tall.

Olajuwon had never played basketball before. Coach Ganiyu taught him the basics, beginning with a layup. Step with your right foot, then your left, then release. Hakeem couldn't get the footwork down. Then Coach Ganiyu demonstrated proper shooting form, how to position yourself for a rebound, the way to use your pivot foot, and how to flick your wrists to pass the ball. Two days later, Hakeem participated in a tournament, after which Coach Ganiyu placed him on the Lagos State basketball team. That summer, Richard Mills, an American who coached the Nigerian national team, saw Olajuwon play. The boy had grown to 6 feet 11 and was remarkably agile for his height. Mills offered him a spot on the junior national team.[1]

The national team lost to the Central African Republic in a tournament in Angola that fall. After the game, Central Africa's coach, Christopher Pond, sought out Olajuwon. Pond was shocked to learn that he had started playing basketball months earlier and told Olajuwon he could land him a scholarship in the United States. Hakeem had never seen American basketball before, though he was excited about the opportunity to attend an American college. Pond was well connected in the basketball world. He made some calls and set up campus visits for Hakeem.[2]

A few weeks later, Olajuwon departed for the United States. The first school he tried out for was the University of Houston. Coach Guy Lewis saw his potential as he scrimmaged with the Cougars. Less than a year after picking up a basketball for the first time, Hakeem had a scholarship at an elite program in the United States.[3] U of H classes had been in session for a couple months when he arrived in October, so he enrolled for spring semester. Meanwhile, he worked out with the team. "We knew he'd get better," said teammate Clyde Drexler, "because he couldn't get any worse." Lewis decided to redshirt Hakeem for his first season.[4]

Olajuwon watched the Rockets on television and noticed their dominant center, Moses Malone. One night, Cougars assistant coach Terence Kirkpatrick told Hakeem, "You'll play against him this summer." "Really?" asked Hakeem. He couldn't believe Malone played with nonprofessionals. "Yeah," replied Kirkpatrick, "he plays at Fonde."[5]

Fonde Recreation Center is an unassuming one-story brick building just west of downtown Houston. The gym is dark, with dirty windows and no air conditioning in the humid Houston summers. There's one full court, divided by a blue curtain down the middle into two minicourts. In the '70s and '80s, one side held pickup games for anybody who wanted to play. The other was reserved for serious ballers.

The University of Houston basketball team began practicing at Fonde when its facility was under renovation in the mid-1960s. Cougar stars Elvin Hayes and Don Chaney were impressed by the talent there and began attending regularly. In the early 1970s the Rockets showed up.[6] By the time Moses arrived in Houston, Fonde's summer runs were among the best in the country. Many Houston Rockets, including Major Jones, Jacky Dorsey, Dwight Jones, Allen Leavell, Robert Reid, and Alonzo Bradley, were regulars in the late '70s and early '80s, along with college stars, like Ollie Taylor of the University of Houston, Carl Belcher of the University of Texas, George "Stretch" Campbell from Prairie View, and Dave Lattin of the legendary Texas Western national championship team. Tomjanovich, Calvin Murphy, and Elvin Hayes stopped by occasionally, as did NBA All-Stars, like George Gervin and Otis Birdsong, when they were in town.[7]

Angelo Cascio, a short former referee from Louisiana, was the center's evening recreation director and gatekeeper for the main court.[8] He protected the stars from the "rinky dinks," as he called them. College players and professionals weren't guaranteed entrance. "If you wanted to play, you had to go through Moses," said James Clayton, a longtime Fonde employee.[9] Moses would send word to Cascio.

Cascio picked six captains at the beginning of the night and determined which teams played first. Moses was always in the first game. The other captains, who had third, fourth, fifth, and sixth "ups," could select players from the teams that lost. Some nights, only eighteen or twenty players saw action. If someone lost a game, he might not get back on the court, so the competition was fierce.[10] The games started between 5:30 and 6:00 p.m. on Mondays and Wednesdays and ran until the gym closed at 9:00. One team was shirts, the other skins, and they played to 12 by ones.[11] Players called their own fouls, which led to arguments. If Moses called a foul, there was no discussion. Nobody challenged the King of Fonde.[12]

Malone set the tone for the games. "It wasn't pickup," said Olden Polynice, a fourteen-year NBA veteran, "because Moses made it so, because he wasn't out there to have fun per se. He was like, 'This is a workout.' So it was literally like a practice, like an NBA practice or NBA game. It was that intense."[13] Malone held everybody accountable, demanding excellence from his teammates and forcing opponents to match his intensity. One evening, Drexler was taking it to Robert Reid. "You better come on and play 'cause he's busting your ass," Malone told Reid. "And if he's busting your ass now, he's going to bust your ass in the season."[14]

Moses took young players under his wing. Herb Baker was a local kid who tagged along with his parents when they worked out at Fonde. He sprang to 6 feet 9, and when he was sixteen Moses invited him to play with the professionals. Malone taught him how to use his body against smaller players and quickness against bigger ones. Baker went on to play professionally overseas for sixteen years. He had tryouts with NBA teams but never made the cut. Malone always encouraged him to keep working.[15] Moses offered advice and encouragement to countless others. His greatest protégé was Olajuwon.

Hakeem joined his Cougar teammates at Fonde in the summer of 1981. The first thing he noticed were the cars in the parking lot: Mercedeses, Jaguars, and Porsches. Moses wasn't there for the first few weeks because the Rockets were in the Finals. When he arrived, Big Mo showed the young Nigerian no mercy. He shouted, "Be a man!" to Olajuwon as he bullied him in the post.[16] Hakeem was helpless. He'd never played against somebody that strong or quick.[17] He couldn't overpower Malone, so he built his game on agility and deception—spins, fakes, and double and triple pumps.

Off the court, Moses was gentle with Hakeem. The Rockets center poked fun at him in a playful way to make him feel like one of the guys. The two men were about the same size, so Malone arrived at Fonde with suits, pants, and shirts for the youngster. He handed Hakeem a wad of cash and said to let him know if he needed anything. Moses told reporters he was impressed by the Nigerian, which boosted Hakeem's confidence.[18]

Before and after games, Malone taught Hakeem a jump hook and a drop-step countermove. Hakeem grew frustrated with his inability to execute the hook shot. Malone calmly explained that it was a two-part drill. The first part was to make the shot, the second to grab the offensive rebound. If you missed your shot, it was an opportunity to work on your reaction time and grab the board. Rockets guard Mike Dunleavy witnessed Malone's explanation and later used it with players he coached in the NBA.[19]

The most important lesson Hakeem learned from Moses was resilience. "With Moses there were no rests, no breaks," Olajuwon said years later. "He was working every time down the court—scoring, rebounding or just making you feel his body. He would laugh when he slammed into you. If you tried to take a breath, he went by you or over you. There was no stop." While Hakeem's peers spent their summer competing against college players, he was learning from the best big man in the world.[20]

Hakeem and Moses resumed their battles at Fonde in the summer of 1982. One evening, Drexler missed a jumper from left of the free throw line. Hakeem grabbed the offensive rebound, took one dribble, and dunked with his right hand, while pulling Moses to the ground with his left. The players in attendance were so excited, they ran out of the gym. "Oh my God! Hakeem just dunked on Mo!" Moses picked himself up off the floor, looked at Hakeem and said, "About time. About time." Hakeem had learned to fight back.[21]

"Ain't no secrets about playing basketball," Malone said of tutoring Olajuwon. "Who wants the ball more? Who wants the shot? Who wants the rebound? Go get it. Don't matter if you play in the NBA or you're off a plane from Africa. It's the man who's the strongest, the man who won't give up on the play, the man who does more work."[22]

Moses advised Hakeem on whether to leave school early and how to choose an agent. He and Malone grabbed a bite to eat after their teams squared off in the NBA. But they were never close. Olajuwon blames himself. He was raised in a culture that emphasized respecting your elders. He kept Moses on a pedestal and was never able to view him as an equal.[23] Olajuwon won an MVP award and two championships in the NBA. "I would never have accomplished what I did if I did not play against Moses at Fonde," he said before being inducted into the Hall of Fame.

Hakeem wasn't the only Cougar to benefit from playing with Moses. Other members of the team that came to be known as Phi Slama Jama, including Clyde Drexler, Larry Micheaux, Benny Anders, and Michael Young, competed against Malone and the Rockets during the summer. The Cougars always played on the same team and matched up against the pros at Fonde on Mondays and Wednesdays and at the old Robertson Gym on U of H campus on Tuesdays and Thursdays.

Moses hated to lose, and he and his teammates used their superior strength to push around the college kids. They beat the Cougars every time. Games were straight to 12. One evening late in the summer of 1981, the teams were tied at 11. Cougars guard Rob Williams missed a jump shot. Olajuwon grabbed the rebound. He faked right, turned back over his left shoulder, and flipped the ball into the basket. The Cougars won. They turned to Moses and repeated what he'd said to them countless times before, "Get your fucking ass off the court."

Moses demanded a rematch. Again, the game was tied at 11. Moses had most, if not all, of the Rockets' points. Hakeem released a mini hook shot that fell through the hoop. The Cougars won again. "And a couple of things happened that day," said Cougars guard Eric Davis. "I think Moses had a newfound respect for us, and it was like us thanking the master, 'cause he taught us. And that day was the day that we thought we really can win the national championship."[24] The Cougars didn't win a championship, though they came close, reaching the Final Four three times, and the national championship game in 1983 and 1984.

The fun continued after the games. Moses, Hakeem, and Drexler engaged in heated ping-pong battles at Fonde.[25] There was a regular dominoes game in the back of Major Jones's truck in the parking lot, where the trash talk was as animated as on the court.[26] Sometimes the guys grabbed a bite to eat. Moses enjoyed Otto's Barbecue and Hamburgers, where he played Pacman after chowing down.[27] Frenchy's, a takeout fried-chicken restaurant near the U of H campus, was another popular destination. The athletes ran to their luxury automobiles and raced each other to Frenchy's after the games. Moses always won and would be waiting with buckets of chicken for everyone by the time the whole crew arrived.[28]

Malone loved being in the gym. He believed in staying in shape and constantly working on his game. One summer, he went on a Nike trip to China. Moe Vines was surprised to see him walk into Fonde the day he returned. Moses went directly from the airport to the gym. "I told my wife I gotta go to work," he told Vines.[29] For most of the Rockets and Cougars, Monday through Thursday was enough. Not Moses. On Sundays, he and Rob Williams played three-on-three on the concrete court at MacGregor Park.[30] He also participated in a league at the Second Baptist Church with Rodney McCray, U of H star Lynden Rose, and their friend Tony Dale on Saturday mornings.[31]

Big Mo formed a team to compete in tournaments around the country. He named them the Houston Regulars because although most of them played professional ball they were just regular guys.[32] Major Jones, Allen Leavell, Drexler, Chris Morris, Rodney McCray, Ricky Pierce, Terry Teagle, and Robert Reid were some of the Regulars over the years. Moe Vines was the coach.[33] When the Regulars hit the road, they went by the name Moses Malone's Traveling All-Stars and Motorcade or the Houston Regulars Traveling All-Stars and Motorcade. They competed against Dominique Wilkins and his crew in Georgia, George Gervin and the boys in San Antonio, and Mark Aguirre's team in Dallas. There were trips to Shreveport, Louisiana, and the Bahamas.[34] Moses always took care of his boys. When the Regulars were invited to participate in a tournament in Atlanta, the organizers offered to fly Moses first-class. He informed them that he and the Regulars wouldn't come unless they all received first-class tickets.[35]

Ron Foster, the sports director at Fort Hood army base outside of Killeen, Texas, met Malone at a basketball game and nervously asked if he'd come entertain the troops. Malone didn't hesitate. "Yeah, I'll do that," he said. "I respect soldiers." It became an annual summer trip for the Traveling All-Stars and Motorcade. They played softball and basketball on the base. In between, they met with the generals and soldiers, played golf, attended a concert, visited hospitals, and fired M16s at the range. Foster offered to take Moses and his friends out to dinner, but Malone chose to eat with the soldiers instead.[36] He drove around the base in a tank with his head sticking out the top and a big grin on his face, and when the officers band played a song for their guests, Big Mo broke out into a crazy dance that had his teammates in hysterics.[37]

Po Bill's Tournament in Dallas was another annual stop for the Traveling All-Stars. Bill Patterson grew up in Tulsa, Oklahoma. After serving in the army, he barnstormed with Harlem Globetrotters legends Marques Haynes and Goose Tatum. Bill was the first Black salesman for Kinney Shoes, and when the company opened an office in a Black neighborhood in Dallas, Kinney asked him to move there. His wife jumped at the opportunity, believing he was messing around with other women in Tulsa.

One day a friend saw him coming and said, "Oh, that's Ol' Big Money Bill."

Patterson responded, "No, I'm Po' Bill." The name stuck.

Po Bill loved basketball and started a tournament in the late seventies. His friend Frank Fields from Houston called one year and said Moses wanted to enter a team. Bill asked for the team's name.

Fields said, "Houston Regulars Traveling All-Stars and Motorcade."

"Damn, that's a long name," replied Bill.

Moses was the first professional to take an interest in the tournament, and his involvement drew other NBA players, such as Spud Webb, Dennis Rodman, Karl Malone, Mark Aguirre, and John Starks. In later years Richard Dumas and Larry Johnson participated, as did Arkansas Razorbacks Lee Mayberry, Corliss Williamson, and Oliver Miller. Po Bill added a subtitle to his tournament: "The Tournament that Moses Malone Built."[38]

One summer, Moses set up a game for some of the Regulars in a prison where he knew the warden. The guys arrived and had lunch with the inmates, then played a game. The Regulars were up in the fourth quarter when Mo called a timeout and told them they had to lose. He noticed that the inmates were gambling a lot of cigarettes on the action and knew there would be trouble if the Regulars came out ahead. For the only time in his life, Big Mo didn't provide maximum effort. After the game, the Regulars were signing posters for the inmates when Reid felt somebody looking over his shoulder. He turned and saw a man "as big as the guy from the Green Mile."

"Hey man, you good?" asked Reid.

"Yeah!"

"You want an autograph?"

"I don't want no graph."

"You want a picture?"

"I don't want no picture."

"What you want?"

"I want them kicks you wearing."

Reid wore size 14 shoes. He looked at the man's enormous feet and thought he must have been a size 24. He said, "Bro, I'll tell you what, I know a guy with 24s back at the gym I can bring out."

"I don't want. I want them you wearing."

Reid looked around for the warden, but there was no help in sight. He removed his shoes and gave them to the inmate. When they left, he told Moses he was never going back. Then Moses shared the story of the Milkman, whom he played against in prison when he was in high school.[39]

Malone started a Houston Regulars softball team as well, which joined a local YMCA league. Major Jones was the catcher-coach, Moses played first base, and Drexler was the shortstop. Rodney McCray, Jim Petersen, and Allen Leavell were some of the other pros on the team. In later years, Chris Morris, Nick Van Exel, and Robert Horry joined the squad. The Regulars often stayed on the diamond talking shop until well past midnight.[40] Whether it was basketball or softball, after the games they discussed where to meet up later that night.

Houston was booming in the 1970s and early '80s. The city added 670,000 jobs during the '70s. Bank deposits jumped from about $6 billion to $24 billion, and office space grew to 100 million square feet from 30 million. The rising tide included a growing middle and upper class of African Americans. The number of Blacks who counted themselves as professionals or managers tripled from 1960 to 1980, and the amount of Black college graduates in Houston almost doubled between 1970 and 1980.[41]

The growth led to a vibrant nightlife. Faces was the hot spot for Black athletes and entertainers. A tiny club near the Astrodome, it featured a projector that displayed images of famous people on the wall. Moses and his friends were frequent guests, as was the other top athlete in Houston, Oilers running back Earl Campbell. Nearby, Paseo was another popular stop.[42] Sometimes Mo chilled out to reggae music at the Caribana Club or listened to jazz at the Red Rooster.[43]

Malone partied during road trips as well, though he never stayed out late the night before a game. You could find him prowling the hotel lobby in search of breakfast by 7:00 a.m. If he ran into an opponent the night before a game he'd warn, "Get your rest, cause you know I'm gonna bust that ass."[44]

Moses didn't drink alcohol or smoke. He had a sign in his house that read "PLEASE DON'T SMOKE OR I WILL PUT YOU OUT."[45] If he smelled marijuana at a party, he'd leave. Barry Warner, a broadcaster for the Rockets in the late seventies, went out with Moses and Major one night in Phoenix and lit a joint while driving. Moses told him to pull over, took the joint out of his mouth, and threw it out of the car. Then he asked Warner to turn over whatever was in his pockets and discarded that too. "Don't be doing no drugs around Big Mo," he said.[46] Cocaine was the drug of choice for athletes and entertainers at the time. Malone told *Playboy Magazine* in 1984 that he never tried it and never would. Coke was expensive, and that's not how he wanted to spend his money. "Look at me: I'm 6'10"—I'm high enough," he said.[47]

Moses's vice was women. Star athletes confront the endless temptation of women throwing themselves at them at clubs and hotel lobbies. Moses was wary of those women. He preferred to quietly scope out the ones he was interested in, then make his move. Big Mo could be smooth with the ladies. He slowed his speech, annunciated words, and became quite loquacious. Other times, he confidently sidled up to an attractive woman and boldly asked, "Are we fucking?"[48]

Moses and Alfreda moved into a new nine-thousand-square-foot house in Sugar Land, Texas, in 1981 and were married on May 12, 1982. Their second son, Michael Earle, was born two years later. Big Mo still pursued other ladies, both in Houston and on the road. It would be an ongoing issue in his marriage.

15

Straight Cash

The 1982 All-Star Game took place on January 31 at Brendan Byrne Arena in East Rutherford, New Jersey. "You want to win this game," Moses said, "because it's nice to have $2,000 (the winners' share) instead of $1,000. You can have a lot better night out on the town with $2,000 instead of $1,000."[1]

Pat Riley coached the West squad. His center with the Lakers, Abdul-Jabbar, was voted the starter over Malone. Moses had 12 points and a team-high 11 rebounds in a close contest, when Riley sent him to the bench early in the fourth quarter for the remainder of the game. The West lost by 2 points. "That made the big fella mad," said Robert Reid.[2] Malone took out his anger on the rest of the league. He began with a career-high 53 points and 23 rebounds against the San Diego Clippers in the Rockets' first game after the All-Star break, then followed that up with 45 points and 20 rebounds against the Suns and 47 points against the Kings.

The *Houston Chronicle* published an article on February 11 in which writer Neil Hohlfeld noted that Malone's recent hot streak had come at the expense of "centers incapable of slowing a man of half his talent." The Rockets played the SuperSonics that night, and Hohlfeld suggested their big man, Jack Sikma, would be a true test for Malone. Sikma was an All-Star and the second-leading rebounder in the league.[3] Moses scored 38 points and grabbed 32 rebounds, including an NBA record 21 offensive boards (still an NBA record), while holding Sikma to 16 points and 3 rebounds.

Moses averaged 40.1 points on 60.2 percent shooting and 19 rebounds over seven games. His numbers for February were 38.1 points and 17.3 rebounds, while shooting 55 percent and playing 44.6 minutes a night. "Naw, I'm not the greatest player in the game today," Malone said. "There are a lot of guys who could do this if they were in my situation. I'm not the greatest player, but one thing I do want to be remembered for, that I have always tried to be the greatest worker."[4]

His teammates knew better. "I think if Moses went out on the court one night and jumped over the backboard, I think I'd probably take it in stride," said Allen Leavell. "What's left to surprise you after the way he's been playing?"[5]

Between December 12 and April 6, the Rockets went 36-17, finishing 46-36 with a matchup against the SuperSonics in a first-round miniseries. Moses looked fatigued after playing at least forty-four minutes in thirty of the Rockets' previous thirty-eight games, and the Sonics prevailed in three games, with Sikma outplaying him in the decisive one. Malone averaged 31.1 points (second to George Gervin) and 14.7 rebounds (first in the NBA) for the season and was named MVP for the second time. The greatest player in basketball was about to become the most coveted free agent in NBA history.

A new phase in free agency went into effect the previous summer. Teams no longer had to compensate a player's former team for signing him. Instead, the old team had a "right of first refusal," which allowed it to match any offer the player received. There was concern that wealthier franchises like the Lakers and Knicks would buy championships by signing players to contracts that small-market teams couldn't afford. Malone would be a test case.

The only adornment in the office of Rockets GM Ray Patterson was a Moses Malone poster, one of a series produced by Nike in the late 1970s and early 1980s to promote its foray into basketball sneakers. The image is a play on the biblical Moses, with Malone parting a sea of orange basketballs. He's holding a ball in his right hand and a staff in the shape of Nike's swoosh logo in his left.

"It's so good, so symbolic of the whole franchise," Patterson told Ed Fowler of the *Houston Chronicle*. "The guy loves to play basketball more than anybody I know." Patterson explained that some athletes use their celebrity as a platform to espouse views on religion, politics, or other topics. Moses's focus never drifted from the game.

The GM was certain Houston would retain the MVP, telling the *Houston Chronicle* in February 1982, "It's not a case of whether the present ownership can afford him, it's a matter of there being no alternative. Houston will not lose him. That doesn't mean I'll be around or the Maloofs will be around. Moses Malone transcends any ownership, general managership or coaching. There are enough people in this city who won't let him leave." Patterson added, "If we start next year without Moses, we might as well forget it. We're dead."[6]

Moses had no interest in becoming a free agent. Houston was home, and he would have preferred to avoid the speculation over where he'd sign.[7] As early as 1980, he instructed Lee Fentress to work out an extension with Houston. Fentress met with Rockets owner George Maloof in November 1980. After ten days of negotiations, the agent believed the parties were "pretty damn close to a deal" just before Maloof died suddenly of a heart attack on November 29.[8]

George was replaced by his twenty-four-year-old son Gavin, and Malone's extension talks were put on hold.[9] Fentress and Patterson discussed a new contract early in the 1981–82 season, then agreed to break off negotiations in January so Moses could concentrate on basketball.[10] Fentress grew frustrated by what he perceived as differing views within the Maloof family about selling the team.[11] Several weeks after the end of the season, on or about June 4, the Rockets finally made Moses an offer reported to be worth anywhere from $1.6 to $1.9 million for three to six years, depending on which options he chose. It was too late. Free agency began a few days later, and Moses felt compelled to test the market.

Malone's free agency unfolded against the backdrop of leaguewide economic uncertainty. The NBA was a small operation with just thirty-one employees and total operating expenses of $2.4 million. The Rockets' Finals series in 1981 aired on tape delay outside of Boston and Houston.[12] Cable television was just getting started, and the NBA's new deal with CBS was for $88 million, mere peanuts compared to the $2.4 billion contract the NFL signed with the three major networks.[13] Corporations were reluctant to invest in a league with a perceived drug problem that many deemed "too Black."

Teams were dependent on gate receipts for income, and sixteen of the twenty-three franchises were losing money.[14] The league created a Special Committee on Problem Franchises, which, among other things, explored the possibility of reducing the number of teams.[15] "There was a lot of skepticism about how long the NBA would survive," said Russ Granik, who became deputy commissioner in 1984.[16]

The league's collective bargaining agreement expired the summer Malone became a free agent, and the owners were determined to push back after massive gains by the players. Concerns about escalating salaries due to the right of first refusal were well founded. NBA salaries reached a high point in 1981–82, at 63.9 percent of the league's total revenue, up from 56.7 percent the year before.[17] The main culprits were Lakers owner Jerry Buss and Cleveland Cavaliers owner Ted Stepien.

Buss purchased the Lakers in 1979 and set out to construct a team to match his flashy image. He found the perfect leading man for "Showtime" in a charismatic rookie named Earvin "Magic" Johnson. Buss signed Johnson to a twenty-five-year contract worth $1 million per year in the summer of 1981. The owner inked Mitch Kupchak, a scrappy forward who'd never been a starter in the NBA, to a ten-year contract worth $800,000 per year and expressed his intention to sign Moses the following summer.[18]

Ted Stepien was as unsophisticated as Buss was suave. Within months of buying the Cavaliers in 1980, he made racist remarks about players and fans and began dealing first-round draft picks like they were Mounds bars on Halloween. The league imposed a moratorium on the Cavaliers' ability to make trades and later passed what became known as the Stepien Rule, prohibiting teams from trading future first-round draft picks for consecutive seasons.[19] The Cavaliers went 28-54 and lost $3 million in Stepien's first season. In the summer of 1981 he shelled out huge sums of money for mediocre players, signing James Edwards to a four-year, $3 million offer sheet and Scott Wedman of Kansas City to a five-year, $4 million deal and offering forward Bobby Wilkerson double what the Bulls had offered.[20]

Executives of other teams were perturbed by the Lakers' and Cavs' spending. "So far it has been some kind of disaster," said Bullets GM Bob Ferry of the right of first refusal. "The market value of the players has not been proportional to their abilities." NBA owners proposed the first salary cap in North American sports to curb the escalation of salaries and maintain competitive balance. Larry Fleisher, the general counsel of the players association, accused the owners of colluding to not sign players in the summer of 1982. A week before training camp, fifty-one of the sixty-four veteran free agents were unsigned, and only three of the first-round picks from that June's draft had deals.[21]

Still, it only took one renegade owner to spend the cash necessary to secure the reigning MVP. A short list of teams could afford Moses, including the Lakers, 76ers, Knicks, Nets, Bulls, and SuperSonics. The Sonics removed themselves from the discussion, and the Bulls and 76ers had quality centers. Buss remained quiet after declaring a year earlier that he would pursue Moses.[22] L.A. won the 1982 championship without Malone, and incoming general manager Jerry West was concerned about his fit with the Lakers' fast-paced offense.[23]

Moses had yet to receive an offer when he was named MVP on June 15 and expressed his frustration. "The way I look at it, I should have never become a free agent in the first place," he said. "I think if everything had been done the right way, the Rockets would have gotten into serious negotiations last summer and had me signed to a new contract before last season even started." Malone added, "I'm the only man ever to win the MVP that ain't got a job."[24]

That same day, Maloof sold the Rockets to a local Ford dealer named Charlie Thomas for a reported $11 million. At the NBA's annual summer meetings held in mid-June, the Knicks, Lakers, and 76ers declared themselves out of the running for Malone. Nets coach Larry Brown expressed the prevailing opinion around the league when he said, "I don't see Moses playing anywhere except Houston next season."[25]

Harold Katz, a lifelong 76ers fan from South Philadelphia, made his fortune on the weight-loss company Nutrisystem and purchased the Sixers from Fitz Dixon in July 1981. "Dixon ran it as a hobby, and he had very little involvement with the team," Katz said. "I don't think sports should be treated as a hobby. It's a business, and I intend to run it as I run my other businesses." Katz was demanding of his employees, oversaw every aspect of the business, and was notoriously cheap, leading to stories by team employees about what they called "Katzonomics." Like most professional teams, the 76ers laid out a pregame spread in the press room. Katz didn't think reporters should eat on his dime and replaced the meals with pretzels. He fired the team's cheerleaders and confiscated credit cards Dixon had given the assistant coaches and trainer for entertaining and dining on the road.[26]

Katz was extremely knowledgeable about basketball for an owner and talked hoops with assistant general manager John Nash after the games. On one occasion, he told Nash to name the twelfth man on each team. Nash said they'd have to agree on one through eleven first. Katz suggested that he'd name one through eleven, and Nash would name the twelfth, and they did.[27] The owner possessed a satellite dish long before the device was common and watched college games late into the night to scout players. Philly assistant coach and scout Jack McMahon sat in the first row along the baseline every time he scouted a televised tournament because he knew Katz would be watching and wanted to make sure the owner saw him.[28] Katz quizzed McMahon about college players and held workouts for draft prospects at the basketball court at his house.[29]

On August 27 the 76ers traded their starting center, Darryl Dawkins, to the Nets. The man known as Chocolate Thunder had tremendous talent and charisma but was always clowning around. Katz, who built his fortune on hard work, was frustrated by his center's inconsistent effort. Dawkins's lackluster performance in an April game in which the 76ers were thoroughly outrebounded by the Celtics was the final straw.[30]

Two days after trading Dawkins, Katz flew to Lake Tahoe with his wife. On the way, he decided to pursue Malone.[31] As soon as he landed, he called Nash (GM Pat Williams was out of the country) and told him to set up a meeting with Malone's people. Fentress was in New York for the U.S. Open, and Moses was set to fly out of New York to Europe on Wednesday, so they scheduled the meeting in Manhattan.[32]

Tim Malloy, a group sales director for the 76ers, picked Malone up at the airport for a secret physical exam to make sure the big fella was healthy before the Sixers signed him. Malloy thought Moses resembled an octopus as he squeezed his 6-foot-10-inch frame into the front seat of Malloy's 1977 Toyota Corolla liftback. Malloy drove to Veterans Stadium, where the team's offices were and where the Phillies were set to play a home game that night. As Malloy slowed down at the circular driveway near the offices, a fan yelled, "Hey, check that car, that looks like Moses Malone is in that car." Another fan chimed in, "That *is* fucking Moses! Yeah, he's in there! Hey, hey!" The fans were so excited that they started to rock the car back and forth. "I felt like I was in Beirut," said Malloy. Moses laughed. "I could walk down the streets of Houston and nobody would say anything," he said. "Here I can't even slip into town."[33]

Fentress, his associate David Falk, Malone, Katz, Nash, and Larry Shaiman, the 76ers' team attorney, met at the Grand Hyatt Hotel on 42nd Street in New York City at 7:00 p.m. on September 1 to discuss a contract.[34] Katz decided he wanted Sixers coach Billy Cunningham to meet with Moses first to make sure the center would fit with the team's culture and style of play. Cunnigham was golfing at Pine Hurst in North Carolina with Dean Smith and Larry Brown when somebody from the pro shop informed him that he needed to fly to New York immediately. He hopped on a plane from Raleigh to Newark Airport. The coach flagged down a cab at Newark, but when the driver told him the ride to the Grand Hyatt would cost $70, he took a bus instead. Cunningham arrived at the hotel close to 8:00 p.m. and walked into the meeting to hear the parties discussing a contract worth $2 million per year. He couldn't believe he worried about spending $70 of the team's money on a taxi.[35]

Cunningham explained to Malone that the 76ers played at a faster pace than he was accustomed to and he'd be less of a focal point on offense with more talent around him. Moses said he understood. He simply wanted to fit in and help the 76ers win a championship. The coach was satisfied. Katz was impressed that Malone asked several questions about the team and none pertaining to money.[36]

Fentress, Falk, Shaiman, and Katz worked until 2:00 a.m. to hash out an offer sheet. Everything they agreed to was written in longhand. When the two sides reached an agreement, Moses read the contract.[37] "No 'ferred. I'm not having no 'ferred!" he exclaimed. He was referring to deferred income. The money had to be up front. The parties reworked the deal to meet his demand.[38]

The offer sheet was worth as much as $13.2 million over six years if certain incentives were met, which would have made Moses the highest paid athlete in the history of North American team sports.[39] Julius Erving, who reportedly made $900,000 per year, had been the highest paid 76er, and Abdul-Jabbar was believed to be the highest paid player in the league with an annual salary between $1.1 and $1.2 million.[40]

The business center at the hotel didn't open until 6:00 a.m., so the parties waited until then to make copies of the offer sheet. The Rockets had fifteen days to match the offer once they received it. Nash rushed to the team office in Philadelphia, called Ray Patterson to inform him of the offer, and sent Marlene Barnes, a team secretary, on a plane to Houston to deliver a copy in person.[41] Moses ensured that his childhood friend, Mitch Malone of WSSV radio in Richmond, broke the story.[42] Then he, Alfreda, and Moses Jr. flew to Amsterdam. Katz held a press conference later that day to announce the signing.

Julius Erving was in China on a goodwill tour with other NBA players, including Celtics forward M. L. Carr. Boston and Philly were rivals, and Carr poked fun at Erving when word reached China that the 76ers traded Dawkins. He knew the 76ers couldn't beat the Celtics without a center. Erving fell into a funk. Boston's young forwards were a year older, and they were about to add Scott Wedman. The Lakers, who'd just beaten Philly in the Finals, selected James Worthy with the first pick in the draft. Philadelphia was falling behind in the arms race. When the players landed in Hong Kong a few days later, there was a message waiting for Erving at his hotel. The 76ers had signed Malone to an offer sheet. Carr heard the news too. When he saw Erving in the lobby, he shook his head and said, "You guys just won the title."[43]

Rockets spokesman Jim Foley announced that Houston would match the contract and either keep Malone or trade him. Patterson wanted to keep the star center. "Moses made our franchise," he told Frank DeFord a few years earlier. "We were going down the tubes, and we wouldn't be in Houston today if Tom [Nissalke] hadn't kept after me to make that deal."[44] Charlie Thomas wasn't willing to pay anybody that much money. "Christ, Ray, I paid $12 million for the whole goddamn team," he told Patterson, "And now you want me to pay that for one player."[45]

Nash wanted to call the Rockets' bluff, believing that Thomas wouldn't match, though as the deadline grew near Katz decided to make a trade with Houston. He was concerned the Rockets would match. It would've been devastating for them to let the MVP walk without receiving anything in return. Katz also felt it would be detrimental to the league to sign a star away from a new owner.[46]

Katz flew to Houston and arrived at Thomas's house on the afternoon of September 14. The two discussed a trade late into the night. The sticking point was the Cavaliers' first-round pick in the 1983 draft, which the 76ers had acquired in a 1977 trade for Terry Furlow. The Cavs had the worst record in the league in 1981–82 and were expected to be at the bottom of the standings again. The 1983 draft was projected to include potentially three franchise centers in Ralph Sampson, Patrick Ewing, and Sam Bowie. Thomas insisted there'd be no deal without that pick, which he needed to acquire a new star and assuage the fan base's anger over losing Malone.

Katz returned to Philly in the morning without an agreement. Upon landing, he instructed his lawyers to contact Thomas's lawyers and work out a deal that included the pick.[47] The two sides agreed on a trade of Caldwell Jones and the Cleveland pick for Moses. "In the 37-year history of the league there have been only four dominant players," Patterson said after trading one of them, "Wilt, Russell, Abdul-Jabbar, and Mo."[48]

The 76ers scheduled an introductory press conference, but their plan hit a snag when Moses found out that Jones was in the trade. The two were close friends from their time together with the Spirits of St. Louis, and Caldwell was a major reason why Moses wanted to play in Philadelphia. He told Williams he wasn't going through with the deal. Williams called Katz, and the owner calmed Malone down.[49]

The 76ers held the press conference at Veterans Stadium as fans arrived for a Phillies game that night. A spontaneous chant of "Mo-ses, Mo-ses" broke out throughout the concourse. "They wouldn't have paid Moses the money if they didn't think Moses was worth it," said Malone. It was the first time sportswriter Bill Livingston heard an athlete speak in the third person, and he didn't know what to think of it.[50] Malone would make a habit of it.

Coaches and executives around the league were shocked and concerned by the size of Malone's contract. Pistons GM Jack McCloskey called it "catastrophic for the league."[51] There would be a trickle-down effect on salaries, and small market teams worried about competitive balance. Less than a year later, the NBA and the players association agreed on a salary cap.

FIG. 1. Petersburg had a vibrant civil rights movement. Here, Black students from Peabody High School protested the relegation of their school to a junior high when the schools integrated. Copyright *Richmond Times-Dispatch*.

FIG. 2. Moses Malone with classmates Deborah Tompkins and Catherine Parham (*left*) at Petersburg High School. Copyright *Richmond Times-Dispatch*.

FIG. 3. They called Malone "Sweet Moses" at Petersburg High School, where he led the Crimson Wave to Virginia state championships in 1973 and 1974. *1974 Petersburg High School Yearbook*, Petersburg Public Library.

FIG. 4. Moses (*third from the left*) and his teammates at Five-Star Basketball Camp listening to Coach Tom McCorry. Malone never looked people in the eye when they spoke to him. Courtesy of Five-Star Basketball Camp.

FIG. 5. Five-Star director Howard Garfinkel called Malone the only player who was "too good for the camp." Courtesy of Five-Star Basketball Camp.

FIG. 6. Moses is seated next to his mother, Mary, on Moses Malone Day in Petersburg in 1974. Lefty Driesell appears to be handing something to Mary. Photograph by Bill Lane. Copyright *Richmond Times-Dispatch*.

FIG. 7. Lefty Driesell, the charismatic coach of the University of Maryland, won the recruiting battle for Moses. Here he is entering Cole Field House. Courtesy of Special Collections and University Archives, University of Maryland Libraries.

FIG. 8. Moses admiring the trophies he won at Petersburg High School. He committed to attend the University of Maryland before deciding to skip college. Photograph by Don Rypka. Copyright *Richmond Times-Dispatch*.

FIG. 9. Moses prior to a press conference on August 29, 1974, to announce his signing with the Utah Stars of the American Basketball Association. Photograph by Robert Houston, Associated Press.

FIG. 10. Moses became the first modern player to jump from high school to professional basketball. He made the All-Star Game as a rookie with the Utah Stars. Photograph by Gary Burns. Copyright *Richmond Times-Dispatch*.

FIG. 11. Moses drove around Petersburg in a Mercedes the summer after his rookie season in the ABA. Photograph by Don Rypka. Copyright *Richmond Times-Dispatch.*

FIG. 12. Moses Malone was known as the Chairman of the Boards for his dominance on the offensive glass. The Celtics were one of his favorite victims. PCN Photography/Alamy.

FIG. 13. Moses bounced around several teams before finding a home with the Houston Rockets. Courtesy of Special Collections and University Archives, University of Maryland Libraries.

FIG. 14. Moses Malone and Julius Erving needed each other to win a championship with the 76ers in 1983. Associated Press.

FIG. 15. Moses wore goggles during the second half of his career after suffering an eye injury in 1986. Photograph by Al Messerschmidt, Associated Press.

FIG. 16. Moses loved hanging out with his buddies. Here he is with Tony Dale (*center*) and Major Jones (*right*). Courtesy of Tony Dale.

FIG. 17. Moses met the mother of his youngest child, Leah Nash, in March 2006. He initially told her he was a janitor. Courtesy of Leah Nash.

FIG. 18. Moses enjoyed coloring and reading with his third son, Micah, who was born in May 2009. Courtesy of Leah Nash.

FIG. 19. In 2006 the Houston Parks and Recreation Department named the court at Fonde Recreation Center after Malone. Photograph by the author.

FIG. 20. Several of Moses's friends attended his statue unveiling at the 76ers' training complex on February 8, 2019 (*left to right*): Tony Dale, Ed Gholson, Herb Baker, Kevin Vergara, and Major Jones. Courtesy of Tony Dale.

FIG. 21. Moses's three boys posing with his statue on February 8, 2019 (*left to right*): Michael, Micah, and Moses Jr. Courtesy of Leah Nash.

FIG. 22. Charles Barkley called Moses "Dad." Here is he posing with Moses's youngest son, Micah, with a photograph of Moses in the background. Courtesy of Leah Nash.

16

Time to Go to Work

Julius Erving was the prized jewel of the NBA-ABA merger, though it wasn't clear what team he'd play for when his New York Nets joined the NBA in 1976. The Nets were forced to pay a $4.8 million territorial fee to the Knicks in addition to the $3.2 million to join the league. To make matters worse, Erving claimed that Nets owner Roy Boe had promised to renegotiate his contract if the leagues merged, a claim Boe denied. Boe didn't have the money, anyway.

Erving held out of training camp in the fall of 1976, and Philadelphia's GM Pat Williams called Nets GM Bill Melchionni to express his interest in the star forward. A few days later, Melchionni called back ready to talk. Williams drove to the estate of Fitz Dixon, the 76ers' new owner. "Fitz, there is a player available from the other league," he said, pausing for effect. "And his name is Julius Erving."

Silence. Fitz didn't know anything about basketball. He finally asked, "Now tell me, who is he?"

"Uh, well, he's kind of the Babe Ruth of basketball," Williams replied.[1]

Williams provided more detail. Erving hailed from Long Island and attended the University of Massachusetts. The dunk was outlawed during his college career, so only his teammates knew how high he could soar. The shackles came off at the legendary Rucker Park in Harlem, New York, where kids hung from trees and gathered on rooftops to witness "the Doctor." There were spectacular dunkers before Erving, though he brought the aerial artistry of the streets to the mainstream. Erving's friend Leon Saunders dubbed him "the Doctor" in high school, and Bob "Chopper" Travaglini, the Virginia Squires' trainer, changed it to "Dr. J" during training camp in 1971.[2]

Erving wasn't simply a dunker. He glided past defenders and used his massive hands to finish around the basket. Doc was also a tenacious rebounder. He won the ABA MVP award in each of the league's final three seasons and led the Nets to championships in 1974 and 1976. But the most captivating basketball player in the world operated in relative obscurity in the ABA.

Dixon's interest grew as Williams told the tale of the Doctor. Finally, he asked how much Erving would cost. Williams said it would take $3 million to acquire him and another $3 million to sign him.

"Are you recommending this?" Dixon asked.

"Yes sir, I am," replied Williams.

"Fine and dandy, then. Let's do it," he said.[3]

Erving's star power exploded in the NBA. He led the Sixers to the Finals in his first season and immediately became the face of the league, a mantle he embraced. Doc set the template for future ambassadors of the game. "He [Erving] was the classiest player I ever met," longtime 76ers employee Harvey Pollack once said. "In 50 years in the NBA, he was the classiest by far." Doc signed every autograph, delivered thoughtful answers to each interview question, and always had time for kids. John Kilbourne, the 76ers' strength and conditioning coach, was driving Erving out of The Forum in L.A. after practice one day when a bunch of kids gathered around the vehicle. Doc asked Kilbourne if he had anything to do that day. Kilbourne said no. Doc climbed out of the car, talked to the kids for a while, and signed autographs. "I saw him do that over and over again," Kilbourne said.[4]

The one thing missing from Doc's résumé was an NBA title. His 76ers advanced to the Finals three times during his first six seasons in Philly, losing on each occasion to a team with a great big man. Erving needed Malone, and Malone, who'd been carrying a mediocre Rockets team for years, needed Erving.

Moses saw Julius play for the Squires in Richmond while in high school. It was a revelation. Erving became one of his heroes. Doc first set eyes on Malone when the nineteen-year-old played his first professional game against Doc's Nets at Nassau Veterans Memorial Coliseum in the fall of 1974. The Nets ownership asked Erving to welcome Malone to the league. Doc took the microphone and said, "Well kid, you know you've been swimming around in shallow ponds for a long time. Now it's time for you to step into the deep water in pro basketball. And I hope you can swim."

Moses flashed a confident smile. By the time Moses joined the Sixers, Doc knew "that he could not only swim in the water, but he could do the back stroke, he could do the freestyle, he could do the butterfly, he could do the breaststroke. He could swim any way that people could swim."[5]

Reporters wondered how the two previous MVPs (Erving in 1981 and Malone in 1982) would mesh. Could they put their egos aside for the good of the team? Malone set the tone at his introductory press conference, stating, "Y'all know who the leader is. Dr. J is the leader. Moses is just enjoying the show."[6] He expressed the same sentiment to Cunningham the night he signed his offer sheet and repeated it several times over the following months.

Erving was equally deferential, accepting that for the first time since ninth grade he wasn't the best player on his team.[7] "I'm second in command on that team," he said years later. "I'm the captain, but Moses is really driving the ship."[8] Doc was perplexed by questions about whether the two stars could coexist. They played different positions, and Moses didn't demand the ball.[9]

Erving and Malone took pressure off each other. At thirty-two, Doc could no longer soar as high as he had in his ABA days. Malone picked up some of the offensive burden, allowing Erving to choose his spots. Moses had more room to operate in the post than he had in Houston as teams were forced to respect Erving's scoring ability, and Doc absorbed much of the spotlight that Moses abhorred.

The 76ers were more than a two-man show. "They had almost an All-Star team as a starting lineup," said Dan Issel. Maurice Cheeks provided a steady hand at the point of attack. The soft-spoken floor general set up his teammates and frustrated opposing point guards with dogged defensive pressure. At the other guard spot, Andrew Toney was entering his prime as an elite scorer in his third season. He'd been dubbed "The Boston Strangler" for his spectacular performances against the Celtics, including 34 points at Boston Garden in Game 7 of the 1982 Eastern Conference Finals.[10] "With the exception of Michael Jordan, I have never been more afraid of an opponent at the shooting guard position than Andrew Toney," wrote Larry Bird in his autobiography. "To me, there wasn't much difference between the two when it came to the sheer ability to score."[11]

The fifth starter was twenty-six-year-old rookie Marc Iavaroni, who spent his first few professional seasons in Europe. He split time at forward with sixth man Bobby Jones, a quiet, born-again Christian who played with reckless abandon and was the team's defensive stopper. Jones, like Cheeks, Doc, and Moses, would be inducted into the Basketball Hall of Fame. Toney would've joined them if his career hadn't been ruined by chronic foot injuries.

NBA training camps in the 1980s were communal events. The 76ers stayed in a hotel with roommates. After practice, they went out to dinner as a team, then hung out at the hotel bar. Players didn't come to camp with entourages, and their eyes weren't glued to cell phones. It was a great bonding opportunity.[12] The 1982–83 76ers were a tight bunch. Several of the core players had been together for years. Moses fit in immediately with everybody from Erving and Cheeks to John Kilbourne, the strength and conditioning coach. Malone and Kilbourne had shooting contests after practice with the loser paying for lunch. Naturally, Malone always won, and Kilbourne picked up the tab, even though he made $25,000 a year compared to Malone's $2.2 million.[13]

"Time to go to work" was Moses's mantra that season, and his teammates followed his lead. Jones was on the European tour that Malone embarked on the day he signed his offer sheet. "I played with him on that tour and was blown away by how hard he worked," said Jones. "We'd play a game in Amsterdam, then drive to Germany, have two hours sleep, and he would just kill these guys."[14] Pat Williams called Malone "a seven-foot Pete Rose."[15] "I've never seen a grown man sweat so much," Erving wrote in his autobiography. "There is water dripping off him everywhere. It's puddling on the floor. We're hydroplaning in Moses's sweat, splattering it up into the seats and onto the backboard."[16]

Moses informed rookie Mark McNamara early in training camp that he was never going to let him score in practice. He wasn't joking. The rookie had heard that superstars take it easy in practice. "I was like, 'Cross that one myth off the list, the first day of practice,'" he told writer Gordie Jones.[17] Some days, Cunningham allowed the veterans to sit out practice, but Moses never skipped a day of work. He competed as hard as always, talking trash and banging down low with the rookies.[18]

Malone's teammates quickly discovered that he was extremely misunderstood. Doc Rivers, who played with him in the late eighties and early nineties explained why in his book *Those Who Love the Game*:

> Moses is *not* a dumb guy. He is not a "problem player," either. He has been a leader everywhere he has played, he has willingly taught younger players, and has worked harder than anybody. But because he speaks in black slang that white reporters don't understand, he is mocked as being stupid. And his feelings get hurt, and he acts cranky, and the press gets cranky right back and the next thing you know all everyone knows about Mo is that he's a "problem." It's all wrong.[19]

It wasn't merely reporters who questioned Malone's intelligence. Some front office members of the organizations he played for believed he wasn't very bright. His teammates knew better.

Superior basketball intelligence is one of the qualities of great players, and Moses, concluded Erving, possessed a "brilliant mind."[20] Hall of Famer Sidney Moncrief spent one season with Moses late in their careers and determined that Malone processed information on an elite level.[21] He studied the game, poring over film of his opponents in the locker room before such film work was commonplace.[22] Malone anticipated what was going to happen on the court before anybody else. He knew what angle a shot would carom off the rim and sensed when the double team was coming. He was aware of where each of his teammates were supposed to be at all times, often directing them on the court, and had a firm grasp of his opponents' strengths and weaknesses.[23]

Moses was always the first Sixer in the shower after practice and games. Then he'd wrap himself in a towel, sit in a chair in a centralized location and cool down. As each player exited the shower, he critiqued their game. "Doc, you had such and such on ya and you should have taken him left more cause he was all the way on your right hand." He had tips for Cheeks, Toney, and everyone else.[24]

Moses's intellect was evident off the court as well. His childhood in the Heights taught him how to size up a person in an instant. He had a remarkable memory and a mathematical mind. Moses would look up his stats in a newspaper and immediately calculate how many rebounds he needed over the remaining twenty or thirty games to reach the per-game average necessary to receive a bonus.[25]

Moses also had a sharp sense of humor. Sure, he pulled childish pranks and told corny jokes. He'd call a teammate, pretend to be somebody else and tell the person to meet him somewhere.[26] When examining his bill upon checking out of a hotel in Milwaukee, he turned to the cashier and said, "I only want to check out, I don't want to buy no hotel."[27] However, he could also lead someone down a path, prompting the person to ask a specific question about what was assumed to be a serious conversation, then spring a punch line.[28]

He cut the tension in the locker room with his playful nicknames and biting one-liners. He called McNamara "Tank" after the comic-strip character and joked that the Dodge Colt driven by Kilbourne was "a Matchbox car."[29] After Cheeks scored 32 points early in the season, Moses poked his head through a throng of reporters and said, "You've got a lot of explaining to do Cheeks. How does a point guard score 32? Explain that to me Mo."[30]

Moses and Andrew Toney jawed back and forth, with Moses poking fun at his teammate's wardrobe. If Toney arrived in the locker room wearing a porkpie hat, Moses would ask, "Where you going? You going to the disco?"[31] When teammates joked that Malone threw the ball off the backboard to pad his rebound stats, he said he did that because if he threw it out to Toney, it would never come back. He had a better chance of retrieving it off the backboard.[32]

Big Mo enjoyed messing with the rookies. Every year, he and athletic trainer Al Domenico handed them movie tickets instead of boarding passes for their first road trip.[33] Malone made the rookies run errands for him, though he also bought them dinner and took them out on the town.[34] He took particular interest in McNamara, pushing the rookie on a daily basis. He'd count how many shots McNamara made at practice and inform him when they were done.[35] McNamara was also Malone's favorite target. The rookie was responsible for transporting the team's videotape machine during road trips. Malone ran off with the machine at the Milwaukee airport. "Excuse me, but a very large black guy just swiped your suitcase," a bystander told McNamara.[36]

On at least one occasion, Moses went too far. The Sixers were in the locker room in Houston during the 1982 preseason when a rookie who was a long shot to make the team arrived wearing a white blazer. Moses said, "Man, you're bleeding. You're bleeding."

The guy checked himself and asked, "What are you talking about?"

Moses said, "You got blood all over the back of your jacket, man."

The rookie asked, "What are you talking about?"

Moses said, "You cut man, you cut."

Malone's teammates were hysterical. It was a cruel joke. The player was cut soon after.[37]

Moses could take a joke too. His unique voice and mispronunciations were fair game for teammates. Everybody who played with him did their own Moses impression. He called referees Jake O'Donnell "Jack" and Jack Madden "Jake." Madden, in response, started calling Moses "Wilt."[38] While with Houston, Malone and Slick Watts argued over the details of a story. Moses told Watts he must have "amonesia" instead of "amnesia." He once requested "pesto bisto" rather than Pepto Bismal from the trainer for his stomach and after a tough loss asked, "Who's gonna scape the goat?" instead of "Who's going to be the scapegoat?"[39]

Teammates took their shots at Malone, though the big man always had a comeback in the holster. When Iavaroni complained after an exhibition game that Moses stole a couple of rebounds from him, Moses replied, "Shut the fuck up. They pay me to get 10 or 12. They only expect you to get 2."[40]

In his second season in Philly, Moses raced rookie Leo Rautins home from the airport after road trips. One night, Malone nearly drove Rautins into the median of the Schuylkill Expressway. The rookie looked over to see Moses laughing in his truck as he zoomed by. As Rautins approached his exit, he saw his teammate pulled over on the side of the road. Moses ran out of gas. Rautins had to get him more. This time the veteran, not the rookie, would be the butt of the joke. Rautins arrived early for shootaround the next morning prepared to roast Moses in front of their teammates. As soon as he walked into the facility, Moses said, "Leo, that's my pit crew. That's my pit crew." He turned the whole thing around. "He could talk shit with the best of 'em," said Rautins.[41]

The joke was on Moses when he left practice in late October of his first season in Philly to find that somebody had broken into his Cadillac Seville in the parking lot at St. Joseph's University and stole his dry cleaning. He told Erving, "When I see people walking around Philly with my big-collared shirts, I'm going to recognize my stuff." He looked for his clothes for days. Eventually, Doc said, "Mo, it's gone. Forget about it. You gotta concentrate on basketball. Welcome to Philly—you gotta lock your car up."[42]

Moses's humor eased the tension for a team with huge expectations. The reigning MVP joined a squad that advanced to the Finals months earlier. Anything less than a championship would be deemed a failure. Billy Cunningham managed those expectations in his sixth season as coach by dispensing with the notion that they were under immense pressure. "We've been to the Finals twice in the last three years and lost a seven-game conference final to Boston in the other," said Cunningham. "What worse pressure could I feel in my seat?"[43]

Cunningham grew up in Brooklyn and played college ball at the University of North Carolina. Nicknamed "the Kangaroo Kid" for his leaping ability, he was the sixth man on the Sixers' 1967 championship team and named ABA MVP in 1973. A year after retiring, he was hired to coach the 76ers in November 1977. Cunningham admired Red Holzman, coach of the 1970 and 1973 Knicks championship teams, for his ability to leave the game behind when it was over. Cunningham couldn't do that.[44] He took the losses too seriously. The coach often appeared disturbingly pale on the sidelines during the playoffs, prompting people within the 76ers organization to worry about his health.[45] "Billy was a perfectionist," said Earl Cureton. "We could win ten in a row and lose a game, and he'd go absolutely crazy. He'd come in the locker room, he'd scream, he'd yell."[46]

Early in his coaching career, Cunningham was primarily a backslapper, relying on assistant coach Chuck Daly for x's and o's. In time, he became more of a teacher who emphasized defense.[47] The Sixers enjoyed playing for him. They respected his pedigree and knowledge of the game. The coach was an excellent communicator, was approachable, and sought the advice of his veterans.[48]

In the first few games, Moses answered any questions about chemistry. He controlled the paint on defense, allowing the 76ers to run. Cunningham ran the offense through Erving and Toney down the stretch, with Moses crashing the offensive boards. Malone turned the Sixers' biggest weakness, rebounding, into a strength. At midseason, he had more offensive rebounds, 240, than Caldwell Jones and Dawkins had combined over the entire 1981–82 season, at 232.[49]

Malone's impact was evident against Philly's main rivals. Kevin McHale noted that the 76ers had a different attitude with Malone after the Sixers center played fifty-six of fifty-eight minutes in a double-overtime win over the Celtics. Weeks later, Malone broke the Lakers' back with 3 offensive rebounds and putbacks in the closing minutes. "I mean, I've seen Kareem so many times, and we've never had anybody who could neutralize him. Now we do," assistant coach Jack McMahon told Phil Jasner of the *Philadelphia Daily News* after the game.[50]

Philly won 50 games faster than any team ever, beginning the season 50-7. Malone, Erving, Cheeks, and Toney made the All-Star Team. Before the game, Erving exchanged pleasantries with Marvin Gaye, who performed his celebrated rendition of "The Star-Spangled Banner." And that, Julius recalled, "really set the stage for a great game. . . . I was loose, and the game was like we were out on the playground."[51] Doc scored 25 points and won the MVP award.

Cunningham believed his team could have won 70 games, though they suffered injuries late in the season, and he pulled back the reins down the stretch.[52] They went 8-8 in their last sixteen games, for a record of 65-17. Moses was named MVP for the third time, becoming the first player to win the award in back-to-back years for different teams. But he and his teammates would be judged by the playoffs.

17

The Promised Land

Julius Erving and the 76ers won the first two games of the 1976–1977 Finals against the Portland Trail Blazers, then lost four straight. After the season, management hired the SonderLevitt advertising agency to develop an ad campaign for the team. It came up with the slogan "We Owe You One," in reference to the Finals loss, and the Sixers plastered it on billboards and promotional material for the 1977–78 season.[1] The debt would remain unpaid for years.

Philadelphia lost in the Eastern Conference Finals in 1978 and the conference semifinals in 1979. In 1980 the 76ers returned to the Finals, only to be eliminated by a 42-point, 15-rebound performance by rookie Magic Johnson in Game 6. The Sixers jumped out to a 3-1 lead over the Celtics in the 1981 conference finals, then lost the last three games by a combined five points. They returned to the conference finals the following season. Once again, they took a 3-1 lead over the Celtics, only to lose the next two, though this time the Sixers prevailed in Game 7. They had homecourt advantage against the Lakers in the Finals and believed they were the better team. But they came up short, losing in the Finals for the third time in six years.

The heartbreak in the locker room was unforgettable. Erving cried for the only time in his career and the first time since his brother Marvin died of lupus in 1969.[2] The 76ers had the highest winning percentage in the league from 1976–1982 but hadn't won a championship. All the while, the We Owe You One campaign hung like an albatross around the team's neck.

Harold Katz, who purchased the Sixers in the summer of 1981, saw Erving crying and said, "Doc, you're not going to cry anymore." The owner vowed to make changes.[3] Enter Malone, whose psychological impact was as significant as his play. "When you lose in the finals," Lakers coach Pat

Riley said, "it takes a tremendous toll. You lose a little bit of your basketball life. They had a lot of guys who had tasted nothing but the pain, and that's bad. Getting Moses was the best move they could have made. It rejuvenated them. They went out and said, 'With Moses, we're going to win it this year.'"[4]

Cunningham knew something was wrong during a game against the Knicks on April 10 because Malone didn't grab an offensive rebound for the first time all year.[5] His right knee began hurting when he banged it in a game against Detroit on March 20, though he didn't tell anybody until Cunningham asked him what was wrong late in the Knicks game.[6] The diagnosis was tendonitis, and Moses sat the final four games of the season. The 76ers had a bye in the first round, which provided him with an extra week to heal.

Malone was so tough that his teammates didn't contemplate the possibility he wouldn't play in the playoffs.[7] Moses returned to practice on April 20, four days before the Sixers' second-round matchup with the Knicks. According to Cunningham, Moses was lying in the trainer's room after practice when the coach asked him what he thought about the playoffs. Moses replied, "Fo, Fo, Fo," Mosesspeak for "Four, Four, Four." The Sixers had to win three best-of-seven series to secure the championship. Cunningham interpreted Malone's quote to mean that they were going to sweep all three rounds, something that had never been done. "From your mouth to God's ears," the coach replied.[8]

The quote appeared in the *Philadelphia Inquirer* and *Philadelphia Daily News* the next day, written as "Four, Four, Four," not as a blaring headline or grand proclamation but tucked away in the middle of articles. The following day, Malone explained the line to Phil Jasner of the *Daily News*. "I ain't saying we're gonna sweep everybody in four games," he said. "I'm just saying, if we have an idea of winning the championship, the best thing to do is win it as fast as we can."[9]

Other versions of the story emerged. John Kilbourne remembered George Shirk of the *Philadelphia Inquirer* asking Moses how he felt about the playoffs while the big man was getting into his car after practice. Moses rolled down the window, said "Fo, Fo, Fo," and drove away.[10] Jack McCaffery of the *Trenton Times* and Roy S. Johnson of the *New York*

Times claimed Moses said "Four, Four, Four" in the locker room at the Spectrum.[11]

According to McCaffery, Malone said it matter-of-factly. The writer's interpretation was that Moses was simply stating that they had to win four games in three rounds, not necessarily that they wouldn't lose one. Malone's words weren't a rallying cry for his teammates or used as bulletin-board material by opponents. Some reporters wondered if he even said them. It's also possible that he said them more than once, which would explain the various accounts. Bill Lyons of the *Inquirer* had the final word years later: "If he didn't say it, he should have."[12]

The quote appeared as "Fo, Fo, Fo" for the first time more than a week later in a headline for an article in the *Philadelphia Daily News* after the 76ers swept the Knicks in the first round.[13] The line captured the simplicity of Malone's vernacular and approach to the game. As the Sixers cruised through the playoffs, it took on a life of its own. "It turned into Babe Ruth pointing into the bleachers and hitting a home run there," Marc Iavaroni said.[14]

Moses played along as the line morphed into legend, though he resented that the words were changed to match his colloquial style.[15] He was sensitive about his speech impediment and aware of the racial undertones to the way some reporters covered him. The altered spelling was reminiscent of writers quoting early Latino baseball players in broken English, like when Roberto Clemente reportedly said, "I no feel gud."[16] Malone's southern, Black vernacular had not yet penetrated mainstream culture through rap music and other mediums, and "Fo, Fo, Fo" reinforced the perception that he and those who spoke like him were unintelligible at best and unintelligent at worst.

Despite Malone's bravado, Cunningham remained concerned about his star. Moses's other knee, the left one, began hurting after his return to practice on April 20. Trainer Al Domenico determined that Malone had fluid in the knee. Moses could barely walk the next morning, and equipment manager Jeff Millman drove him to see team physician Dr. Michael Clancy.[17] Big Mo almost crumbled to the ground as he exited Millman's car.[18] Publicly, he insisted he'd play, though privately he doubted he'd be ready for Game One.[19] After practice the day before the first game, he estimated that he was at 70 to 75 percent.[20] Erving reasoned that "Moses at 70 percent was still better than most centers."[21]

Malone pummeled the Knicks in Game One, with 38 points and 17 rebounds over 38 minutes in a 76ers victory. Dr. Clancy and Knicks center Marvin Webster noted that Big Mo didn't attack the offensive glass with his usual tenacity, though he impacted the game in other ways, including knocking down several jump shots.[22] After the game, Knicks coach Hubie Brown said,

> Of course he was going to play. Moses never sits down [in a big game]. We knew he was going to play. Go back over Moses Malone's career. Moses Malone never misses [a game] on his volition, and when he plays, he's going to play great, hard no matter what his condition is. That's why he's a super talent. That's why all the professional sports need people like him, *all* the sports because pain is not a factor [with Malone]. With him, winning and his performance are factors. He's a major catalyst. There are very few people in all of professional sports that are major catalysts. He's right at the top of the list.[23]

The 76ers fell behind by 20 points early in the second half of Game Two, then went on a 22–1 run sparked by Malone, who finished with 30 points, 17 rebounds, and 3 blocked shots in 45 minutes. Philly swept the series in four close games. The man teammates called Mozilla totaled 125 points and 62 rebounds, compared to 60 and 36 from New York's centers, Bill Cartwright and Marvin Webster, combined.

Next up for the 76ers was a talented Milwaukee Bucks team that swept the Celtics in the previous round. Don Nelson's squad was led by perimeter players Marques Johnson and Sidney Moncrief, though the Bucks were thin at center. Dave Cowens had to shut it down midway through the season, leaving thirty-four-year-old Bob Lanier and his arthritic knees to try to contain the MVP.

Bobby Jones blocked a Brian Winters shot in the closing minute of Game One to secure the win, and Malone led the way with 26 points in a Game Two victory. The series moved to Milwaukee for Game Three on Saturday afternoon. Philly trailed, 78–71, with 9:57 left in the fourth quarter. Cheeks scored 7 consecutive points to tie the game, then Doc brought home the victory with 11 points in the final eight minutes, to put the 76ers up 3-0.

Game Four tipped off less than 24 hours later. The Sixers led by two heading into the fourth quarter, then appeared to tire late in the game, and the Bucks pulled out a 100–94 victory. "Okay," Moses said, "so it will be fo . . . *five* . . . fo."[24] The Sixers closed out the series in Game Five. In the final minutes, the sellout crowd at the Spectrum chanted, "We want L.A. We want L.A." They received their wish. The Lakers finished off the Spurs in the Western Conference Finals to set up a rematch of the 1982 Finals.

The Lakers-76ers series was a star-studded affair that featured four of the five biggest draws in the game: Doc, Moses, Magic, and Kareem. (Bird was the fifth.) The contest would hinge on the battle of the big men: Moses and Kareem. Abdul-Jabbar was the preeminent player of his generation. Many, including Erving, believed him to be the greatest of all time. Born Lew Alcindor in Harlem, New York City, he became the most sought-after high school player in the country after a stellar career at Power Memorial Academy. Alcindor played for John Wooden at UCLA, where he led the Bruins to an 88-2 record and three championships in three seasons. When the NCAA outlawed the slam dunk after his freshman year, the 7-foot-2 center developed a skyhook, the most unstoppable shot in the game.

Alcindor was drafted by the Bucks first overall in 1969 and teamed with Oscar Robertson to win a championship in 1971. Afterward, he announced that he'd changed his name to Kareem Abdul-Jabbar. Four years later, he was traded to L.A., where he won championship rings in 1980 and 1982. By the 1983 Finals, Kareem had a record six MVP awards and was less than a year away from passing Wilt Chamberlain as the NBA's all-time leading scorer. He turned 36 during the 1983 postseason, though was still at or near peak form. The center averaged 21.8 points per game during the regular season and ratcheted that up to 26.5 against the Spurs in the conference finals. When the Lakers needed a bucket, they still threw the ball inside to No. 33.

Moses respected Kareem and knew he'd be measured by how he performed against the Laker great. He'd had some of his best games against Abdul-Jabbar. "He [Malone] used to always say, 'Oh, I love playing against

Kareem, I just love it,' said Erving. 'Everybody thinks he's the man, but he never beats me.'"[25]

The Lakers were shorthanded in the Finals. James Worthy broke his left shinbone during the last week of the regular season and missed the playoffs. Bob McAdoo was severely hampered by a torn hamstring, and Norm Nixon played through a separated left shoulder.[26] Still, any team with Magic and Kareem was dangerous.

Several fans arrived at the Spectrum for Game One dressed in the garb of the biblical Moses, staff and all. A banner read, "Moses Parts the Lakers" and signs implored Big Mo to lead the Sixers to the promised land. Malone scored 27 points and snatched 18 rebounds in a Sixers 113–107 victory. Kareem amassed 20 points, but just four rebounds, and the Lakers' center was so fatigued late in the game that Pat Riley switched 6-foot-8 Mark Landsberger onto Moses.[27] Malone was too strong for the forward. "Landsberger's like a little grinding machine they put on your knees," he said. Moses was limited to 24 points in 31 minutes in Game Two due to foul trouble, though the Sixers won again, 103–93. This time Riley tried defending him with another scrappy forward, Kurt Rambis, who was equally ineffective.

The series shifted to Los Angeles for Game Three. Like the first two games, the Lakers led at halftime. The score was tied at 72 at the end of the third quarter, when Malone and the 76ers ran over Kareem and company. Philly began the fourth quarter on a 14–0 run. The Lakers clawed back to within six, 90–84, with 4:40 to play. Moses lowered his head and charged past Kareem, who helplessly fouled him as he completed the basket. The three-point play gave Philadelphia a 93–84 lead. A minute and a half later, Malone rumbled past Abdul-Jabbar for another three-point play, and on the 76ers' next possession he converted a short scoop shot. His defense was equally impressive. He pushed, shoved, and leaned on Kareem, preventing him from scoring a field goal for a span of thirty-one minutes, from late in the first quarter until deep into the fourth.[28]

In all three games, Malone had a relatively quiet first half, then gradually wore down whomever Riley threw at him. "He has the talent that you normally find dispersed throughout several different individuals," said Rambis. "To his credit, he seems to get stronger and stronger as the game goes on. He seems to smell the blood of everybody else getting tired and seems to gain strength from it. He draws from that tiredness that's in everybody else. He has you fighting, not only him, but your own body that's telling you that you can't do it anymore."[29]

Cunningham received a scare when he arrived at practice the day before Game Four. Moses had taken an elbow to the chest during Game Three, and Domenico informed the coach that his center was having difficulty breathing. He needed to be taken to the hospital. Cunningham walked over to Malone to see how he was doing. "Don't worry, Coach; Kareem doesn't want to see me anymore," Moses said.[30]

The Lakers fought desperately in Game Four. They took a 16-point lead in the third quarter and led by 11 at the start of the fourth. Philly outscored the Lakers 10–2 in the first few minutes of the quarter. "We were like a big train coming," Moses said. "They knew a big train was coming."[31] Doc took over with the 76ers trailing 106–104 and a little over two minutes remaining. He deflected an Abdul-Jabbar pass, recovered the ball, and raced down the court for a dunk. A minute later, he converted a three-point play to give the 76ers a 109–107 lead. Then he nailed a dagger from the top of the key with 40 seconds remaining. Cheeks raced down the court and dunked the ball as the clock expired. The 76ers swept the Lakers and were NBA champions.

Moses finished Game Four with 24 points and 23 rebounds, including 9 points and 10 boards in the fourth quarter.[32] Big Mo averaged 26 points and 18 rebounds for the series and was named Finals MVP. He outrebounded Abdul-Jabbar 72–30 over the four games. After that, the line around the NBA was that "Moses liked Kareem in his coffee."[33]

The 1982–83 76ers are remembered as one of the greatest teams in NBA history. The 2000–2001 Lakers and 2016–2017 Warriors are the only other teams to win a championship with only one playoff loss. Katz had "Fo, Fi, Fo" inscribed in the Sixers' rings, along with "perseverance," in recognition of the times they fell short, and R&B band Pieces of a Dream released a song titled "Fo-Fi-Fo" later that year.[34]

The Sixers celebrated in the locker room after winning the championship. Even the teetotaling Malone grabbed a bottle of Cordon Rouge and started chugging. "This champagne's stopping Moses more than the Lakers did," he told Bill Livingston of the *Philadelphia Inquirer*.[35] Earl

Cureton introduced a friend to Moses. "I want you to meet Al Capone Malone—he steals basketball games," he said.

Malone responded, "That's me, the gangster of basketball."[36]

He mugged for the cameras as he stepped onto a small podium with CBS's Brent Musburger and Dr. J. Moses took the opportunity to praise others, most notably Erving. "I remember seeing Doc back in the ABA, saw him win two titles there," he said. "When I came to this team, it was to win a title with him. I want to be remembered a long time from now as a guy who played on a championship team with Doc."[37]

At the team celebration later that night, Malone turned to Katz and said, "Mr. Katz, you'll be hearing from Mr. Fentress in two days." Katz turned white. "Just kidding," Moses said and started laughing.[38] He earned about $2.9 million for the season, including bonus and salary.[39]

An estimated one million people turned out for the parade on June 2. The team boarded a flat-walled, glass-bed truck that wound through the heart of the business district, down South Broad Street, all the way to Veterans Stadium. The caravan stopped in front of the Bellevue-Stratford Hotel a few blocks from city hall. Moses said a few words to the crowd, including a follow-up to "Fo, Fo, Fo": "We gotta repeat, and peat, and peat," he said.[40] A group of construction workers watching from a rooftop lifted their lunch pails to salute their hero.[41]

18
Reluctant Superstar

Malone was in high demand after winning back-to-back MVP awards and leading the 76ers to a championship. He appeared on the cover of *Sports Illustrated* and sat down for an interview with *Playboy Magazine* (for which he was reportedly paid $40,000).[1] People looked at him differently, though he never changed the way he viewed himself. "And you know what," said Jim Lynam, who coached him in Philly, "he was as content in his own skin as anybody who ever walked planet earth."[2] Moses viewed the accolades and fame as temporary distractions from his goals. "Once you establish yourself that you that great ball player, you're not gonna work for the effort to get better," he said years later.[3]

Big Mo had a complicated relationship with fame. Not long after the championship season, he and Floy Johnson were hanging out in front of his house on a beautiful day. Moses Jr. was shooting hoops in the driveway. Big Mo picked up a basketball and held it in the palm of his hand as he surveyed his luxury automobiles and enormous home. He turned to Floy and dreamily said, "I owe all of this to basketball."[4]

Yet Moses was loathe to recognize the role others played in his lifestyle. His success on the court was the result of skill and hard work. The money that followed was generated by the media and fans. While he enjoyed the perks of celebrity, such as skipping the line at a club and his choice of women, he resented the loss of anonymity that came with it. He'd leave a venue because of attention from fans, when his fame was the only reason he'd been admitted in the first place.

Moses usually denied requests for autographs and photographs. If he was in a relatively quiet place without many people around, he might be receptive. But if a fan approached him while he was walking through an airport he'd say, "No, no, no, no, no."[5] He was skeptical of adults' motives and generally more willing to accommodate kids.

Moses's friend Mel Hughlett recalled stopping at a car wash with Moses and Jacky Dorsey. A man walked over and said his little brother, who was an avid sports fan, was sick in the hospital. His brother would be so excited if the guys signed autographs for him. The man provided a blank sheet of paper and a pen. Mel and Jacky signed and handed the paper to Moses. He looked at it for a while, turned it over and examined the other side before signing. Later that afternoon Moses noted that the piece of paper could have been a blank check.[6] He was always wary of people trying to take advantage of him.

Franklin Edwards received a taste of life as a superstar when he roomed with Moses during training camp in 1982. Fans knocked on their hotel room door at 2:00 a.m. When Edwards answered, they asked him to get Moses's autograph for them.[7] It can be exhausting for celebrities to be bombarded by autograph requests every time they're in public. They can't possibly accommodate every fan. Still, friends cringed when Malone told off autograph seekers. He'd be furious if somebody slipped him a piece of paper while he was eating. "Get that fucking piece of paper out of my face," he'd say. "Don't you see me fucking eating? I'm with my boy. We here trying to eat, not here trying to sign autographs. Get the fuck out of my face."[8]

Moses hobnobbed with celebrities and hit up trendy clubs, though he felt most comfortable around old friends and familiar establishments. He had no use for people with big egos and remained loyal to buddies from high school and friends he met when he first moved to Houston. He ate at Frenchy's, Whataburger, and McDonald's and walked around in track suits.[9] Malone didn't hesitate to attend a party in one of Houston's poorer neighborhoods. When traveling with friends, he'd ask what hotel they were staying at and join them even though he could afford more luxurious accommodations.[10]

Moses was perplexed by the concept of being a superstar. Basketball is a team sport. A player's success is attributable to his teammates, he reasoned. He treated the twelfth man on the roster the same way he treated Erving, and that sentiment extended to the people he encountered away from the game, like janitors and construction workers.

Malone had already won an MVP award in Houston when he and his Rockets teammates disembarked from the team bus at Cleveland Hopkins Airport. The players wore suits and ties on the road. An elderly white woman approached him and said, "Excuse me sir, can you get my bags for me?" She thought he was a porter. Moses grabbed the woman's bags and carried them to the gate.[11]

"I don't know, I just had this bias towards superstars," said Fred Roberts, who played with Moses toward the end of his career. "I thought they just wanted to be treated special. They thought they were special. But that wasn't him at all, not at all."[12] He never complained about accommodations or requested special perks. Some stars arrive fashionably late. Malone was always respectfully early.

His teammates revered him precisely because he didn't ask for it. In the locker room, he was rarely the center of a conversation, but happy to chime in with a one-liner or anecdote. Mike Newlin recalls Moses as one of the greatest teammates he ever had because "he didn't fail you. He never failed to do his job. Whatever that job was, he did it in spades, and he never failed to do it. You can say that was an anchor."[13]

The bond between teammates was sacred to Malone, who cherished those relationships long after his playing days. C. J. Kupec was a teammate with Moses in Houston during the 1977–78 season, after which he played professionally in Italy and Switzerland. In the summer of 1982, Moses and some NBA players participated in a game in Italy. Kupec attended and approached Moses, who was surrounded by a throng of reporters. He and Malone weren't teammates for long and hadn't been close, but upon seeing his former teammate, Moses stopped the press conference, walked over to Kupec and said, "C, how you doing?" The two spent several minutes catching up.[14]

Of course, Moses was happy to escape the horde of journalists. "He was the most humble guy in the world," said Hughlett. "You could talk to him about anything, but the topic he was least comfortable with was Moses Malone."[15] Big Mo was fiercely protective of his privacy, which was challenging after he led the 76ers to the promised land. The Philly press grew accustomed to lines like "No comment," "No interviews on Tuesdays," and "I don't do interviews in Denver." Moses didn't talk to reporters at shootarounds or before games.[16] He dutifully answered basketball-related questions after games, though as soon as a reporter tried to penetrate his personal world, he shut down.

Ray Didinger of the *Philadelphia Daily News* wrote a profile on Malone during the 1983 playoffs. He asked Malone for an interview. Malone told him to talk to somebody else. Didinger said, "But the story is about you." Malone shook his head no. Didinger persisted. "But the people in Philadelphia don't know much about you."

"I was in Houston six years," Malone said. "They don't know me there either. I like it that way."

"Why?" asked Didinger.

Malone shrugged. "Just do," he said.[17]

Fentress asked Moses to talk to Didinger. No luck. Cunningham and Katz did the same, but Moses refused. Didinger asked Alfreda to talk to him. She said she'd ask Moses if that was okay. The next day she told Didinger, "Moses wants his private life kept private. I'm sorry."[18]

Didinger interviewed David Pair, Moses's close friend from high school, who still resided in the Heights, for the profile and mentioned that some people found Malone to be aloof. "When the season is over," said Pair, "Moses comes back here. He says, 'Let's get something to eat.' So we go to the Fish House. That's the place we went fifteen years ago. All you can eat for $3. Last year, we went and Moses ate twenty-four pieces of fish. Ran the poor waitress half to death. After that, we rounded up the old gang—Jimmy Snake and that crowd—and we played ball. Moses was there in the school yard fooling around. Does that sound like a guy who's aloof?"[19]

Pro Hayes, Malone's high school coach, told Didinger that Malone didn't trust anybody because people had been trying to take advantage of him since he was in high school. Nissalke, his coach with the Stars and Rockets, noted that Malone was discarded by several teams at a young age. The result, both coaches concluded, was an unwillingness to reveal himself to reporters.[20]

Every great player endures aggressive recruiting pitches, invasion of their privacy, and other obstacles on the path to stardom. Malone's journey was unique in that he was the first modern player to jump directly from high school to the pros. Coaches and teammates spoke about how seamless that transition was for him. Perhaps it was more emotionally complicated than they realized, creating a professional athlete who struggled with a significant aspect of his job, communicating with the press. His natural introversion and sensitivity undoubtedly played a role as well.

Regardless of the reason, Malone's reticence was often interpreted as rude by reporters. Jack McCallum, the longtime *Sports Illustrated* scribe, didn't hold back in his assessment of Moses in his 1992 book, *Unfinished Business*. "He was a selfish, complaining, nearly unintelligible brute of a man who seemed to speak in a language decipherable only to himself, although the word 'Moses' could be picked up quite often," wrote McCallum.[21]

Even with teammates, Moses maintained his privacy. "It's like he's part of a group, but then not part of a group," said Mark McNamara. "He comes in when he wants to and leaves when he wants to."[22] Many who shared a locker room with Moses adored him though felt like they didn't really know him. He didn't engage in intimate conversations or confide in teammates about personal problems. Malone attended parties but never hosted and only welcomed close friends into his home.

"You just don't get it," David Stern told a group of employees. "We're not just a sport. We're Disney."[23] Stern saw the NBA as an entertainment property when he succeeded Larry O'Brien as commissioner on February 1, 1984. He forged a path forward for the struggling league through force of personality and innovative marketing. The commissioner realized that the players—tall, thin, and soaring through the air without a helmet, hat, or much clothing to obscure their faces and bodies—were the stars and marketed them as such. Instead of the Lakers coming to town, it became "Magic Johnson and the Lakers."

Moses Malone was nobody's Mickey Mouse. The three-time MVP sat on the sidelines while some of his peers emerged as the faces of the league. Magic was a willing ambassador in the mold of Erving, happy to comply with all interview requests. Bird was prickly, particularly early in his career, and like Malone had no interest in stardom, though he garnered enormous attention as the lone white superstar in an increasingly Black league and through his rivalry with Magic. Stern found his leading man in Michael Jordan, a handsome, charismatic, gravity-defying assassin, who entered the league months into the commissioner's tenure. With the assistance of brilliant marketing by Nike and other brands, Jordan's star power circled the globe and carried the NBA with it.

Stern envisioned All-Star weekend as the NBA's Super Bowl, an opportunity to showcase his stars and the league. The NBA held its first Slam Dunk Contest in 1984. Two years later, the three-point contest was introduced. Those and other events drew advertising dollars, and the weekend-long festivities evolved into a destination where former and current players, entertainers, business executives, and advertisers mingled.

The NBA also had the foresight to align itself with seismic cultural developments. Cable television provided greater exposure for the game's stars. The NBA signed a deal with the newly established USA Network to air Thursday night games in the late 1970s.[24] ESPN was founded in 1979 and would become a destination for games and highlights.

The league cross-promoted its product with the emerging genre of rap music, which encapsulated the beats and rhythms of basketball and shared common roots in America's inner cities. It was fresh and stylish and jived with the cutting-edge image Stern attempted to portray. The NBA used Kurtis Blow's song "Basketball" in promotions. As Pete Croatto noted in his book *From Hang Time to Prime Time*, "rap's emergence was aided by acceptance of blacks in mainstream culture. Michael Jackson, Bill Cosby, and Eddie Murphy achieved massive popularity around the same time in three separate realms of pop culture."[25] Those icons made Black basketball players more palatable to white America as well.

Transcendent stars, marketing ingenuity, and cultural shifts boosted the popularity of the NBA in the United States and abroad during the second half of Malone's career. An influx of endorsement money followed, creating a massive revenue stream for the league's stars. Moses's share of the sponsorship pie wasn't commensurate with his accomplishments. The big man who mumbled through interviews and wouldn't smile for the camera wasn't an ideal pitchman and had no interest in being one. Fentress suggested several times that his client see a speech therapist to improve his marketability, but Moses refused.[26]

Malone signed endorsement contracts with MacGregor, for a Moses Malone basketball; Anheuser-Busch; and an athletic sock company, though his most lucrative deal was with Nike.[27] Had he made the jump from high school twenty-five years later, he would have signed a massive shoe deal before stepping foot on an NBA court, but sneaker sponsorships were a new concept in the mid-70s. Moses wore Adidas during his two ABA seasons, then moved to Converse upon joining the NBA. He switched to Nike around 1980 because Converse wouldn't supply him with matching warm-ups and sneakers. "I didn't go to Nike for any contract," he said. "My negotiation was for a warm-up suit. I've been wearing Nike ever since."[28]

Phil Knight founded Blue Ribbon Sports in 1964 as a track-shoe company and changed its name to Nike in 1971 in honor of the Greek goddess of victory.[29] The company released its first basketball sneakers in 1972 and 1973 with the Bruin and Blazer, respectively.[30] It increased its investment in basketball in 1977 by signing eighty college coaches.[31]

That same year, Nike hired Peter Moore as creative director. Moore designed an innovative line of hoops posters to showcase the company's talent. They began as promotional items in sneaker stores and eventually made their way to the bedroom walls of young basketball fans.[32] The first one depicted Darrell Griffith, the high-flying guard for the Utah Jazz, as a mad scientist holding a basketball that had split in half, with his nickname, Dr. Dunkenstein, prominently displayed.[33] There was a classic depiction of George "Iceman" Gervin dressed in all white sitting on an ice throne. The poster of Moses parting a sea of basketballs was released in 1980.

Still, Converse ruled the basketball sneaker world in the early 1980s, with Johnson, Bird, and Erving under contract. Adidas ranked number two. Then Nike introduced a sneaker called Air Force 1 in 1982 that changed the game. It was the first basketball shoe to include the revolutionary air technology, essentially a pressurized air bag that acts as a cushioning system in a shoe.[34]

Nike rolled out Air Force 1 prior to the 1982–83 season. The advertising campaign featured a poster of the Original Six—Moses, Bobby Jones, Jamaal Wilkes, Calvin Natt, Mychal Thompson, and Michael Cooper—posing in front of a plane at sunset, donning white flight suits and white AF1s with silver swooshes.[35] Moses, the most accomplished of the six, became the face of the sneaker. "Once Malone brought us to the promised land, everybody in Philly was like, 'Yo, I got to get those. I got to wear them,'" said Anthony Gilbert of *Sole Collector* magazine.[36] From there, they spread to New York and other cities.

The air technology was well received by professionals and amateurs. The extra cushioning was particularly beneficial to street ballers who were jumping, starting, and stopping on concrete playgrounds. Prior to the Air Force 1s, they wore three or four pairs of socks to absorb the shock. The AF1s enabled them to use one.[37] The shoes gained street credibility due to their functionality and sleek design and became the first basketball sneaker to cross over to an everyday shoe that could be worn to school, the club, or even church.[38]

Moses wore a low-top model that became a cultural touchstone. The sneaker's simple, clean look (the air bubble was not visible as on later Nike models) made it an ideal canvas for personalization. Nike released over 1,700 color combinations in the decades to follow, including countless special editions from renowned artists. Rappers Eric B. and Rakim wore them on album covers, and in 2002, Nelly wrote a song about them.[39] Nike released a limited-edition version of the sneaker in honor of Malone in the early 2000s.

Moses's collaboration with Nike extended beyond Air Force 1. He was the brand's highest-paid basketball player and first to appear in a commercial. The spot featured him alone in a gym, putting up shots and grabbing rebounds, sweating profusely. Moses spoke in a painfully slow voice, "At the age of fourteen, I discovered the secret: pick the one thing you do best and work at it. So, while every other kid was trying to be the next Iceman, I would hit the boards. Because I figure if you ain't got the ball, you can't shoot the ball." It ended with an exhausted Moses, hands on his knees, as "Nike" flashed on the screen. The commercial is comically primitive in retrospect, though it served as a steppingstone for a brand that would soon soar on Jordan's wings.

Malone shot more Nike commercials, including one with Charles Barkley and other NBA players competing in a game of three-on-three in a dingy gym. He also appeared in a print ad with Barkley in which both were dressed in space-aged black and silver outfits. Many years later, Malone participated in one of LeBron James's first Nike commercials, called Book of Dimes. Bernie Mac played a pastor who preached the gospel of a young phenom named LeBron James. There was a choir of female players, including Sue Bird, Dawn Staley, and Lisa Leslie. On stage was a collection of NBA legends in Nike track suits, among them Jerry West, George Gervin, and Moses, welcoming LeBron to the congregation of Nike basketball.[40]

Moses enjoyed being part of the Nike family. Every summer, the company flew its college coaches to a retreat at an exotic destination. Moses was one of the few players to regularly attend. He and the coaches played golf and relaxed by the pool. Mitch Buonaguro, the coach of Fairfield University, remembered Moses "picking up the coaches' kids like they were footballs" and tossing them into the pool.[41]

Nike hired Howard White, the coach who recruited Moses to Maryland, as a field representative shortly after signing Malone. The two men grew close and spoke a few times a week. Moses also developed relationships with Nike athletes Gervin, Barkley, and Jordan. Whenever Jordan's team visited Malone's he spent the day at the Malone house, playing cards with Moses and Nintendo with Moses Jr. while Alfreda cooked dinner. At night, Moses and Michael hit the clubs.[42]

Nike signed Moses to a lifetime contract. In the fall of 2003, it flew him to Sacramento to deliver advice to LeBron before his NBA debut.[43] Moses filled a room in his house with Nike apparel and invited select friends to pick out what they wanted. He brought warm-ups to Fonde for the players he and Floy coached in a pro-am league, then asked Floy to hand them out when he wasn't around. The players knew where they came from, but Moses didn't want the attention.[44]

19

Fat and Lazy

The Sixers faced the obstacles of fatigue, injuries, and complacency in their quest to repeat as champions. Their biggest external threat was the Celtics, which improved in the offseason with the acquisition of guard Dennis Johnson, MVP of the 1979 Finals. Hatred ran deep between the two teams. One year they met in an exhibition game in Knoxville, Tennessee. Only one restaurant was near the arena. After the game, the Celtics arrived first. The 76ers walked in later. The two groups stared each other down, then the Sixers said, "We ain't eating," and walked out.[1]

The Celtics were intent on reclaiming alpha status in the Eastern Conference when the two teams met in an exhibition game at Boston Garden on October 17, 1983. Three minutes into the game, Celtics forward Cedric Maxwell fired the ball at Moses's head after Malone bumped him following a rebound. Malone tackled Maxwell. A minute later, Bird and Iavaroni exchanged punches. Celtics general manager Red Auerbach ran onto the court, removed his glasses, walked up to Malone, and said, "Hit me, you big SOB. Go ahead, I'm not big. Hit me, you SOB."[2]

The Sixers began the season 13-3, yet the players and Cunningham sensed something was off. They weren't playing with the same intensity as in the championship season. The Sixers lost to the Pistons, 120–116, in Detroit on November 9. After being startled awake by telephone calls at 5:00 a.m. the next morning, they caught a 7:10 flight out of Detroit. They landed in Philadelphia at 8:30, began practice at 9:30 at St. Joe's, and didn't leave the floor until 11:00.[3] It was the first time Cunningham held a practice the morning after a game. Still, their effort level continued to vacillate. The low point was a 111–73 loss to the Knicks at Madison Square Garden. It was their fifth loss in eight games and dropped their record to 24-10.[4]

Moses hurt his knee in training camp, then suffered repeated ankle injuries. He sprained his right ankle a few weeks into the season and the left one against the Pistons on December 21. He severely reinjured the left ankle during a January 24 loss to the Knicks, forcing him to miss nine games. Moses returned to the lineup on February 17 against the Nets, though the ankle was far from healed. He wore a plastic cast to protect it. His teammate Leo Rautins wore the same cast that season and could barely walk in it, never mind play ball. He marveled at Moses "playing like an animal" with the cast on.[5] The cast and injury affected Malone's lateral movement and explosiveness, impacting his performance.

As Moses went, so went the Sixers. Philly lost 5 out of 6 games in late February and early March, amounting to 13 losses in 19 games. On February 29 Moses accumulated just 11 points and 5 rebounds while being outplayed by the Jazz's second-year center Mark Eaton. A few nights later, he was unable to dominate journeymen James Edwards and Rick Robey in a loss to the Suns.[6] Katz had seen enough. The owner chewed out Malone and the team in the locker room after the Suns game. He "basically called Moses a bum and said the team's not worth shit," recalled Rautins.[7]

Katz shared his thoughts with reporters in a hotel lobby hours later. "Is Moses Malone worth $2 million this year?" he asked rhetorically. "No. The answer is absolutely no," Katz said. He admitted that Malone might still be recovering from the ankle injury, though it was impossible to know because Moses didn't communicate with the team doctor, trainer, or Cunningham. Malone hadn't been in top form prior to the injury either.[8]

Katz's frustration dated back to the start of training camp when Moses arrived overweight and out of shape.[9] He ran the mile on the first day of camp over half a minute slower than the previous year, coming in at a little over seven minutes. Malone had more commitments than usual during the offseason, resulting in the longest layoff of his career.[10] There were a couple of Nike trips, a radio advertisement for Fuji Film, and a trip to the White House for a state dinner in which he was paired with astronaut Sally Ride. "Now that was something," Malone said. "I was one seat away from the president. I never would have thought, growing up in Petersburg, that I'd ever be having dinner with the president."[11] Katz was also annoyed that Moses went to L.A. to shoot a Nike commercial, then visited Houston, rather than receiving treatment in Philly, while sitting out the All-Star Game due to injury.[12]

Malone avoided the press for days after Katz's comments, then refused to address them.[13] In a rare public comment, Alfreda told *Ebony* that the criticism of Moses was hurtful. "I'm sitting there every night looking at his ankle almost double its size," she said.[14] Katz's words appeared to provide a spark for the Sixers, which won thirteen of the next fifteen games, and by the end of March, Moses was delivering vintage performances.

Despite the turmoil and a disappointing regular season, Philadelphia won 52 games, second-most in the Eastern Conference. Even in a down year, Moses led the league in rebounding and was named to the All-NBA Second Team. The 76ers appeared to be rounding into form as the playoffs began and, based on their talent and pedigree, were considered a threat to win another championship. They were a heavy favorite in the first round against a New Jersey Nets team led by guards Michael Ray Richardson and Otis Birdsong.

New Jersey stunned the Sixers in Philadelphia in Game One, 116–101, holding Moses to 4 points in the second half. They stole Game Two as well, as their two centers, Mike Gminski and Darryl Dawkins, combined for 27 points and 22 rebounds, compared to Malone's 25 and 22. The 76ers won both games in New Jersey to even the best-of-five series, setting up a decisive Game Five in Philly. Philadelphia was up a few points with five minutes left when the team ran out of gas. Cunningham pushed every button he could think of but couldn't propel his team across the finish line.[15] The Nets won by three points to knock out the defending champions. Their centers outscored Malone 112–107 in the series.

Cunningham believed the team was mentally and physically exhausted. The players advanced to the Finals three times in four years (1980, 1982, and 1983) and reached Game Seven of the conference finals in 1981.[16] Management and some of the players felt that a degree of complacency crept in after winning the championship. Cunningham had said the championship was "more relief than anything," and a poster made of Moses and Doc said, "Paid in Full."[17]

The 76ers had three first-round picks in the 1984 draft, including a lottery pick, which they received from the Clippers in 1978 in exchange for World B. Free. The Clippers won just 29 games in 1983–84 and were in play for the number one pick. On the last Saturday of the season, they won, and the Rockets lost, taking the 76ers out of the coin flip for a shot at Hakeem Olajuwon or Michael Jordan. Houston won the top pick for the second year in a row after trading Malone and opted for Olajuwon a year after selecting Ralph Sampson. The 76ers settled for the fifth pick.

Katz and Pat Williams set their sights on a pudgy forward out of Auburn University named Charles Barkley. "The Round Mound of Rebound" was undersized for a power forward, though made up for it with exceptional athleticism. The 76ers were concerned about Barkley's weight, work ethic, and confrontations he'd had with Coach Sonny Smith at Auburn, but there was no denying his talent.[18] Barkley, who weighed close to 300 pounds, lost 10 pounds in the weeks before the draft at the 76ers' request.[19]

The NBA's new salary cap went into effect for the 1984–85 season. Teams at or above the cap could only offer their first-round pick $75,000 for one year, after which the player would become a restricted free agent. When Barkley's agent Lance Luchnick informed him of the rule, Charles replied, "I didn't leave college for $75,000." He gorged himself, putting on about 20 pounds in two days before the draft to discourage the Sixers from selecting him. Williams was alarmed. Katz was furious.[20] They drafted him anyway.

Williams performed a stand-up routine about Barkley's weight for reporters after the draft. "When he walks down Broad Street, it'll instantly become a one-way street," the GM said. "When he goes swimming, you gotta worry about him getting harpooned." And lastly, "He came in yesterday wearing a form-fitting poncho."[21]

Barkley continued the behavior that drove Coach Smith crazy at Auburn, showing up teammates at practice. On one occasion, he slammed a teammate to the ground and dropped the ball on him.[22] The 76ers called a players-only meeting during a losing streak that season. As captain, Doc went down the line asking his teammates if they had an opinion about what was wrong with the team. Leon Wood, another first-year player, adhered to the notion that it was better for rookies to keep their mouth shut and passed on the chance to speak. Rookie or not, Barkley wasn't going to pass up an opportunity to speak his mind and stated that the offense should run through him and Moses. "Doc, no disrespect," he said, "I think you're getting up there in age." Wood was shocked to hear his fellow rookie speak that way to the great Dr. J.[23]

Barkley first met Malone soon after he was drafted. Charles visited his agent in Houston and made a stop at Fonde. "Hey fathead, welcome to the team," Malone greeted him. Barkley was Malone's rookie that season. He was required to carry the veteran's bags and fetch him a drink whenever he wanted one, whether it was at a club or in the middle of the night.[24]

Charles suffered a rare crisis of confidence during his rookie season. He was coming off the bench and frustrated about his playing time. He voiced his concerns to Nike's Howard White. White convinced Barkley to seek advice from Moses.[25] Barkley and Malone lived in the same building, so the rookie went up to the penthouse and knocked on Malone's door. He asked Moses why he wasn't playing more. Moses looked him up and down and said, "You're fat and lazy."

Malone told Barkley to lose 10 pounds and began working with him before and after practice. He even ran outside with the rookie in the rain at a track near their building. Moses showed Charles how to execute a drop step and tricks of the trade, like stepping on an opponent's toes when he's getting ready to shoot.[26] Charles dropped down to 290. Moses told him to lose 10 more, and he obliged. Moses said 10 more, then 10 more. Eventually Charles trimmed down to 250 pounds.[27] His play improved. The Sixers traded Iavaroni, and Cunningham inserted Barkley into the starting lineup.

Moses stayed on top of him. Charles ordered pizza to his apartment one day. Moments later there was a knock on his door. "You got pizza in here," said Big Mo. "You can't lose weight eating pizza."[28] Barkley didn't know how Malone knew about the pizza.

Moses took a softer approach with Charles when necessary. During training camp, he advised the rookie to "watch out for the freaks," referring to the women who would be throwing themselves at him, and provided words of encouragement when Barkley was frustrated with Cunningham.[29] Malone and Erving taught the rookie how to dress like a professional and took him on a $25,000 shopping spree.[30]

Malone and Barkley poked fun at each other. "I consider myself ugly," Barkley told a reporter, "but I consider Moses uglier."[31] Charles looked at the stat sheet in the locker room after every game and clamored about his rebounding totals, knowing that Malone resented the competition.[32]

Barkley has repeatedly stated that Moses was the most important person in his basketball career because he taught him how to work hard. He could never understand why a superstar like Moses took such an interest in a fat kid from Leeds, Alabama, though he was eternally grateful. "Moses filled a gap in my life that had burdened me since my father abandoned my family," Charles said. He began calling Moses "Dad."[33]

Barkley often spoke of Malone's influence, though Malone kept their relationship to himself as Barkley emerged as one of the league's top players. "He never said anything about what he did for me," Barkley said. "Most guys, when they mentor a young player like that, they go around saying, 'Yeah, that was me. I did that.' Not Moses. He never told anybody. And that was the best part."[34]

Moses returned for the 1984–85 season healthy and in top shape. He rediscovered his MVP form, and the 76ers looked like championship contenders again. Malone and Barkley overwhelmed teams on the boards as the Sixers won thirteen-consecutive games in late December and early January, pushing their record to 33-6. They faded a bit down the stretch due to injuries. Moses sprained both ankles late in the season, and Erving, Toney, and Clemon Johnson were also banged up.[35] Cunningham's team won 58 games, finishing 5 behind the Celtics in the Atlantic Division. The 76ers knew the path to the Finals ran through Boston.

Philly defeated the Bullets in the first round of the playoffs and swept an excellent Bucks team in the second round, setting up another matchup with the Celtics in the conference finals. The two teams exchanged blows again early in the season in an altercation that began with Bird and Erving. Dr. J was known for his cool, calm demeanor, but on a Friday night in November at Boston Garden, the Doctor lost his temper.

Erving and Bird had a friendly relationship. They'd participated in Converse and Spalding commercials together. Bird was in the middle of a three-year MVP reign, while Erving was slowing down in his fourteenth season. Bird torched Doc on November 9, accumulating 42 points on 17 of 23 shooting midway through the third quarter, compared to just 6 for Erving. Bird accompanied his shooting display with a verbal assault that intensified in the second half. "Larry started saying he was done, he was washed up," recalled Bird's teammate Robert Parish. "Larry started saying he was the better player, that there's only one man that could guard him and that was God."[36]

With about six minutes remaining in the third quarter, Doc cut from the left wing toward the middle of the floor. Bird threw an elbow, which grazed Erving's temple, and was called for a foul. The two legends exchanged words in front of the press table. Then Erving cupped Bird's waist with his right hand and reached for his throat with his left. Bird shoved Erving's face in response. Barkley and Malone grabbed Bird from behind and held him as Erving unleashed punches at Bird's head. They eventually tackled Bird to the floor, and Malone ended up scuffling with M. L. Carr. "Larry earned that ass whoopin'," Parish told ESPN's Jackie MacMullan years later. "He earned it from his words."[37]

The Celtics won that game by 11 points, and the teams split the season series 3-3, creating tremendous buzz for the Eastern Conference Finals. The matchup proved to be disappointing. Philly looked old and a step slow as it fell to Boston in five games. Dennis Johnson held Toney under wraps, and Parish matched Malone with 17 offensive rebounds for the series. Cunningham resigned a few days later.

Moses led the league in rebounds for the fifth consecutive season. He was selected to the All-NBA First Team and finished third in MVP voting behind Bird and Magic, both of whom had surpassed him as the greatest players in the world. He and that Sixers team would never reach such heights again.

20

The Breakup

Cunningham noticed that Moses's game was slipping during the Eastern Conference Finals. The center played well by most players' standards, averaging 18.2 points and 13.4 rebounds against arguably the greatest frontcourt in basketball history, though he looked worn down and connected on just 40.5 percent of his shots. The effort was there, but Moses wasn't able to access that extra gear that propelled the Sixers to a championship a couple years earlier. "There were situations where he normally would just freaking dominate. And he just couldn't do it," Cunningham recalled.[1]

Moses was only thirty years old, typically still a player's prime, though he had a ton of mileage on his legs after eleven professional seasons, including two in which he led the league in minutes played. He was still one of the top ten players in the world and one of the two best centers in the game, along with Olajuwon, but his MVP days were behind him.

Cunningham was replaced by Matt Guokas, his teammate on the 1967 Sixers championship team who had served on Cunningham's staff for a few years. Guokas was more even-keeled than his predecessor and was well liked around the league. "If you could not get along with Matt Guokas, something was wrong with you," said Pat Williams.[2] The coach inherited the difficult task of shepherding a team of veterans in decline. The 1985–86 season would be Bobby Jones's last. Dr. J averaged less than 20 points per game for the first time since high school, and Toney played just six games due to stress fractures in his feet that would end his career.

Malone's knees bothered him during the preseason, and he looked so sluggish that new assistant coach Jim Lynam expressed concern to Guokas and Katz. They told him not to worry; Moses would be ready when the season started. Sure enough, Big Mo manhandled Patrick Ewing, the first pick in the 1985 draft, in his NBA debut a few nights later with 35 points and 13 rebounds in an opening night win against the Knicks. "Moses wore my butt out; he kicked my ass," said Ewing years later.[3]

The 76ers were inconsistent, and Malone clashed with his new coach. On February 1 the Sixers lost in Oakland to a Warriors team that had lost eight games in a row. Philly looked lethargic, particularly on the defensive end. It was the team's third loss in a row and fourth in five games, dropping its record to 30-18. Malone fumbled a rebound of a Warriors free throw late in the game, and Guokas pulled him at the next stoppage of play with a little over a minute remaining and the 76ers trailing by 7. Moses believed the coach was trying to embarrass him and yelled at Guokas as he walked off the court. The two engaged in a heated exchange as Moses took a seat on the bench.[4] "You should have been there the night in Golden State when Mattie [Guokas] jerked him in and out of the lineup," Barkley recalled years later. "Mo said, 'I'm gonna kill him. I'm gonna kill him. I'm gonna kill him, and I'm gonna kill [owner Harold] Katz.'"[5]

After the game, Guokas criticized Malone's defense. The two men had a long talk after the next practice. Guokas explained that he was fishing for an effective lineup down the stretch, and Malone dismissed the altercation as "just something that happened" though was unwilling to say that he had put it behind him.[6] Disputes between players and coaches are common over the course of a pressure-packed eighty-two-game season. They're often insignificant, and both parties move on, though sometimes such arguments are indicative of a deeper issue. Malone and Guokas's disagreement was symptomatic of a player and team struggling with aging.

Meanwhile, Malone's relationship with Katz was deteriorating. When the owner questioned whether Toney was hurt and threatened to suspend him for not attending practice, Moses backed his teammate. "My standpoint is, if the guy says he's hurt, I believe the man," Malone said. Moses pointed out other instances when the owner criticized injured players, including himself. "When I was hurt," Malone said, "they criticized me, and I had a swollen ankle. If Andrew says he's hurt, I'm with him 100 percent." Moses also suggested that the team's slide since the championship and recent poor play was a result of insecurity in the locker room due to the players' lack of faith in management. He lamented the departure of some players from the championship team and was incredulous that Erving, whose contract expired at the end of the season, hadn't been given a new deal. Moses hinted several times during the season that he wanted a contract extension, even though he had two years left on his deal, which didn't sit well with Katz.[7]

Moses suffered a fractured orbit of his right eye during a game against the Bucks on March 28, 1986, when Milwaukee center Randy Breuer inadvertently caught him with a right hand.[8] Dr. Jack Jeffers, an ophthalmologist at Wills Eye Hospital, determined that Malone would risk further damage by playing. Big Mo was done for the season.[9] He'd been voted a starter in the All-Star Game and averaged an impressive 23.8 points per game, but there were signs of decline. His 11.8 rebounds were the lowest average of his NBA career and ended his five-year streak of leading the league. In fact, he ranked second on his own team in rebounding behind Barkley. His shooting percentage fell for the fifth-consecutive season to a then career-low 45.8 percent, and he was noticeably less active on defense.

Perhaps most telling, the Sixers excelled in his absence, winning the first six games after his injury, before losing the final game of the season. Their offense was less predictable and moved at a faster pace, relying on the young legs of Barkley and rookie Terry Catledge. The 76ers disposed of the Bullets in the first round of the playoffs and pushed an experienced Bucks squad to seven games in the second round without Malone. People inside the organization began to wonder if the team was better without him.

Moses and Doc were guests on Brent Musburger's halftime show during CBS's coverage of Game Four of the Finals between the Rockets and Celtics. It was a rare public appearance for Malone, whose teams' public-relations staff generally passed over him for promotional events in favor of more eloquent teammates. Musburger asked Malone about the possibility of him being traded. "What Harold [Katz] wants to do is up to him," Malone said. "If he thinks the team is playing better without me, that's up to him."[10] Moses added that his chances of remaining with the team were fifty-fifty and that if he was traded, he'd prefer to go to the Dallas Mavericks or San Antonio Spurs.[11]

The 76ers hadn't been shopping Malone, though Pat Williams's phone began to ring after Malone's TV appearance. Moses's quotes kicked off a frenetic two weeks for the organization.[12] In addition to fielding calls for Malone, the 76ers were interested in dealing the first pick in the 1986 draft, which they had acquired from the Clippers in 1979 in exchange for Joe Bryant.

There wasn't a consensus No. 1 pick as in the three previous years, with Ralph Sampson (1983), Hakeem Olajuwon (1984), and Patrick Ewing (1985). Brad Daugherty, a skilled 7-footer from the University of North Carolina, was the presumptive choice, though he'd been plastered with the dreaded "soft" label.[13] Talented centers Chris Washburn, William Bedford, and Roy Tarpley were either suspected of drug abuse, alcohol abuse, or both. The 76ers crossed sharpshooter Chuck Person off their list because he'd clashed with Barkley at Auburn.

The most intriguing prospect was a physical marvel from the University of Maryland named Len Bias, whose athleticism drew comparisons to Michael Jordan. Jack McMahon, the 76ers' director of player personnel, vetoed drafting him. "There's something about him I don't like," McMahon said when the front office was discussing which players to interview.[14] (Bias died of a cocaine overdose two days after the Celtics selected him with the second pick, and Washburn's, Bedford's, and Tarpley's careers were marred by addiction, resulting in the 1986 draft becoming known as "the drug draft.")

The 76ers worked out Daugherty at Katz's house. They liked him but weren't convinced he'd be a star.[15] If they kept the pick, he'd be the choice, but they explored trade options. Daugherty needed time to develop, and with Erving nearing the end of his career, Katz wanted to compete for a title immediately. Williams, Nash, and McMahon contacted nearly every team in the league about trading the first pick for a player or players who could help them win right away.[16]

About a week before the draft, the Pistons offered Philadelphia Bill Laimbeer, Vinnie Johnson, Kelly Tripucka, and the No. 11 pick for Moses and the No. 1 pick. The Sixers were more intrigued by an offer from the Bullets that centered around big man Jeff Ruland and forward Cliff Robinson. The Bullets initially inquired about Malone and the No. 1 pick, with the intention of selecting local hero Len Bias, though the Sixers preferred not to include the pick. The teams discussed several players and ultimately settled on a framework of Ruland and Robinson for Moses, Terry Catledge, and two first-round picks.[17]

Then it was decision time. Were the 76ers really willing to part with a three-time MVP who led them to a championship a few years earlier and was still one of the elite centers in the game? Malone had clashed with Guokas, publicly criticized Katz, and was asking for an extension with two years remaining on his contract. The owner was also irked that Moses didn't attend the team's playoff games. Moses believed he'd be too tempted to play if he was in the arena.[18] Malone's play was slipping. His plodding post play epitomized what had become an old and slow team. Philadelphia excelled in his absence with Barkley emerging as a superstar in the postseason, averaging 25 points and 16 rebounds a game. Charles and Moses occupied the same turf on the low block, though Barkley operated with greater efficiency, connecting on 58 percent of his field goal attempts. Charles even outrebounded the Chairman of Boards. He was the future of the 76ers.

Guokas wanted to transition to a more up-tempo offense, which didn't fit Malone's style of play. The acquisition of Ruland and Robinson, 27 and 26, respectively, would improve the aging squad's quickness and athleticism. Additionally, Ruland operated out of the high post, which would free up the low block for Barkley.[19] Katz publicly referred to Moses as "an old thirty-one" because he entered pro ball at such a young age. Management knew his value would decrease as he continued to decline and neared free agency. If they were going to trade him, this was the time to do it.[20]

The major question from Philly's perspective was Ruland's health. The two-time All-Star averaged 22.3 points and 12.3 rebounds while leading the league in minutes per game during the 1983–84 season, though he appeared in only 67 of 164 regular-season games in the two subsequent seasons. The center suffered a strained right shoulder during the 1984–85 campaign, forcing him to miss all but thirty-seven games. In 1985–86, he fractured his right foot and later tore cartilage in his left knee, limiting him to thirty games. It was the knee that caused concern. Ruland underwent arthroscopic surgery on March 31 and returned to action for the Bullets-76ers playoff series.[21] Bullets GM Bob Ferry indicated that Ruland passed a team physical, and his injuries were not chronic.[22] Ruland believed he was healthy as well, based on a stress test he underwent. "My [surgically repaired] left knee was stronger than my right one," he said years later.[23]

On Monday, June 16, the day before the draft, the Bullets sent out a telex to the rest of the league stating that they expected to acquire the twenty-first pick and that any team interested in it should call them. The Cavaliers knew the pick belonged to Philadelphia, and scout Ed Gregory called Jack McMahon of the 76ers to inquire about its availability. When McMahon refused to trade the Cavs the twenty-first pick, Gregory proposed dealing Roy Hinson, a long, bouncy twenty-five-year-old forward who averaged just under 20 points per game that season, for the No. 1 pick. McMahon countered by asking for the eighth pick in addition to Hinson, but Gregory held firm. McMahon said he'd get back to him.[24]

Katz, Guokas, assistant coach Jim Lynam, GM Pat Williams, assistant GM John Nash, and McMahon met in a conference room at Veterans Stadium on the evening of June 16 to discuss the trade proposals for Malone and the No. 1 pick. Katz excused himself from the room and asked the basketball experts to vote on the deals.[25] The group felt it was time to move on from Moses and believed Daugherty would create a logjam in the post with Barkley and either Moses or Ruland.[26] Guokas liked the idea of adding three players twenty-seven or younger who could get up and down the floor.[27] The vote was unanimous in favor of the two trades. Katz was reluctant to deal Moses but ultimately went along with the recommendations of his basketball experts and approved the trades. Williams went back to the Cavs and convinced them to throw in $800,000 with Hinson for the first pick.[28]

The trades were announced the next day at the draft; however, there was one final hurdle before they became official. Ruland had to pass a customary physical examination with the 76ers. Michael Clancy, the team physician, examined the center and refused to give him medical clearance. His knee was damaged. Katz believed it would be disastrous to call off the deal and bring back an enraged Malone. He searched for a more optimistic second opinion and found one. The trade went through. Ruland's knee began to hurt and swell during the exhibition season. He played two regular-season games, then was shut down until January when he played three more for a total of five games before being forced to retire due to a torn meniscus in his knee.[29]

Nash called Moses the night before the draft to inform him that he'd been traded. Katz phoned him the next morning. Malone was upset. He'd grown close to his Philly teammates.[30] He was also furious with Katz for not calling him immediately and accused the owner of "lying to the press" by claiming that he wanted to be traded.[31] He continued to lash out at the Sixers' owner at his introductory press conference with the Bullets a week later, calling him "a psycho." "Dealing with Harold was really a problem," Malone continued, "and I'm looking forward to shutting his mouth up I-95." Malone believed Katz was cocky for trading him to another Eastern Conference team and vowed to make him pay for it.[32]

The 76ers players were crushed. "The perception that our team is better or more cohesive without Moses is wrong," Erving said. "If Moses had been healthy in the playoffs, we would have beaten Milwaukee and also been the only real challenge to Boston. Moses was the real cog in our wheel. Take him out, and it leaves the spokes hanging." Toney stated the pervasive opinion in the locker room that they couldn't compete for a title without Malone.[33]

No teammate was more distressed than Barkley. "For me personally, the trade was devastating," he wrote in his book *Outrageous!* "Mentally it screwed me up a great deal for some time because in losing Moses I lost another father figure, someone who was more important to me than anyone in my life other than my mother and grandmother." Barkley believes the trade was the beginning of the end of his career in Philadelphia.

Opposing players and executives didn't understand the trade either. "I don't know why they did that," Larry Bird said. "Jeff and Cliff are good, but Moses always scared the heck out of us."[34] Sixers season-ticket holders flooded the team's phone lines with angry rants.[35] The trade of the No. 1 pick turned into a disaster as well. Hinson spent one-and-a-half forgettable seasons in Philadelphia, and Daugherty became a five-time All-Star. Pat Williams left the organization as planned the day after the draft to join a group dedicated to bringing an expansion franchise to Orlando.[36] "After all that, it was a good thing I was getting out of town, because it just wasn't safe for me in the City of Brotherly Love anymore," Williams said.[37]

21

Come On Down!

Chuck Douglas was a twenty-four-year-old video coordinator and scout in his second season with the Bullets. He was watching videotape of the team's next opponent at the Capital Centre at 10:00 p.m. on a weeknight in November when his phone rang. He picked it up.

"Hey, Chuck, this is Moses."

"Moses who?" asked Douglas.

"Moses Malone."

"Yeah, right," said Chuck. Chuck barely knew Moses. There was no way the team's new star player would be calling him on his direct line at 10:00 p.m. Douglas assumed it was one of his friends playing a prank.

"Yeah, okay, what do you want, *Moses Malone*?" Chuck asked.

"I just got back in town, and I need to get some shots up. You need to let me in the gym," said the voice on the other end.

"Oh, you gotta get some shots up," said Chuck in a snarky tone.

"Yeah, I gotta get some shots up."

"Alright man, I got a lot of work to do . . . whoever this is," said Chuck. Then he hung up.

Ten seconds later, the phone rang again. Chuck answered.

"Chuck, why did you hang up on me?"

"Who is this?" asked Chuck.

"I told you, it's Moses Malone."

It really was Moses. He'd just returned from a trip to Philadelphia to see his eye doctor. The trainer or equipment manager would typically open the gym for him, but they were on the road with the team. Chuck hopped in his car and drove the twenty minutes to Bowie State University where the team practiced. Moses was waiting for him when he arrived. "Hey man," said Malone, "one thing you don't do, you don't hang up the phone on Big Mo."

Moses worked on his shot for over two hours, until close to 1:00 a.m. The man had three MVP awards and a championship ring, and he was one of the highest paid players in the game, yet he was still motivated to practice alone until well past midnight. In his thirteenth season, he was always the first player to arrive at practice and the last to leave. Malone was determined to prove to Harold Katz and anybody else who doubted him that he was still an elite player.[1]

Moses shined on a young Bullets team coached by Kevin Loughery, averaging 25.1 points and 11.8 rebounds through the first twenty-five games. He didn't have the talent around him that he'd grown accustomed to in Philadelphia and could no longer carry a mediocre team the way he had in Houston. The Bullets were 12-13 when they rolled into Philadelphia for Malone's first game against his former team on Christmas Day.

Moses's stance on Katz had softened since the trade. "Harold's a great guy," Malone said. "He gave me a six-year contract. I just didn't like the way he traded me when I got hurt. My feelings were hurt when I got injured and I didn't get a chance to come back and prove that I could still play the game after I fractured my eye."[2]

Barkley discussed how much he missed Moses. "Nobody can keep a team loose like he did," said Charles. "He's one of the nicest people I've ever played with; one of the few people I know making $2 million dollars a year who isn't a jerk." A reporter pointed out that Moses was the highest salaried employee in the Washington area. Barkley replied, "He's the best rebounder in Washington, ain't he?"[3]

Moses danced around a question about whether he was happy in Washington. Alfreda provided insight into his psyche during rare public comments. "He misses a guard like Cheeks," she said. "And he misses the guys. He had a lot of close friends when he was playing in Philadelphia. He has fewer friends here. There was a bond there."[4]

The Bullets were Malone's team from the moment he entered the locker room. There wasn't a Dr. J or Barkley to share the spotlight. Big Mo had an aura about him, though he remained unassuming. Deniz Hardy, the director of community operations, was bombarded with requests for Malone to make appearances at community and charity events. Malone rarely turned him down. Hardy typically turned to Moses for events involving children. Moses had a way of making them feel like they were the stars.

Hardy would meet Moses at his home, and they'd drive to events together. Moses let Hardy pick which of Malone's cars to drive in. Hardy always chose the Maserati. The first time he entered the Malone home, he spotted one of Moses's MVP trophies sitting on top of a television console, a T-shirt belonging to one of Moses's boys draped over it. "It was so casual," recalled Hardy. "His whole life seemed so casual."[5]

Life in the NBA is full of drama: teammates competing for playing time and sometimes for women; players dissatisfied with their contract, number of shots, or both; coaches paranoid about losing their jobs; feuds with opposing players; and complaints about referees. Moses enjoyed watching it all unfold in the locker room, quick with a quip if so inclined.[6] He created a nickname for each Bullet. Ennis Whatley was "the Maid Killer."[7] Darwin Cook was "Darnell," and Mark Alarie, who joined Washington the following season, was "the Book Reader."[8] Cook called Moses "Big Sexy," which always made Malone laugh.[9] Moses Jr. and Michael were a regular presence in the Bullets locker room. Malone introduced his sons as "Harvard and Yale."

Moses scored 28 points and snatched 21 rebounds while leading the Bullets to a 102–97 victory over the Sixers on Christmas. He followed that up with 39 and 17 in the teams' second meeting. "[H]Akeem is considered the best center in the game today, but he doesn't know as much as Moses," said Erving after the game. "Akeem is younger, perhaps physically able to do more things, but when you combine the physical and mental aspects of play, Moses is the man."[10]

Malone posted 41 and 20 against the Kings two nights later and dropped 50 points on the Nets in April. Washington scribes penned homages to the old warrior. Not only was he playing great ball, but he also brought credibility to a rudderless franchise and set a standard for the young players with his work ethic and willingness to play through pain. The day before the Bullets played the 76ers in early March, Malone was wearing a neck brace, evidence of an injury he suffered the night before. While his teammates practiced at Bowie State, he was in traction in the locker room. Still, he was in the starting lineup the next night.[11] Moses was named to the All-NBA Second Team, but he had little help in Washington. The Bullets won 42 games and were swept in the first round of the playoffs.

Manute Bol resembled a stick figure. Dark skinned and 7 feet 7 inches, he weighed barely 200 pounds. Bol was raised in Turalei, a village in the swamplands of southern Sudan, as a member of the Dinka tribe. His father was a cow herder, and Manute lacked a formal education.[12] In accordance with tribal rituals, six of his bottom teeth were removed with a chisel when he was eight years old, and four incisions were cut all the way around his head with a sharp knife at fourteen.[13] Bol family lore included a story about Manute killing a lion with a spear in defense of his village.[14]

In the summer of 1983 Don Feeley, former coach of Farleigh Dickinson University, coached a one-month clinic for the Sudanese national team in Khartoum. It was there that he discovered Manute. The young man was illiterate and didn't speak English. Feeley brought him to the United States, where Manute ended up playing college ball at the University of Bridgeport in Connecticut. After one season, he was selected by the Bullets in the second round of the 1985 draft.[15]

Bol's English consisted of curse words, African American slang, and lines he picked up from television. One day at practice, apropos of nothing, he hollered, "Dudley Bradley, come on down! You're the next contestant on *The Price Is Right*!"[16] He called a fly swatter a "fly spear" and a vacuum cleaner a "train for his rug." When he had a stuffy nose, he said that his "left nose was broken."[17]

Bol led the league in blocked shots as a rookie, averaging 5 in just twenty-six minutes per game. He landed endorsement deals with Nike and Church's Chicken and appeared on *Late Night with David Letterman*. The public was fascinated with the wiry African, and Moses was no exception. The two big men competed one-on-one after practice, and Malone taught Bol the nuances of the game.[18] At night, they hit the clubs. Manute chugged beers while Moses sipped a soft drink. They sat next to each other in the airport and on the bus. Big Mo often poked fun at his new friend. A woman asked Malone for an autograph in the airport, then inquired as to whether Bol, who had his hands in his pockets, was a player too. "No, he's a stickup man," said Malone.[19]

In Malone's second season in Washington, the comedy routine of Moses and Manute added a third member, 5-foot-3-inch Muggsy Bogues. The point guard's improbable climb began in the projects of Baltimore, where he was hit with a stray bullet at the age of five. He witnessed a man get shot in the head on the basketball court and another beaten to death with a baseball bat.[20] In addition to his dire surroundings, Bogues had to overcome the assumption of coaches at every level that he was too small to succeed in a big man's game. He led a Dunbar High School team that included future NBA players Reggie Williams, Reggie Lewis, and David Wingate to two undefeated seasons, then thrived at Wake Forest University. Washington selected him twelfth in the 1987 draft.

The Bullets treated Muggsy and Manute, the tallest and shortest players in NBA history, as a novelty act. Manute wore No. 10, so they assigned Muggsy No. 1, to represent the scale of 1–10. The two appeared in photo shoots together.[21] Muggsy befriended Moses and Manute. One day, when the Bullets were fooling around at practice, Muggsy blocked Manute's shot. Their teammates hooted and hollered. Bol was embarrassed and chased after Muggsy. Such shenanigans were common between them, and Moses was often at the center of it, egging Manute on, then erupting in laughter as the African pursued Muggsy.[22]

Moses looked out for Muggsy, whom he called "the Baltimore Pimp" because of his flashy wardrobe. The point guard wore alligator and snakeskin suits and fur coats. Muggsy was Malone's rookie, though the veteran didn't haze him. He taught Bogues the business of basketball and the importance of remaining even-keeled. "Avoid the newspapers," Malone said. They could be detrimental to a young player's confidence. Moses also served as a sounding board when the rookie was frustrated by his lack of playing time. "You know I was facing a lot of challenges anyway," recalled Bogues. "And for him [Moses] to be able to walk me through it and give me that type of guidance was priceless for me, which allowed me to have a fourteen-year career in the NBA. Without him, I might have been lost."[23]

Of course, Moses teased Muggsy. Ford released a car called the Festiva in 1987. It was a small automobile, like a Toyota Prius, and the company hired Bogues to promote it. They even made special model Muggsymobiles. Moses couldn't stop laughing when Bogues pulled up next to his Rolls-Royce at practice in a Festiva. "Woah, the little kit mobile," joked Malone. "You got the little kit mobile coming over here."[24]

Bogues, Malone, and Bol often went out to dinner and rolled up to the club together. They walked side-by-side through airports to the amusement of bystanders. Before teams used charter planes, the Bullets flew commercial airlines. Some veterans received first-class seats. Youngsters like Bol and Bogues were confined to coach. Moses was overjoyed at the sight of the league's tallest and shortest players sitting next to each other in the back of the plane.

The summer after Malone's first season in Washington, Manute married a Dinka woman named Atong. Alfreda threw her a wedding shower and welcome party at a local restaurant. She invited the Bullets players and executives and their spouses. Bullets vice president Garnett Slatton and his wife were surprised to find Alfreda collecting $25 from guests at the door. Moses was making over $2 million per year.[25]

Malone had a complicated relationship with money. It can be disorienting for a person who grew up in extreme poverty to make millions of dollars per year. Such accumulation of wealth typically occurs over generations. Athletes like Malone are unaccustomed to managing money and must navigate the requests of family and friends. Many blow through all of it.

Moses was willing to spend on certain luxuries, particularly deluxe automobiles, though he was generally tight with his money. "Listen, I enjoy money. You got to know how to enjoy it though," he said. "A lot of people enjoy it the wrong way. They spend it." Malone knew his earning years were limited and wanted his basketball income to last for the rest of his life.[26]

"Make a dollar, spend a quarter," was one of his lines.[27] He began saving when he entered pro ball, eating at fast-food restaurants and pocketing the rest of his per diem. He taught Robert Reid to place his leftover per diem in a Ziplock bag every day. By the end of the season, he'd have thousands of dollars.[28] Malone had old television sets in his house, generally wore Nike workout clothes instead of designer outfits, and stayed at the Marriot, not the Four Seasons, when traveling on his own dime.[29]

He wasn't close with Slatton, but whenever the Bullets' VP traveled with the team, Moses joined him for breakfast so he wouldn't have to pay. Slatton charged it to the team.[30] After his career, the retired players association hosted an event in Malone's honor at the Mercedes-Benz Club in Houston. Moses pulled up in his Bentley. When the valet asked him for $20 for parking, he refused. "Man, I'm the star of the show tonight," said Malone. "Why I gotta pay $20?" Mike Jones, a friend who was with him, looked at the cars lining up behind them and encouraged Mo to pay. Moses refused. Eventually, he was admitted for free.[31]

Malone was shrewd with his money. While with the Rockets, Del Harris took several of the players to the Dominican Republic one summer. They joined their funds to exchange the local currency for American money. Moses struck out on his own and found a better rate. Harris asked him why he pursued a deal on his own without waiting to see what the coach could arrange. "Don't want no money that doesn't have George Washington's picture on it," Malone said.[32]

Moses allowed Lee Fentress's agency to invest his money. He didn't trust many people, so it spoke volumes that he remained with the agent from the time he left high school until his death. Early in Malone's career, Fentress kept him on a monthly allowance. Big Mo went to a jewelry store with his Rockets teammate Mike Dunleavy and spotted a watch he liked. He called Fentress and told him he needed money. Fentress declined. Malone had spent his monthly allotment. Moses handed the phone to Dunleavy and told him to tell Fentress that if he didn't give Moses the money for the watch he'd be fired. Fentress held firm.[33] The only significant financial dispute between them was when Malone wanted to buy a Rolls-Royce. Fentress believed it was ostentatious and beneath him.[34]

Moses appreciated Fentress's loyalty, and it was reciprocated. When Fentress split with Donald Dell and ProServ in 1983 to form Advantage International, Malone went with him. Advantage later changed its name to Octagon Financial Services. "Moses was the beginning and foundation of our basketball group," said Frank Zecca, managing director of Octagon, who handled Malone's finances for over twenty years. "He was the building block for all the guys we handle today, whether it's Chris Paul or Steph Curry."[35]

Moses was an informed investor who read the *Wall Street Journal* and followed the stock market, sometimes doling out stock tips to friends.[36] In meetings with his advisors "his comments were on point, really on point, but he didn't have to win the point," said former Advantage marketing director Gary Stevenson.[37] Some athletes think they know everything and insist on directing their investments. Many of them lose their money. Moses knew what he didn't know. He deferred to the expertise of his advisors, though he monitored every aspect of his portfolio, meeting regularly with Octagon staff. On at least one occasion, he brought in outside accountants to audit Octagon.[38] "He knew where every penny was," said former coach Billy Cunningham.[39] Malone's money was tied up in real estate; partnerships in shopping centers, office buildings, and warehouses; as well as oil and gas.[40] A robust nest egg was waiting for him when he retired.

The 1987–88 season, Malone's second in Washington, was frustrating for Malone and the Bullets. Management turned over the roster, with the major addition being Bernard King, the league's leading scorer in 1984–85, who missed the two previous seasons with a devastating knee injury. Coach Loughery preached balance on offense with three potential 20-point scorers in Moses, King, and Jeff Malone.[41]

The Bullets began the season 4-10, and Malone's frustration boiled over after a loss to the Hawks on December 12. "This is the [least] I've been in the offense since I've been in the NBA," Moses said. "I'm getting one shot every six, seven, eight minutes. I've never been in this situation before. In Philadelphia, if I was a zero for 10 in a game they'd still come to me." Malone may have been willing to accept fewer shots if the team was winning, but he couldn't abide his reduced role as the losses piled up.[42]

Loughery was fired on January 3, with the Bullets 8-19. He was replaced by Wes Unseld, who had moved to the bench that season as an assistant coach after years in the front office. Unseld was "Mr. Bullet," a former MVP and member of the 1978 championship team. He was more laid-back than Loughery, though Moses clashed with him as well. Malone had 11 points and 10 rebounds in nineteen minutes in a loss to the Mavericks on February 17. "To tell you the truth, if I don't play, we can't win," he said after the game. "I think it's a shame that an All-Star center can't get shots and can't get time and we're 11 games under .500. It's like I'm a substitute on this team." Unseld said his center needed to demonstrate that he deserved to play more than nineteen minutes.[43]

Moses was right, the Bullets couldn't win without him. Washington was 17-8 in games in which he led them in scoring and 16-3 when he scored 25 or more.[44] He was the only player on the roster capable of dominating. However, he'd put on weight and was unable to perform at an elite level on a nightly basis. Unseld pulled him late in games when the team went to a trapping defense, which led to further complaints from Malone.[45] Washington finished 38-44 and was bounced from the playoffs in the first round again.

The NBA and players association agreed to a new collective-bargaining agreement in April that included the introduction of unrestricted free agency that off-season.[46] Moses would be an unrestricted free agent for the first time in his career. Fentress and the Bullets had been discussing an extension since the previous summer. Malone wanted a four-year deal. Owner Abe Pollin was unwilling to commit to that many years.[47]

The local press turned on Malone. The Bullets were 80-84 during his time in Washington, and he argued with two coaches. Malone had begun to sit out practices because of his aching knees and developed a reputation for being a selfish player. Jeff Malone recalled that when Moses was double-teamed in the post, he'd throw it out to Jeff's feet, low enough that he didn't have time to retrieve it and shoot and would have to throw it back to Moses.[48] The losing may not have been Malone's fault, but he wasn't the solution. Slatton and GM Bob Ferry convinced Pollin that it was time for the Bullets to rebuild. They announced that they were no longer pursuing Malone.[49]

The Atlanta Hawks called Fentress on the first day of free agency and offered Moses a three-year deal.[50] Other teams expressed interest, though Moses signed with Atlanta. He was excited to play for a contender again.

22

Superstar in Decline

During his time with the Rockets, Moses and his teammates were at the check-in counter of the Detroit Metropolitan Airport when a Hare Krishna member approached Moses and asked, "Brother, would you like a free book of our faith of Hare Krishna?"

Moses said, "Yes, thank you." He took the book and walked away.

The man asked for a donation.

"No, you said it was free," replied Malone.

"No, no, we need a donation. That's how we do it. Can I get a donation?"

"No, you said the book is free. Big Mo got the book for free."

"Well, I want my book back."

"You said it's free. My book now."

The man followed Moses all the way to the gate. "Give me some money or give me my book back," he said.

Moses refused to do either. The man offended his sense of honesty, and Moses, who could be maddeningly stubborn, refused to yield to the social norm. That stubbornness carried over to the basketball court.[1]

Like all great players, Moses was driven by immense pride in his ability and work ethic. That pride pushes superstars to overcome the odds and reach the pinnacle of their profession. It's also the reason they're typically the last to accept that their game is slipping. When accompanied by stubbornness, pride can lead to discord in the locker room. Longtime NBA coach and broadcaster Jeff Van Gundy navigated that dynamic in New York with Patrick Ewing, prompting him to conclude that "the hardest thing to coach is a superstar in decline." Atlanta's coaches would face that challenge with Malone.

Moses still produced 20 points and 10 rebounds nightly. He believed he should be a focal point of the offense and play close to forty minutes per game. While his numbers were impressive, obviously his play had been in decline for years, and in some situations he was a liability on the court. The drop-off was most evident in Moses's leaping ability and stamina. He couldn't spring for rebounds like he could in his younger days and was no longer a threat to block shots. He'd become slow to respond to double-teams, often fumbling the ball as he attempted to kick it out. Moses tired easily and was less effective on the second night of back-to-back games. Late in his tenure in Washington, the once indefatigable Malone began skipping practices due to fatigue. He'd leave a gold Rolex on his wrist after changing into warmups to signal to Coach Unseld that he needed a break. When Unseld saw the watch, he'd suggest that Moses work out on the bike instead of practicing.[2]

Moses's balding head and the protective goggles he'd worn since his eye injury made him look older than thirty-four. The enduring image of him late in his career was hunched over, hands on his knees, goggles pushed up on his head, as he waited to shoot free throws. The buckets of sweat pouring off his face came to symbolize a tired old warrior, rather than a lithe young buck bouncing up and down the court.

Fred Carter, Malone's assistant coach with the Bullets, believes that many players go through what he calls "skill shock." They don't know how to remain effective when their skills decline. Malone, Carter noted, was able to adapt because of his high basketball IQ. He understood positioning and timing and began using deception, rather than springy legs, to draw fouls.[3] He developed a jump shot, which enabled him to score as his athleticism dwindled. Still, he was a step slow on defense and less efficient on offense. His decline accelerated over his three seasons in Atlanta, to the frustration of Moses and his coaches.

Jon Koncak arrived an hour and fifteen minutes early for the first day of training camp in 1988. The fourth-year center prided himself on being one of the first at practice. He walked into the Hawks' training room and saw Moses sitting on the training table, reading the *Wall Street Journal* while the trainer taped his ankles. Moses put down the paper and clearly said, "Hey, Jon, it's great to be here." Koncak and Malone hadn't communicated as opponents. The image he had of Malone was the one portrayed by the media: gruff, moody, unapproachable, and difficult to understand. "I vividly remember, I was just shocked. Here is this guy—

everything I'd heard about him, thought about him, was 180 wrong," recalled Koncak.[4]

Dominique Wilkins knew Moses well. The Hawks' star forward befriended Malone at All-Star Games and believed he could help Atlanta win.[5] Wilkins, a majestic dunker whose unparalleled mix of athleticism and power earned him the nickname "The Human Highlight Film," received a litany of individual awards: All-Star Games, Slam Dunk Contest victory, scoring title, and selection to the All-NBA First Team. As he approached his thirtieth birthday, Dominique was hungry for team success.

The Hawks won 50 or more games every year from 1986 to 1988 but bowed out in the second round of the playoffs each time, the last of which in devastating fashion. Atlanta had the Celtics on the ropes, 3-2, with a chance to close out the series at home. Boston eked out Game Six by 2 points, setting up an epic shootout between Wilkins and Larry Bird at the Boston Garden. "It was like two gunfighters waiting to blink," recalled Celtics forward Kevin McHale.[6]

The game was tied at 86 with 10:26 to play when the stars took over. Bird scored 9 points over the next two minutes. Nique responded, tying the game again at 99. Both scored 11 points over the final six minutes. Wilkins finished with 47 on 19 of 23 shooting, but it wasn't enough. The Celtics won, 118–116, behind 34 from Bird, including 20 in the fourth quarter.[7]

Only three Hawks averaged double digits in the series: Wilkins, Doc Rivers, and Kevin Willis. Randy Wittman, the starting shooting guard, averaged 8.9 points per game and was held scoreless in Game Six. Tree Rollins was an excellent defensive center and a leader in the locker room, but he scored a total of 53 points over eleven playoff games and was outscored 14–4 by Parish in Game Seven.

The Hawks were a strong defensive team with a star player and great depth. They needed more firepower. Atlanta traded Wittman and a draft pick to the Sacramento Kings for Reggie Theus, a talented shooting guard who had been a 20-point scorer on losing teams. Then they signed Moses. "Winning a championship is my only goal this season," said Wilkins. "Moses makes it possible."[8]

Several media outlets proclaimed the Hawks title contenders. Some reporters wondered if Moses, Theus, and the returning players could sublimate their egos in pursuit of a championship. Malone believed pondering that was silly, noting that he accepted a reduced role in Philadelphia as the reigning MVP; he'd have no problem doing the same in Atlanta. Just as he stated the 76ers were Doc's team, he declared Atlanta Dominique's.[9]

The early results were promising. Atlanta won 20 of its first 29 games. Malone, who lost 15 pounds in the offseason, was the lightest he'd been in years, and his impact was evident. In the second game, he poured in 17 points and grabbed 13 rebounds in the second half of the Hawks' victory over the Bucks.[10] It took seventeen games for him to pass Rollins's scoring total from the previous season. Malone's dominance around the basket took attention away from Wilkins, freeing him to operate in more one-on-one situations.

Moses realized about twenty games into the season that something was off with the team. They were winning, but the effort wasn't consistent, and the players were talking back to Coach Mike Fratello.[11] Mike was excellent with x's and o's, though he wasn't a great communicator in the locker room and was wound as tight as a candidate on election day.[12] The 5-foot-7 Fratello was a screamer, and in his sixth season with the club, many of the players had begun to tune him out.[13]

Rivers wrote in his book, "I remember Moses Malone saying once to him on the sideline during a game when Mike was yelling at him, 'Mike, what you are saying is probably right. But there's a better way to tell me. I've got three kids [actually two] sitting up there in the stands, watching you yell at me. I'm a man, Mike. Treat me like one.' At the time I thought, 'Dang, I got two kids up there myself. Mo is right.'"[14]

Wilkins and Fratello argued frequently. The star screamed at the coach on the court during a win over the Pacers in December.[15] By Christmas, Moses had enough of Fratello as well.[16] He walked off the court during one game and said to Theus, "You better come get your boy," about Fratello. "You better come get him. He's talking to the wrong motherfucker. You better come get him." Malone barked in Fratello's direction, "Don't talk to me. Don't talk to me."[17] He and the coach exchanged words during halftime of a game later in the season.[18]

Friction with Fratello wasn't the only problem. Power forward Kevin Willis was lost for the season with a broken foot. Theus missed defensive assignments and deviated from the offense.[19] The Hawks' energy level was inconsistent, and they didn't gel as a unit. While Malone took pressure off Dominique, he also occupied the block where Nique liked to post up.[20] The Hawks went 9-10 in the six weeks prior to the All-Star break, and nobody considered them a championship contender heading into the second half of the season.

Despite the turmoil, Malone felt comfortable around his teammates. He enjoyed holding court at the back of the team bus, cracking teammates up with stories from his career. Steve Holman, the team's broadcaster, asked Dominique what Moses talked about on the bus. "I don't know," said Wilkins. "All we know is when Moses laughs, we laugh."[21] The players sat in the same seats after every game. If a new teammate sat in somebody's seat, the guys would say, "Moses, tell the man about his seat." Mo would say, "Boy, get the *hell* out of the man's seat!"[22]

Moses remained a mystery to others in the organization, though they generally liked him. He called Holman "Radio Man" during his entire three years in Atlanta. "I'm not sure if he knew my name," recalled the broadcaster. Moses referred to Arthur Triche, who worked in public relations, as "PR Man." About halfway through his first season with the club, Triche asked Moses if he knew his name. Malone replied, "Yeah, Arthur, I know your name. I call you PR man."[23]

It was reminiscent of an exchange in the 76ers locker room during Barkley's rookie season. Barkley was angry about something Stan Hochman of the *Philadelphia Daily News* wrote. "Who *is* Stan Hochman?" he asked.

Moses, who was known to avoid reporters, didn't skip a beat. "Short guy," he said. "Gray hair. Dresses nice. Never know where the man is fucking coming from."[24] It was spot on.

Moses was generally quiet in the locker room and may have appeared aloof, but he was keenly aware of his surroundings. Teammates compared him to E. F. Hutton. When he spoke, they listened.[25]

Malone addressed the Hawks' issues during the All-Star break. He implored his teammates to work harder on defense and suggested they were lacking the killer instinct to put teams away. He still believed they could compete for a championship if they played hard and loose and accepted their roles. "We've got the guys to win," he said, smiling. "But you can't have all chiefs and no Indians."[26] Atlanta won seven of eight games after the break, then lost five of the next seven. They made one final push, winning nine-consecutive games in April, and finished the season at 50-32.

Atlanta faced Milwaukee in the playoffs, a team it beat all six times during the season. Game Three of the series was particularly memorable. The score was tied in the closing seconds. Theus dribbled near half court as the clock ran down and appeared to lose track of time. Rivers ran over, snatched the ball away and heaved it toward the basket at the buzzer. Atlanta lost in overtime.[27] A few nights later, the Hawks dropped the decisive fifth game on their home court, despite 25 points and 16 rebounds from Moses. The game was a microcosm of their season, with impressive stretches that they couldn't sustain. The season was a colossal disappointment.[28]

The Hawks ran back much of the same team in 1989–90, with the hope that the return of Willis and subtraction of Theus, who was selected by the Orlando Magic in the expansion draft, would improve chemistry and production. The plan was doomed to fail. Fratello was a lame duck coach in the last year of his contract, and the discontent in the locker room turned to rebellion. Moses lashed out at the coach publicly after playing just fifteen minutes in a win over Golden State on November 18. It was a reasonable decision by Fratello. Moses had been hobbling on a sore foot and turned the ball over 6 times in limited action; furthermore, Atlanta won the game easily without him.[29]

Malone's anger peaked over a month later in Philadelphia. He believed Fratello was trying to embarrass him against his old team when the coach benched him for the final twenty-one minutes of a nine-point loss. Fratello addressed the team in the locker room after the game. Then Moses said he had something to say. "That little motherfucker is not gonna fuck with me," he started. "You fucking don't know what you're doing," he told Fratello. "I'm a professional. I come to play. And for you not to fucking play me in front of my old team—" Fratello attempted to assert his authority by stepping toward Malone. "I would not fucking take one more step," Moses said.[30] Forward Antoine Carr and assistant coach Cazzie Russell held Malone back. Teammates had never seen him that angry.[31]

It's not unusual for a player to tell a coach to "fuck off" in the heat of the moment, but to dress one down in front of the team is rare. Koncak hadn't seen anything like it in his eleven-year career. A couple of days later, Hawks president and GM Stan Kasten addressed the team. He said that he spoke to Moses, who acknowledged he was wrong, and that they put the incident behind them.[32] It was open season on Fratello after that. Cliff Levingston mimicked the coach during a game after being criticized for missing a defensive assignment. Willis stalked off the court, glaring at Fratello when he was substituted out.[33] The team went into a tailspin. Fratello finished the season, though it was clear he was done in Atlanta.

The Hawks traded for Kings guard Kenny Smith in February 1990. Smith was excited to join the team. The club had talent, and he'd heard great things about Fratello. He believed he was going to make the playoffs for the first time in his career. Instead, he discovered a team that was "entirely dysfunctional." Smith wrote in his book, *Talk of Champions*, "We had players who didn't want to be there and players who didn't respect one another. A number of players did not treat Coach Fratello with respect. I'd been on bad teams in Sacramento, but never one that couldn't function as a unit. It seemed to me that most of the issues stemmed from the fact that the Hawks had simply played together for too long. They were tired of one another. Players would curse one another out during games, even curse out Coach Fratello. I had never seen anything like it, not at Archbishop Molloy, not at the University of North Carolina, and not in Sacramento."[34]

Kasten hired Pete Babcock to replace him as general manager in March. Babcock concluded that the team had been together for too long and advanced as far as it could.[35] It was time to rebuild. The players performed as if their days in Atlanta were numbered, bumbling their way to a 41-41 record, and missed the playoffs for the first time in five years.

Moses averaged 18.9 points and 10 rebounds per game. His streak of twelve consecutive All-Star Games ended. "It's okay," he said, "I'll always be No. 1 to myself."[36] The press blamed him for the team's failures. "The man who complains loudest and most often of their failure to stop the opposition is himself the worst defensive player on the roster," wrote beat writer Jeffrey Denberg. Moses was slow on his defensive rotations and refused to box out, something that wasn't necessary when he had hops like a kangaroo, but now led to easy putbacks for the opposition.[37] He led the league in offensive rebounds but ranked a lowly thirtieth in defensive boards, which hindered the Hawks' running game.[38] His unwillingness to pass out of double-teams and high turnover rate were more glaring as he became less effective.

The team had other problems. There was dissension in the locker room. Starting guards Doc Rivers and John Battle missed significant portions of the season with injury, and Willis didn't have the impact expected. Yet Malone had clashed with four coaches over the past five seasons. He was at least part of the problem.

The Hawks attempted to trade Moses in the offseason. A couple of teams expressed interest but were unable to absorb his large contract under the salary cap.[39] Atlanta returned the same nucleus for the 1990–91 season with Bob Weiss as the new coach. Weiss was an amateur magician who enjoyed doing tricks for the players. He could pull a quarter out of Malone's ear on a team flight but couldn't turn back the hands of time.

Moses scored 2 points in the team's eighth-consecutive loss on November 27, prompting Weiss to replace him in the starting lineup with Koncak. The coach tried to put a positive spin on the move. "I decided to try Moses in a Kevin McHale–type role," he said, referring to the great Celtics forward who served as a sixth man for much of his career. The reality was that Malone had been benched.[40] Moses refused to comment on the move. Privately, he was furious that he was demoted in favor of Koncak, a player he believed had a poor work ethic.[41] "He thought he should have been playing," said assistant coach Johnny Davis. "It was just not a good time for him."[42]

Big Mo was in the final year of his contract and knew his NBA future depended on his willingness to accept the change and adapt to his new role. At thirty-six years old, he continued to be the first player at practice, putting in work on the exercise bike before teammates arrived.[43] He mentored young players, like rookie Rumeal Robinson, and provided a boost off the bench, earning praise from Weiss.[44] Atlanta finished 43-39 and lost in the first round of the playoffs. Management decided not to re-sign Moses, opting to focus on youth.

Big Mo didn't depart quietly. He called his teammates selfish, complained that management wasn't appreciative of his contributions, and said his family was embarrassed that he was benched. He also expressed disappointment that he wasn't presented with a game ball or standing ovation after breaking Wilt Chamberlain's record for consecutive games without fouling out.[45] His pride made him sound petty. Jack McCallum opined in *Sports Illustrated* that "Malone will be remembered as a complaining ball hog whose image grew increasingly tarnished as his career wore on."[46]

23

Endings

Alfreda Malone played the traditional female role of caring for the home and children. She supported Moses's career by participating in team charity events, such as the Bullets' annual fashion show.[1] When he played for the 76ers, she sent Christmas cards to each member of the organization, a sweet gesture that resonated with the staff.[2] Every time Moses switched teams, she designed their new home. Moses and Alfreda enjoyed working out together, swimming, going to the movies, and listening to their jazz collection.[3]

Moses loved Alfreda, though expressed to friends that he wished he'd waited until he was older to get married.[4] The union had been rocky from the start, due in large part to his infidelity. Whether on the road or out with friends in Houston, he constantly pursued other women. Alfreda was a bright woman and aware of Moses's transgressions. She'd threatened to leave him over his infidelity and finally filed for divorce on September 18, 1991.[5]

The divorce petition included extremely disturbing accusations of physical and verbal abuse by Moses. Mrs. Malone claimed that on February 15, 1991, Moses hit her in the head, then pointed a gun at her head and stated he'd kill her if she called the police. She stated that the same morning, he shot a BB gun in the house and told his sons that when they returned from school, their mother would be lying dead on the kitchen floor. That night, Moses allegedly hit Alfreda, kicked her, and locked her out of the bedroom. According to Alfreda, he hit her in the back with a belt months later.[6]

In May 1992 Alfreda filed a second affidavit with the court alleging further abuse, most notably a violent episode on or about December 21, 1991, during which the 6-foot-10, 250-pound Malone allegedly held Alfreda over a balcony several stories high and threatened to throw her off. He then proceeded to beat her on the face and head. She claimed Moses threatened to kill her on multiple occasions in front of their children, prompting Moses Jr. to ask her whom he and his brother would live with if Moses followed through on his threats.[7] Alfreda's attorney, Judy Przyborski, described one of the threats in graphic detail: "He told her he would cut her up and douse her in gasoline and set her on fire if it would stop her from going through with the divorce." The judge issued a peace bond, forbidding Moses from going near Alfreda.[8]

In the divorce hearing that took place in September 1992, Alfreda testified that their ten-year marriage had been filled with adultery and abuse. Moses denied hitting his wife or threatening to kill her, claiming that Alfreda made up the allegations to hurt his reputation and earning potential.[9] "Why should I kill my wife?" he asked on the stand. "I love my wife." Moses confided to those close to him that he still loved Alfreda and wanted to work things out. He tried to stop her car to talk on the way to the courthouse one day. The next day, she arrived with two bodyguards.[10] Alfreda's friends and family testified that they'd seen bruises on her on numerous occasions, including a black eye after the alleged December incident. When shown photographs of Alfreda's face taken after the incident, Moses once again denied hitting her, and said, "she's very easy to get bruised."[11]

It's difficult to reconcile the allegations of abuse with the rest of Moses's life. Teammates and friends knew him to be a "gentle giant," kind and caring toward others. He had no history of violence, nor were there any allegations of abuse from other women before, during, or after his marriage. Moses was a complicated and private man. He may have been troubled in a way that those around him never realized.

Alfreda was granted sole custody of twelve-year-old Moses Jr. and eight-year-old Michael. Moses was allowed to take the kids one weekend a month and for a few one-week periods during the summer. He was required to pay $3,000 per month in child support. Moses kept the house in Sugar Land, with Alfreda and the kids relocating to League City, Texas. The couple's estimated $10 to $12 million in assets were split in half. Most notable was their impressive collection of automobiles. Alfreda received a 1992 Mercedes 500, 1990 BMW 750IL, 1988 Jaguar 2 door sedan XJ-SC, 1983 Rolls-Royce, and 1989 Chevrolet Suburban. Moses retained the 1979

Mercedes 6.9, 1983 Mercedes 380SE, 1986 Ford Bronco, 1987 Ferrari 412, 1991 Cadillac Limousine, and 1989 Lincoln Continental Mark VII.[12]

Moses was arrested a few months after the divorce for violating the peace bond. Alfreda alleged that he illegally entered her home, damaged her property, and threatened to kill her. He claimed that he went to the house to drop off posters for his boys and that Alfreda wasn't even there at the time.[13]

Despite the acrimonious divorce, Moses still loved Alfreda, and friends believe he would have taken her back until she married another man for a brief time.[14] Their relationship fluctuated between friendly and adversarial over the next two decades. Big Mo remained in contact with Alfreda's relatives, attending Gill family gatherings and hanging out with her cousin Kirk. He even spent some holidays at Alfreda's parents' house with Alfreda and their boys.[15]

Moses was a member of the Milwaukee Bucks at the time of his divorce. He didn't discuss the developments with his teammates other than to warn them to save their money and to occasionally complain about how much Alfreda asked for in child support. He believed she'd spoil the kids and use the remaining money for herself.[16] "I ain't fucking paying that so my kids can wear alligator shoes," he said. When Malone left the team during training camp in September 1992 for the divorce hearing, Bucks forward Frank Brickowski put a shoebox labeled "Moses Malone Divorce Fund" in his locker. All the guys threw in a few bucks. Moses appreciated the joke.[17]

Del Harris knew he wouldn't be vice president and coach of the Bucks had it not been for Moses. Harris's early success with the Rockets led to several opportunities. He returned the favor by signing Moses to a two-year contract worth about $3.6 million in the summer of 1991. Malone insisted on a clause in the contract allowing him to play basketball whenever he wanted in the off-season. He still loved the game. Harris believed Big Mo could help in two areas where the Bucks struggled the previous season: rebounding and getting to the foul line. Moses would be in the starting lineup and share minutes with backup Danny Schayes.[18]

Harris stepped down as coach after seventeen games. The Bucks were 8-9, though they'd had an easy schedule. Harris determined that the team wasn't a contender and would benefit from losing games to increase their odds of landing Shaquille O'Neal or Alonzo Mourning in the draft lottery. He had coached a rebuilding team in Houston the season after the Rockets traded Moses and was unwilling to endure that agony again. Harris remained in the front office and hired assistant coach Frank Hamblen as his replacement on the bench.[19]

Moses played all eighty-two games and averaged 15.6 points and a team-high 9.1 rebounds. "He played hard, and he was serious about the game," said teammate Fred Roberts. "Some guys get to the end of their careers and they're not as serious anymore. Moses was very serious. He wanted to be a good player and an important part of our team." Unfortunately, the Bucks went 31-51.[20]

Moses missed the first four days of training camp in 1992 due to his divorce hearing. He felt pain in his back and side during his first day of practice. The pain began the previous season, and Moses thought it was a pulled hamstring. It turned out to be a herniated disk.[21] Malone rested for a few weeks in the hope of avoiding surgery. After returning to practice for two days, he decided to go under the knife.[22]

The surgery, as well as a locker room full of faces not much older than his son, forced him to come to grips with his basketball mortality. Mike Dunleavy, his teammate with the Rockets, was his new coach, and several of his teammates grew up idolizing him during his glory days with the 76ers. "I was in awe of him," recalled Blue Edwards.[23] Unable to play, Malone fostered camaraderie in the locker room. He insisted on the entire team eating together on the road and had a regular dice game with teammates Dale Ellis, Alvin Robertson, and Lester Conner.[24] The youngsters looked to Malone for guidance, and he was happy to provide it. He taught rookies Todd Day and Lee Mayberry how to work hard and take care of their bodies.[25]

Moses loved teasing his younger teammates and occasionally entertained them with stories from his career, often punctuated with a corny joke. He liked to tell the tale of another Hall of Famer he played with who told him about a night in a hot tub with a beautiful girl. "She was screaming and screaming," said the player. "Was the water too hot?" Malone asked.[26] If one of the young Bucks said or did something funny, Moses wouldn't let him forget, referencing it repeatedly for weeks.[27] "He was my favorite teammate," recalled Frank Brickowski, who spent thirteen years in the NBA.[28]

Moses began practicing with the team after the All-Star break, though a strained calf slowed his return to the lineup. He suited up for the first time on March 29 after missing the first sixty-six games and participated in eleven games that season. At thirty-eight, his days as a high impact player were over.

Malone returned to the 76ers in the summer of 1993, for his twentieth professional season. He and Harold Katz had long since squashed any animosity stemming from the trade to Washington. Philadelphia was a young team that had just drafted Shawn Bradley, a 7-foot-6-inch center, with the second pick. He, like Malone, took an unconventional path to the NBA, playing one year of college basketball at BYU before spending two years as a missionary in Australia. Sixers GM Jim Lynam and coach Fred Carter wanted Malone to mentor Bradley, who was just two years old when Moses turned pro, while backing him up at center. It was a role Malone embraced. "As a player, you can be older, but you got to have the kid in you," Malone said. "I still have my love for the game."[29]

It was a challenging season for the 76ers, who endured a fifteen-game losing streak on the way to a 25-57 record. Moses served as a quasi captain, encouraging teammates to keep their heads up and continue working hard as the losses piled up. He played cards on the plane and bus and dusted off some of his practical jokes.[30] Bradley and other young players learned what it required to be successful in the league from witnessing Malone's hard work. The veteran woke up early, worked out on the exercise bike and swam every morning to keep his back loose, even on game days. Warren Kidd, a twenty-three-year-old rookie, tried to emulate Malone's routine but couldn't keep up.[31] Malone also provided Bradley with tips about the game. "We told Shawn to listen to everything Moses says, because Moses parted the Red Sea," said Carter.[32]

Moses had a few highlights with the Sixers. He led the team in points and rebounds (18 and 12, respectively) in just nineteen of minutes of action in a win over the Bucks in December. That game, he became the fifth player in NBA history to collect 16,000 rebounds.[33] On March 22 he moved into third on the NBA's all-time scoring list, behind Kareem Abdul-Jabbar and Wilt Chamberlain.[34] But his effectiveness was limited. He averaged 5 points and 4 rebounds in eleven minutes of action and missed a string of games with a sore back. The 76ers chose not to bring him back for another season.

Moses wanted one more shot at a championship and found an opportunity with the San Antonio Spurs when the team's young general manager Gregg Popovich offered him a one-year deal. "He has such a work ethic," Popovich said. "He adds a lot on the court and in the locker room as well. I don't care if he's 47 or 21."[35] Moses was brought in to back up one of the next generation's great big men, David Robinson, who played alongside Malone's successor as the greatest rebounder in the game, Dennis Rodman.

Robinson and Rodman couldn't have been more different. Robinson was a devout Christian who didn't curse and who listened to his coaches. Malone admired Robinson's leadership and respected his humility. He encouraged "The Admiral" to be more assertive in the locker room.[36] Rodman was an iconoclast who detested authority and operated on his own schedule. Teammates viewed him as selfish, and his childish antics disrupted chemistry. He defied Coach Bob Hill and engaged in a hostile verbal exchange with Popovich during a team meeting in the playoffs.[37]

Moses played in seventeen games during the first two months of the season, then ruptured a tendon in his leg during practice. The injury required surgery. Malone initially hoped to return for the playoffs, though he didn't make it back.[38] In his final game, Big Mo connected on an 80-foot heave from the opposite foul line as the clock ran out on the first quarter against the Charlotte Hornets on December 27, 1994.[39]

Malone's career was likely over, though there was no farewell tour. Doc Rivers accurately predicted Malone's retirement in his book *Those Who Love the Game*. "It's [the public perception of Malone] all wrong. In Mo's case it's a big shame, because here is one of the greatest players ever to play the game. Ever. But will there be a farewell tour when Moses retires? City after city throwing a Mo party, giving him presents? No way. Nobody's going to give Moses a car every night. Because of the way he has been portrayed, through misunderstanding arising from racial differences."[40]

There was more to it. Moses bore some responsibility for the way he was perceived. It was one thing for him to avoid cameras as a shy nineteen-year-old fresh out of high school, but he was still blowing off writers who asked for a comment about his surgery as he approached his fortieth birthday.[41] Malone also played for many years past his prime, the last few of which, he barely saw the court. Some people forgot how great he was. Of course, Moses wouldn't have wanted a farewell tour anyway.

The mismatched tandem of Robinson and Rodman combined forces to lead the Spurs to a league-high 62 wins. Robinson was named MVP, and Rodman secured his fourth of seven consecutive rebounding titles. The Spurs advanced to the Western Conference Finals, where they faced the defending champion Houston Rockets and their star center Hakeem Olajuwon. Moses instructed Robinson on how to defend his old protege, to no avail.[42] Olajuwon demonstrated he was the real MVP, dominating Robinson over six games, as the Rockets ended the Spurs season on the way to their second-consecutive championship.

Moses never publicly announced his retirement. Two years after his last game, he was still exploring opportunities, hoping to sign with a contender. But he never found the right fit.[43] Malone played twenty-one professional seasons before the days of personal trainers, load management, and private air travel. He represented the end of an era, as the last ABA player to suit up in the NBA. Malone was selected to twelve NBA All-Star teams (and one in the ABA) and won three MVP awards. He retired third all-time in points and rebounds (NBA and ABA combined) and remains the all-time leader in offensive rebounds, by a huge margin.

24

Relentless Friend

Calvin Murphy, Moses's teammate with the Rockets, was arrested in 2004 on charges that he molested five of his daughters. Murphy had a secret life, fathering several children outside of his marriage. The mother of three of those children named him beneficiary of her retirement benefits upon her death. When she died, her children tried to claim the money, and weeks after the $52,408 was awarded to Murphy, they accused him of sexual abuse.[1]

Most people would distance themselves from a person accused of such heinous crimes. Moses stood by his friend. "I know you," he told Murphy. He called Murphy and Murphy's attorney every day offering to testify about his former teammate's character.[2] Murphy was acquitted on all charges.[3]

Malone was cautious about whom he let into his inner circle, though once he formed a friendship, it was for life. Carl Belcher was a 6-foot-eight-inch forward who won two state championships at Kashmere High School in Houston before playing for the University of Texas and Southwestern University. After his junior year in college, he began competing at Fonde and struck up a friendship with Moses. A few years later, Belcher was convicted of aggravated sexual assault and sent to prison.[4] Moses visited him every off-season and brought him sneakers and workout gear.[5]

After his release, Belcher worked as a driver for medical companies, transporting X-rays to radiologists. Malone called him one morning and said, "I ain't got nothing to do. Let me ride with you." Moses went with him into the doctors' offices and took pictures with the staff. "He knew what he was doing," said Belcher. Malone was helping his friend. More doctors began using Belcher's company and requesting his services. His boss thanked Belcher for the business and sent him a bonus of a few thousand dollars.[6]

Franklin Edwards, Malone's teammate on the 1982–83 76ers, called him a "relentless friend." Any time he called Moses, Moses called back immediately. If Moses was in town, he'd call Edwards. On one occasion, Edwards informed Moses that he was going to be in Petersburg. Upon his arrival, three of Malone's friends called Edwards and offered to take him out to dinner.[7]

Malone attended the funerals of his friends' parents and siblings, even ones out of town. When his friend Tony Dale graduated from undergraduate and master's programs at Texas Southern University, Moses was in attendance.[8] Any time a friend threw a party to celebrate a special occasion, Moses was the first one there, typically a half hour early. He lent money to many friends, some of whom never paid him back.[9]

Most basketball players keep in touch with a few teammates after their playing days. Edwards was one of dozens of teammates and competitors that Malone spoke to regularly. He'd drop everything to help a former teammate, whether it was Julius Erving or the guy at the end of the bench. When Darwin Cook and Paul Mokeski asked Moses to attend their respective golf tournaments, Malone immediately answered yes. He didn't ask about compensation.[10]

Moses turned to golf to quench his competitive desire. He and Clyde Drexler played together often, though Clyde was more serious about the game and passed him by.[11] Major Jones was another frequent golfing companion. Mo loved to joke around on the course. "My golf balls are like FedEx," he told his friend Don Wall. "They're all over the place." During a trip to Japan, he purchased exploding golf balls, which he pulled out on the course, scaring Tony Dale.[12]

Moses settled into a regular foursome with Dale, Mike Jones, and former NBA player Ricky Pierce. Big Mo cheated at every opportunity. "We have a story for him on every hole at Hermann Park," said Jones.[13] Moses would shank a ball into the woods, then drop a new ball and claim it was the one he hit. He'd toss a towel over his ball in a sand trap and pick it up while trying to hide from his friends that the ball was underneath it. Moses bragged to other friends that he beat Jones and Dale, and they'd complain that he cheated. The banter was as fun as the golf.[14]

Malone played in numerous charitable golf tournaments and routinely sacrificed money for the benefit of other former ballplayers. If the tournament organizer offered him $20,000 to make an appearance, he'd suggest bringing along three other athletes who he knew needed the money and split the $20,000 four ways.[15] He also provided clothing to former players who he knew were struggling.[16]

If Mo saw somebody on TV that was displaced by a flood or heard about a family that lost their father, he'd have money delivered to them anonymously.[17] "Don't say anything about Big Mo," he'd say.[18] One day, Moses and his friend Adrian Sessum were having lunch at a restaurant when Moses pointed out a homeless man walking past the window. The toes on his shoes were detached and popped up when he walked. After the meal, Malone bought a pair of shoes at the Galleria shopping mall and delivered them to the homeless man.[19]

Moses and Drexler took a motorcycle class together and were nearly kicked out for fooling around.[20] Malone began riding a Harley Davidson and attended an annual motorcycle rally in Galveston, Texas, as well as a few others around the country.[21] He enjoyed going to comedy shows and music concerts. His musical preferences included R&B and jazz, and he often attended shows at the Arena Theater in Houston when old acts like The Temptations, The Manhattans, or Earth, Wind & Fire performed.[22] On the big screen, he preferred westerns. *Blazing Saddles* and Clint Eastwood movies were among his favorites, and he'd hunker down in his house when a *Gunsmoke* marathon was on TV.[23] Big Mo even began wearing a cowboy hat. He spent his Sundays going to church and watching the Dallas Cowboys.[24]

Moses formed Moses Malone Entertainment with his old friend Tony Colbert. It provided management and consulting services for local music groups, including Destiny's Child and the group's manager, Matthew Knowles. Colbert handled the business side, while Moses mentored the artists and used his contacts to gain exposure. Moses and Tony went out to lunch every day. One of their favorite spots was the strip club Treasures. Moses swore it had the best buffet in town. He'd eat his meal, then hang out in the bathroom with Mr. Joe, the guy who shined shoes.[25]

Retirement enabled Moses to spend more time with his sons. He loved them dearly, though had trouble relating to them because they grew up with so much more than he did. He taught Moses Jr. and Michael about the importance of family, respecting God, and how to react if someone came at them. He emphasized that they were not better than anybody else and should help those less fortunate.[26]

It wasn't easy to be Moses Malone's son, especially for Moses Jr., who carried his father's name. People asked Junior why he didn't pass on the name to his first-born son. "I wouldn't want him to grow up with that target on his back," he said, "all the pressure and go through the same type of shit I went through just because of his name. I've seen jealousy, envy and hate my whole life. But yes, it has its pros and cons but, over time I realized the Cons outweigh the Pros."[27]

Big Mo attended many of his sons' games. Moses Jr. was a star basketball player at Friendswood High School and played college ball at University of Houston, Texas Tech, and South Carolina State. Michael opted for football and played wide receiver at Virginia Tech before transferring to Sam Houston State.

Moses could be hard on his boys. When Moses Jr. was fourteen, Big Mo began taking him to play ball at the prison in Richmond, Virginia, when they visited Mary in Petersburg.[28] During a high school playoff game against Texas Wheatley at San Jacinto Community College, Moses Jr. fell to the floor, holding his ankle. His father came down from the stands and hollered, "Get up. There isn't nothing wrong with you. Get up."[29]

The younger Moses was stubborn like his father, leading to confrontations between the two. Moses Sr. and Floy coached Jr. on a pro-am team at Fonde. Junior often ignored his father's instructions, leading Moses to pull him from the game. "My dad, man, he don't know what the fuck he's doing," Moses Jr. complained to Floy on the bench.

"Are you kidding?" Floy replied. "Your father is one of the greatest players in the history of the game."[30]

Michael was more laid-back and had a less combative relationship with his father. Moses had a falling out with the boys toward the end of his life when they sold his game-worn goggles without his permission, but he never stopped loving them.[31]

Big Mo remained connected to basketball in numerous ways. He went to All-Star weekend every year with his old buddies Gholson and Kevin Vergara and sometimes to the Final Four as well.[32] He still spent his summers at Fonde, where he organized the games and participated when he felt up to it.[33] A new group of Rockets were there, including Kenny Smith and Sam Cassell. Big Mo held court for hours, telling stories about the NBA. He instructed the young guys on what to do with their money and how to take care of their bodies. Smith called him "one of the smartest guys I ever met" and followed his advice on how to choose an agent.[34]

Moses was an active member of the National Basketball Retired Players Association (NBRPA). He gave the Houston chapter credibility by attending every meeting and participating in events.[35] Very few superstars were that supportive of the organization. The former players visited a children's hospital every year at Christmastime, put on basketball camps for youth in underprivileged neighborhoods, and served at food banks.[36] Malone particularly enjoyed activities with kids. "Moses was 100 percent a giver—never a taker," said Spencer Haywood, an active member of the NBRPA. He and Moses sang Bob Marley songs on stage in Mexico at the last event they attended together.[37]

Malone was inducted into the Naismith Memorial Basketball Hall of Fame in 2001. "It is an honor to think people consider me a great player," he said. "I never considered myself a great player; I considered myself a hard worker."[38] He selected Julius Erving to introduce him. "Moses Malone—just think of that name," Erving said. "He had to get famous." The Doctor delivered a beautiful ode to his former teammate, focusing on Malone's skills, heart, and intelligence.[39]

Moses began his speech with a joke. "You know, what I'm going to do is, I'm not going to give a long speech, like [fellow inductee] John Chaney did." He reached into his jacket pocket and pulled out a ream of paper that cascaded to the floor, saying, as the crowd laughed. "But, Mr. Chaney spoke so much, our words fade away."

Malone talked about what it took for him to succeed. "If you can think where Moses Malone came from, a small town, Petersburg, Virginia . . . people always said, well, this young man, 6-10, would never make it. Well, I was 6-10 with a lot of heart. And I took a lot of pride and determination to be the best. I can remember the time that me and friends used to go to the playground. We never partied. I'd never go out. We'd just go to the playground."[40]

Petersburg remained a part of Malone. He returned regularly to visit his mother until she moved to Alabama to live with her sister at the end of her life. Mary died in 2012. Moses attended family reunions in Virginia and checked in on his friends when he was in town. "He'd always smile when he'd see you," remembered Morris Fultz. "'Hey, hey, boy. What you doing?'" Fultz said in his best Moses voice. "He was always Moses. He never changed. As great as he got, he would always stop, spend time with you, talk to you, treat you like you're still on the playground at school. He never got to the point where he thought he was better than anybody else. He never got to that level. I never saw that out of him."[41] Moses went back to celebrate the thirtieth anniversary of his 1973 and 1974 championship teams and attended his forty-year class reunion in 2014.[42]

Most Petersburg residents are proud of the man they say "put them on the map," though some believe he should have done more for the city that raised him. Malone worked out a deal with Nike to benefit Petersburg High School through the sale of his jersey and financially supported the first Black-oriented radio station in the Richmond area, MAGIC 99.[43] Who's to say what the proper amount is for an athlete to give back? Many of Malone's friends and classmates who remained in Petersburg believed the city was run by corrupt or ineffective politicians. One friend discouraged Malone from backing a proposed development project for fear that his money would be squandered.[44] Petersburg hasn't so much as named a street or basketball court after Malone.

The 76ers hired Maurice Cheeks as coach in 2005, and Little Mo asked Big Mo to work with the Sixers big men. For three seasons, he flew in for a week or two at a time every month or so. "I'm going to call my father and tell my father I got to chop it up with Moses," said 76ers forward Chris Webber after meeting Malone. The future Hall of Famer grew up watching Moses, and his father was a huge fan. Not all Sixers were as impressed. "I'd had no idea he won three MVPs," said center Steven Hunter.[45]

Moses emphasized rebounding and defense. "It takes an attitude, a bruising attitude that it's going to be tough right there," he told the players. "If you ain't got an attitude about rebounding, you're not going to be a great rebounder. But if you want to do it, you're going to be a great rebounder." Moses demonstrated tricks and positioning around the basket.[46] He worked on a hook shot and spin move with center Samuel Dalembert.[47]

The players enjoyed winding Moses up by asking him how he fared against assistant coach Jeff Ruland or an opposing team's coach. Malone served as a liaison between the players and coaching staff.[48] He also counseled Allen Iverson on how to navigate stardom. "He was able to be that guy—when he knew I was going to explode—to say, 'Come on, young fella.' And I'm, like, 'Well, Mo said calm down. So, I guess I should calm down,'" Iverson said.[49]

Moses enjoyed chatting with opposing players as well. After the 76ers beat the Lakers, he went into the Lakers' locker room to say hello to Kobe Bryant. The Lakers had been thoroughly outrebounded, and Bryant was frustrated by his team's lack of toughness, particularly by center Andrew Bynum. "I don't know what to do with these guys," Kobe said to Moses. "Give Andrew Bynum some raw steak with some gun powder on it and make him mean," said Moses. "That's how they train dogs." Kobe laughed. Moses didn't appear to be joking.[50]

Moses worked out daily on the exercise bike, elliptical, or StairMaster and cut carbs, fried food, and sugar from his diet. Former Sixers GM John Nash was working as a scout with the team and asked Moses, then about fifty years old, if he could suit up and play five minutes a night. "Big Mo can give you fifteen minutes a half," Moses replied.[51]

Cheeks knew his job was in jeopardy as the team floundered during the 2007–08 season. He decided to address the players and asked Moses to say a few words. Big Mo passionately explained what it took to be a champion. Jim Lynam, an assistant who coached in the NBA for thirty years, had never heard a locker room speech like it. "Put it on the top shelf, all by itself," he said.[52] The players were blown away. Cheeks was fired midway through the season, and Malone left at the end of the season.

In March 2006, Moses spotted two ladies talking in a parking garage in downtown Houston. They'd just left a Kem concert, and he was on his way to a jazz club. He struck up a conversation with one of them, Leah Nash, and asked for her number. Moses told her he was a janitor, which was his standard line. She believed him after looking at his old, broken-down Range Rover.[53] Malone owned a host of luxury automobiles, though he often drove a fifteen-year-old Range Rover that cost a lot of money to keep running.[54] The rundown car allowed him to blend in without calling attention to himself. After a couple of dates, Leah, an accountant from Louisiana, caught on that he wasn't a janitor. Soon after, Moses asked her to be his girlfriend. They often went to the movies, and he took her salsa dancing.[55]

In 2009 Leah gave birth to Moses's third son, Micah. Moses didn't live with Leah and Micah, though he visited every day and spent many nights at their home. He left at 5:30 every morning to drive home to Sugar Land because the toll roads were cheaper then. Micah began playing sports through the YMCA at age three, and Moses attended every practice and game. In the evenings, he colored with the boy and read him books.[56]

Moses took Leah and Micah on vacation to Nevis in 2014. He experienced a dizzy spell while there and nearly fainted. More episodes followed. In the summer of 2015 he fainted on the golf course. He told his friends he was just overheated and refused to allow them to call an ambulance. On Tuesday, September 8, 2015, his heart began fluttering while he was working out. He immediately went to the doctor, who couldn't find anything wrong and gave Moses a heart monitor to wear. Malone spent that night at Leah's place and mentioned to her that Darryl Dawkins died a couple of weeks earlier of a heart attack.[57]

Malone had a slew of charity golf tournaments scheduled that summer and fall. He joked with friends that he was on the PGA Tour.[58] That weekend, he was headed to Norfolk, Virginia, to participate in a tournament for the Still Hope Foundation, a charity to benefit single mothers founded by NBA referee Tony Brothers. He always brought his Virginia friends Ed Gholson, Kevin Vergara, and Don Wall to the event.[59]

On Thursday before the tournament, Moses traveled to Springfield, Massachusetts, with Calvin Murphy for the Hall of Fame enshrinement ceremony. His idol, Spencer Haywood, was being inducted.[60] On Friday morning while on the elliptical machine, he talked with Rick Barry about old times and later joked around with Barkley and Bill Walton.[61]

On Saturday Moses and Murphy flew to Virginia. Moses attended a comedy show that night, then hung out with Murphy, Gerald Henderson, Paul Silas, and others at the Waterside Marriot Hotel. At about 2:00 a.m. he reminded everybody to be in the lobby at 6:00 a.m. and told Brothers, who canceled the tournament the previous year due to rain, "Don't you cancel this golf tournament no matter what happens, or I'm gonna kick your ass." Then he went to his room. He called his friend Johnnie White on the West Coast and told him he was very dizzy. White encouraged him to call an ambulance, but Moses refused. He was concerned that the hospital would keep him for several days. He told White he was going to shower, then go to bed.[62]

Sandra White planned the tournament with Brothers. She'd known Moses for over thirty years and immediately knew something was wrong when he didn't show up for breakfast at 6:00 a.m. Moses was always early. Murphy and Wall called his phone—no answer. Sandra gave Wall the key to Moses's room. She was convinced he needed medical attention. Wall unlocked the door, but the latch was closed from the inside. He called Moses's name—no answer. The front desk sent a security man to open the door. Wall, former Redskins safety Alvin Walton, and Sandra followed the man into the room. Moses was lying on the bed with his heart monitor on. He was dead at the age of sixty.[63]

Vergara called Malone's family and Lefty Driesell, whom Moses was supposed to have dinner with that night.[64] Sandra informed Brothers. The sky looked dark and ominous. Brothers considered Moses's comments the night before and decided that Malone would want them to carry on. He pulled Murphy aside to deliver the news. Devastated, Murphy dropped to his knees. Then Brothers informed the rest of the golfers and relayed the conversation he had with Moses. He announced that the tournament would be renamed the Moses Malone Golf Tournament. As soon as he finished speaking, the skies cleared up and the sun came out.[65]

An autopsy revealed the cause of death as an aortic dissection with rupture. Moses's heart appeared to be strong. A piece of plaque broke off and split his aorta, killing him instantly. That type of event typically isn't preceded by the symptoms he'd experienced. He may have had two separate conditions.[66]

Moses was the third 76ers big man from the early-to-mid 1980s to drop dead from heart-related issues. Caldwell Jones died at sixty-four of a heart attack in September 2014. Darryl Dawkins did the same on August 27, 2015, at the age of fifty-eight. Mark McNamara, a 6-foot-11-inch center on the 1983 team, died of a "cardiac event" in 2020 at age sixty, and four years later, Earl Cureton, a power forward on the 1983 Sixers, died suddenly at sixty-six. Studies have concluded that basketball players have a higher incidence of sudden cardiac death (SCD) than athletes in other sports.[67] The National Basketball Players Association and National Basketball Retired Players Association began a joint program in 2016 that provides mobile heart screenings for ex-players.[68]

The funeral was held at Lakewood Church, formerly The Summit, where Moses built his legend with the Rockets. A separate ceremony was held at Petersburg High School weeks later. Several hundred people attended the funeral, including many former teammates, opponents, and coaches. Julius Erving, Clyde Drexler, and Dominique Wilkins made a joint speech at the viewing the night before, as did Floy, who shared the story of how he and Moses met through his teacher.[69] Moses Jr. spoke briefly at the funeral, and Alfreda's cousin Kirk Williams, Howard White, and Charles Barkley delivered eulogies. Barkley said it was bittersweet because he lost his dad, but if Moses's family asked him to speak it meant that his dad was proud of him.[70]

After the funeral, six-year-old Micah said to his mother what was evident to everybody in attendance: "A lot of people loved my Daddy."[71]

Epilogue

Harris Blitzer Sports and Entertainment purchased the 76ers in 2013, and owners Josh Harris and David Blitzer tasked CEO Scott O'Neil with establishing stronger relationships with former players. Moses had been somewhat estranged from the organization for years.[1] The team contacted him several times about retiring his jersey, but he wasn't interested. He wanted other people like Andrew Toney to be recognized as well.[2]

O'Neil grew up in New York as a Sixers fan. "In the backyard with my three brothers, every time we got an offensive rebound, we were Moses Malone" he said. On his bedroom wall, O'Neil even had the iconic Nike poster of Moses parting a sea of basketballs. Moses had returned to Philadelphia for a few events, including sharing a suite with Julius Erving for Iverson's jersey retirement in 2014. O'Neil was anxious to strengthen the relationship between his idol and the franchise.[3]

Fred Whitfield, a longtime Nike executive and the chief operating officer (COO) of the Charlotte Hornets in 2015, asked O'Neil to appear on a panel at a fundraiser he was organizing. Whitfield told O'Neil that Moses, a good friend of his, would be at the dinner. He was surprised to learn that O'Neil and Malone had never met, so he sat them next to each other. They talked for four hours about religion, kids, the ABA, being traded, and a host of other topics. Then O'Neil asked Moses about the 76ers retiring his jersey. Malone resisted. O'Neil asked what the problem was.

Malone delivered the best answer O'Neil had heard an athlete provide in his twenty-five years in professional sports. "Well, it isn't fair," Moses said. "I didn't do this alone. I had coaches, teammates, trainers, even the guys driving the buses. I didn't get here on my own, why should I be recognized?"

It was typical Moses. In 2006, when the Houston Parks and Recreation Department approached him about naming the court at Fonde after him, he said he'd only agree to it if others who helped make Fonde a special place were recognized as well, particularly Angelo Cascio, the center's longtime recreation director. A committee was assembled to create a Fonde Hall of Fame consisting of players and administrators. And Moses Malone Court can now be found in Angelo Cascio Gym.[4]

Every time Moses was paid to participate in an autograph session in Philadelphia, he insisted that each member of the 1982–83 championship team be compensated to attend as well. Franklin Edwards, a bench player on that team, once asked the organizer why he paid Edwards and some of the lesser-known players to appear. Nobody was willing to pay for their autographs. The man informed him that Moses required it.[5]

O'Neil and Malone devised a solution to Malone's concern. The 76ers would retire Malone's jersey with the name of every teammate he played with in Philadelphia on the banner bearing his name and number. Sadly, he died seven months later. Out of respect for his grieving family, O'Neil put the jersey retirement on hold. He didn't want the 76ers to appear opportunistic or exploitative. Then Moses Jr. called the organization and encouraged them to retire his father's number.[6]

The Sixers set a date of February 8, 2019, to honor Moses. That morning, his three sons unveiled a statue of him on Legends Walk outside of the team's training complex in Camden, New Jersey, alongside statues of other 76ers legends, including Julius Erving, Bobby Jones, Maurice Cheeks, Hal Greer, Billy Cunningham, and Wilt Chamberlain. Iverson, who would receive his own statue five years later, was one of the Sixers legends on hand for the ceremony. He walked up to the statue of Moses and patted it on the chest. "He was just an integral part of my life in many ways besides just basketball," Iverson told reporters.[7]

Many of Moses's teammates and friends attended the jersey retirement ceremony at the Wells Fargo Center that night. The Sixers played recorded messages from the team's owners, Billy Cunningham, and NBA commissioner Adam Silver. Julius Erving took the microphone and pointed out that though Moses played for several teams in the ABA and NBA, he chose to be presented as a 76er when he was selected one of the NBA's fifty greatest players. Franklin Edwards used to tell Big Mo that he carried the 76ers on the court. As Edwards watched Malone's No. 2 jersey rise to the rafters with the names of his teammates stitched around the exterior of the banner, he couldn't help but think that Moses was carrying them one more time.[8]

NOTES

Preface

1. Victor Wembanyama, "Victor Wembanyama," interview by J. J. Redick and Tommy Alter, June 21, 2023, in *The Old Man and the Three*, podcast, MP3 audio, 54:00, https://podcasts.apple.com/us/podcast/victor-wembanyama/id1525281746?i=1000617786916.
2. Tania Ganguli, "Victor Wembanyama Has Always Done Things Differently," *New York Times*, October 16, 2022.
3. Garnett and Ritz, *KG A to Z*, 26.
4. Lazenby, *Showboat*, 243, 259.
5. Abrams, *Boys among Men*, 80.
6. Benedict, *LeBron*, 180.
7. Williams, *Ahead of the Game*, 251.
8. Charles Barkley, "Charles Barkley's Basketball Hall of Fame Enshrinement Speech," Naismith Memorial Hall of Fame Enshrinement Ceremony, September 9, 2006, Springfield MA, video, 14:42, https://www.hoophall.com/hall-of-famers/charles-barkley/; and Julius Erving, "Moses Malone's Basketball Hall of Fame Enshrinement Speech," Naismith Memorial Hall of Fame Enshrinement Ceremony, October 5, 2001, Springfield MA, video, 29:12, https://www.hoophall.com/hall-of-famers/moses-malone/.

1. The Heights

1. Frank Deford, "Bounding into Prominence," *Sports Illustrated*, February 19, 1979, https://vault.si.com/vault/1979/02/19/bounding-into-prominence-moses-malone-jumped-from-high-school-to-the-pros-where-he-has-become-the-games-top-rebounder.
2. U.S. Census Bureau, 1940 United States Federal Census, Oscar Hudgins, U.S. Department of Commerce, accessed September 2, 2023, ancestry.com, https://www.ancestry.com/search/collections/2442/records/24805282?tid=&pid=&queryId=2e1a1de4-8233-4c62-ac50-52bb40026a61&usePUBJs=true.

3. Justin William Moyer, "How Moses 'Mumbles' Malone Skipped College to Save His Family—and Rule the NBA," *Washington Post*, September 14, 2015, https://www.washingtonpost.com/news/morning-mix/wp/2015/09/14/how-moses-mumbles-malone-skipped-college-to-save-his-family-and-rule-the-nba/.
4. Clarine Edwards, in discussion with the author, June 9, 2022; and Mario Gray, in discussion with the author, June 13, 2023.
5. Michael Stith, in discussion with the author, March 2, 2024.
6. Gray, discussion.
7. Clarine Edwards, discussion.
8. Arthur Pincus, "A.B.A. Is Stepping Up Search for Talent among Schoolboys," *New York Times*, January 10, 1975.
9. "Moses Malone: From Scared Prep Player to Confident Pro." *Lakeland (FL) Ledger*, March 30, 1975.
10. Ira Berkow, "A Force That Could Stop Malone," *New York Times*, April 24, 1983.
11. George Campbell, in discussion with the author, September 7, 2023.
12. Deford, "Bounding."
13. Moses Malone Jr., "My Dad Use To Tell Me Stories How When He Was A Youngster His Cousins & People Would Drive Past Him," Facebook, January 23, 2021 (account and post deleted; no URL available).
14. Cynthia Kerns, in discussion with the author, April 24, 2023.
15. Deford, "Bounding."
16. Clinton Bufford, in discussion with the author, June 26, 2022.
17. Roger Pegram, in discussion with the author, September 3, 2022.
18. Ray Didinger, "Moses Makes His Private Life Most Valuable," *Philadelphia Daily News*, May 26, 1983.
19. Leroy Cole, in discussion with the author, June 20, 2022; and Patrick Kane, "Hangin' with Mr. Hoopster," *Progress-Index* (Petersburg), July 2, 2011.
20. Deford, "Bounding."
21. Michael Parham, in discussion with the author, May 16, 2022.
22. Hal Miles, in discussion with the author, June 27, 2022.
23. Leroy Cole, discussion; and Kane, "Hangin' with Mr. Hoopster."
24. MacMullan, Bartholomew, and Klores, *Basketball*, 3.
25. David Pair, in discussion with the author, June 8, 2022.
26. Don Wall, in discussion with the author, July 22, 2022.
27. Phyllis Hawkins-Jones, in discussion with the author, November 9, 2022.
28. Linda McNatt, "Historic Community Center Finds New Life as an Urban Farm," *Lancaster Farming*, last modified August 24, 2021, https://www.lancasterfarming.com/historic-community-center-finds-new-life-as-an-urban-farm/article_caaad187-a04c-5c29-97bc-2144f686f13d.html.

29. Pegram, discussion.
30. Moses Malone, "Playboy Interview: Moses Malone," *Playboy*, March 1984, 50.
31. Roy S. Johnson, "Malone's Dominance Grows," *New York Times*, February 19, 1982.
32. Deford, "Bounding."
33. Pair, discussion.
34. Leroy Cole, discussion.
35. Malone, "Playboy Interview," 52.
36. James Jones, in discussion with the author, June 12, 2023; and Ricky Hunley, in discussion with the author, April 4, 2023.
37. Morris Fultz, in discussion with the author, June 5, 2023.
38. Ronald Robinson, in discussion with the author, May 3, 2022.
39. Fultz, discussion.
40. Didinger, "Moses Makes His."

2. Chuck Taylor All-Stars

1. Bufford, discussion.
2. "1730–1985 Petersburg's Tobacco Industry," Historic Petersburg Foundation, n.d., http://www.historicpetersburg.org/1730-1985-petersburgs-tobacco-industry/.
3. Luther P. Jackson, "Free Negroes of Petersburg, Virginia," *Journal of Negro History* 12, no. 3 (July 1927): 365–88, https://www.jstor.org/stable/2714105.
4. Clarence Alonzo Oliver, in discussion with the author, July 16, 2022.
5. "McKenney Library Sit-in," Historic Petersburg Foundation, n.d., http://www.historicpetersburg.org/mckenney-library-sit-in/.
6. Joyce Chu, "'Like Mary and Martha Entertaining Jesus': Family Hosted Dr. King Whenever He Visited Petersburg," *Progress-Index* (Petersburg), January 15, 2023.
7. Francine Cole, in discussion with the author, June 17, 2022.
8. Brown v. Board of Education of Topeka, 347 U.S. 483 (1954).
9. Suan Smith-Richardson and Lauren Burke, "In the 1950s, Rather Than Integrate Its Public Schools, Virginia Closed Them," *The Guardian*, November 27, 2021, https://www.theguardian.com/world/2021/nov/27/integration-public-schools-massive-resistance-virginia-1950s.
10. Adolph H. Grundman, "Public School Desegregation in Virginia from 1954 to the Present" (diss., Wayne State University Dissertations, Paper 952, 1972), 250–51.
11. Fred Van Deventer, "NAACP Urges High School District Plan," *Progress-Index* (Petersburg), February 25, 1969.

12. Harry Kollatz Jr., "Here Comes 'The Judge,'" *Richmond Magazine*, May 20, 2018, https://richmondmagazine.com/news/sunday-story/here-comes-the-judge/.
13. "Peabody High School—the Earliest Publicly Funded High School for African Americans in Virginia," Peabody High School Alumni Association, n.d., https://www.phsnaa.org/history/.
14. Gonzell Phillips, in discussion with the author, April 8, 2023.
15. Bettie Mitchell, "Peabody's Fate Question," *Progress-Index* (Petersburg), October 2, 1969.
16. Mitchell, "Peabody's Fate."
17. Cindy Minton, in discussion with the author, May 4, 2022.
18. Parham, discussion.
19. Fultz, discussion.
20. "Community, Former Students Pay Respects to 'Pro' Hayes," *Progress-Index* (Petersburg), last modified September 9, 2014, https://www.progress-index.com/story/news/2010/05/26/community-former-students-pay-respects/36484694007/.
21. Bufford, discussion.
22. Bernard Wilson, in discussion with the author, April 6, 2023.
23. Mark Thompson, in discussion with the author, April 7, 2023.
24. Bufford, discussion.
25. Fultz, discussion; Bill Nunnally, in discussion with the author, April 19, 2023; and Phillips, discussion.
26. Steven Armstrong, "Peal Can Be Proud of His Former Star," *Progress-Index* (Petersburg), October 6, 1974.
27. Harry Marsh, "Freshman Malone Supplies Height Petersburg Needed," *Progress-Index* (Petersburg), February 25, 1971.
28. Jeff Cohane, "Height, Inexperience Petersburg Keynotes," *Progress-Index* (Petersburg), December 3, 1971.
29. Harry Marsh, "Friend Paces All-Tri-City Team," *Progress-Index* (Petersburg), March 5, 1972.
30. Wilson, discussion.

3. Visitors from the Moon

1. Miles, discussion.
2. Berkow, "A Force."
3. Miles, discussion.
4. David E. Early, "Early Successes Haven't Spoiled Malone," *Minneapolis Star*, April 18, 1974.

5. Thomasine Bolling Hill, in discussion with the author, May 3, 2022.
6. Janice Davis, in discussion with the author, November 8, 2022.
7. Ollie Jarvis, in discussion with the author, April 5, 2023.
8. Nathan Dickerson, in discussion with the author, May 12, 2022; Nunnally, discussion; and Phillips, discussion.
9. Wilson, discussion.
10. Nunnally, discussion.
11. Miles, discussion.
12. Stanley Taylor, in discussion with the author, April 6, 2023; and Fultz, discussion.
13. Ronald Walker, in discussion with the author, April 22, 2023.
14. Ed Robinson, in discussion with the author, June 20, 2022.
15. Pair, discussion.
16. Wyatt Curtis, in discussion with the author, April 20, 2023.
17. Ed Gholson, in discussion with the author, May 17, 2022.
18. Ed Robinson, discussion.
19. "Carl Peal," Story of the Virginia Interscholastic Association (website), July 28, 2020, https://viastory.org/hall-fame/carl-peal.
20. Phillips, discussion.
21. Amir Vera, "City Celebrates Malone's Legacy," *Progress-Index* (Petersburg), last modified January 7, 2016, https://www.progress-index.com/story/news/politics/county/2015/10/25/city-celebrates-malone-s-legacy/32782444007/.
22. Curtis, discussion.
23. Wilson, discussion.
24. Jimmy Williams, in discussion with the author, April 6, 2023.
25. Wilson, discussion.
26. Bill Littlepage, in discussion with the author, July 6, 2022.
27. Ronald Robinson, discussion.
28. Harry Marsh, "Noe Is Different," *Progress-Index* (Petersburg), April 1, 1973.
29. Phillips, discussion.
30. Jimmy Williams, discussion.
31. Jimmy Williams, discussion.
32. Ronald Robinson, discussion.
33. Dan Richards, "Petersburg Blasts Hopewell in Division Final," *Progress-Index* (Petersburg), February 25, 1973.
34. Adrian Sessum, in discussion with the author, June 23, 2022.
35. Ronald Robinson, discussion.
36. Dave Koesters, in discussion with the author, June 7, 2023.

37. Emily Jones, "Moses Malone and Halifax's Brush with Fame," SoVaNow (website), September 17, 2015, https://www.sovanow.com/articles/moses_malone_and_halifaxs_brush_with_fame/.
38. Deford, "Bounding."

4. Five Stars

1. Scott Cacciola, "His Basketball Camp Made Hall of Famers. Now He's One, Too," *New York Times*, September 11, 2021.
2. Will Klein, in discussion with the author, September 8, 2022.
3. Michael Ryan, *Five Star*, 8.
4. Michael Ryan, *Five Star*, 7.
5. Vincent M. Mallozzi, "Howard Garfinkel, Who Discovered and Groomed Top Basketball Talent, Dies at 86," *New York Times*, May 8, 2015.
6. Hubie Brown, in discussion with the author, May 24, 2022.
7. Tate Frazier, "Episode 1: The World According to Garf," November 29, 2021, in *The World of Five-Star*, podcast, MP3 audio, 28:57, https://podcasts.apple.com/us/podcast/episode-1-the-world-according-to-garf/id1584012030?i=1000543346224.
8. Klein, discussion.
9. Hubie Brown, discussion.
10. Klein, discussion.
11. Mallozzi, "Howard Garfunkel."
12. Michael Ryan, *Five Star*.
13. Cacciola, "His Basketball Camp."
14. Hubie Brown, discussion; and Mike Fratello, in discussion with the author, August 24, 2022.
15. Fratello, discussion.
16. Frazier, "World According to Garf."
17. Malone, "Playboy Interview," 52.
18. Fratello, discussion.
19. Tom McCorry, in discussion with the author, May19, 2022.
20. McCorry, discussion.
21. Marc Iavaroni, in discussion with the author, October 3, 2022.
22. Hubie Brown, discussion.
23. Klein, discussion.
24. McCorry, discussion.
25. Dick Vitale, in discussion with the author, November 2, 2022.
26. George Shirk, "Malone Lives by His Instincts," *Philadelphia Inquirer*, February 13, 1983.

27. Tate Frazier, "Episode 2: The Three Discoveries: MJ, Moses and Muggsy," November 29, 2021, in *The World of Five-Star*, podcast, MP3 audio, 34:46, https://podcasts.apple.com/us/podcast/episode-2-the-three-discoveries-moses-mj-and-muggsy/id1584012030?i=1000543346268.
28. Malone, "Playboy Interview," 52.
29. Klein, discussion.
30. Jerry Buterakos, in discussion with the author, September 20, 2023.
31. Campy Russell, in discussion with the author, September 14, 2023.
32. Benny White, in discussion with the author, July 14, 2022.
33. McMullen, *Maryland Basketball*, 52.
34. NBA.com, "75 Stories: Moses Malone," n.d., video, 08:37, https://www.nba.com/watch/video/75-stories-moses-malone.

5. Lefty and the Milkman

1. Eddie Biedenbach, in discussion with the author, December 14, 2022.
2. Didinger, "Moses Makes His."
3. Lefty Driesell, in discussion with the author, March 1, 2022.
4. Alan Goldstein, "Moses Malone: The Bullets' Big Man Shoots for Revenge," *Basketball Digest*, February 1987, 18, https://archive.org/details/sim_basketball-digest_1987-02_14_4/page/18/mode/2up?q=moses+malone.
5. Driesell, discussion.
6. Harmon, *Charles "Lefty" Driesell*, 38.
7. Joe Harrington, in discussion with the author, May 10, 2022.
8. Ungrady, *Tales from Maryland Terrapins*, 140.
9. Dan Steinberg, "Lefty Driesell on the Origins of 'UCLA of the East,'" *Washington Post*, April 19, 2013, https://www.washingtonpost.com/news/dc-sports-bog/wp/2013/04/19/lefty-driesell-on-the-origins-of-ucla-of-the-east/.
10. Ungrady, *Tales from Maryland Terrapins*, 59.
11. McMullen, *Maryland Basketball*, 59.
12. Dave Kindred, "The Case for Lefty Driesell," *The Athletic*, March 29, 2018, https://theathletic.com/167659/2018/03/29/the-case-for-lefty-driesell/?source=user_shared_article.
13. McMullen, *Maryland Basketball*, 59; and Lewis Bowling, "Lefty Time," *Go Duke*, May 11, 2018, https://goduke.com/news/2018/5/11/211715511.aspx.
14. Billy Hahn, in discussion with the author, April 7, 2022.
15. "7 Rent-a-Cars in One Day a Pritchett Mark," *Washington Post*, March 6, 1977.
16. Harrington, discussion.
17. Ken Denlinger, "Malone: His Day Is Here," *Washington Post*, April 17, 1981.
18. Driesell, discussion.

19. Harrington, discussion.
20. Howard White, in discussion with the author, May 11, 2022.
21. "New Mexico Loses Malone," *Albuquerque Journal*, June 21, 1974.
22. Harrington, discussion.
23. Pluto, *Loose Balls*, 324.
24. Bob Ibach, "Petersburg Revisited 110 Years Later," *Evening Sun* (Baltimore), June 14, 1974.
25. George White, "They All Wanted Malone," *Houston Chronicle*, December 14, 1976.
26. Mo Howard, in discussion with the author, September 6, 2023.
27. "Big Business of Sports Recruiting: A Crisis in the Colleges," *New York Times*, March 10, 1974.
28. Bufford, discussion.
29. Didinger, "Moses Makes His."
30. White, "They All Wanted Malone."
31. Driesell, discussion.
32. Pair, discussion.
33. Kevin Sherrington, "Reticent Hall of Famer Moses Malone Helped Save Rockets from Oblivion," *Dallas Morning News*, September 26, 2015.
34. "New Mexico Loses Malone," *Albuquerque Journal*.
35. David E. Early, "Recruiting Pressures Pile Up on Star," *Minneapolis Star*, April 19, 1974.
36. Pair, discussion; and Dickerson, discussion.
37. Pair, discussion.
38. Kindred, "The Case."
39. Pat Putnam, "Don't Send My Boy to Harvard . . . ," *Sports Illustrated*, November 4, 1974, https://vault.si.com/vault/1974/11/04/dont-send-my-boy-to-harvard.
40. Pluto, *Loose Balls*, 323.
41. Bill Tanton, "Are Terps Losing Moses?" *Evening Sun* (Baltimore), April 25, 1974.

6. The Decision

1. Miles, discussion.
2. Minton, discussion.
3. Deford, "Bounding."
4. Early, "Early Successes."
5. Moyer, "How Moses 'Mumbles' Malone."
6. "Malone & Co. Too Much for Manchester," *Progress-Index* (Petersburg), December 13, 1973.
7. Didinger, *One Last Read*, 114.

8. Larry Clark, "Wave Sets Stage for Friday Showdown," *Progress-Index* (Petersburg), January 12, 1974.
9. George Wyatt, "Malone Sets Tournament Records in Wave Victory," *Progress-Index* (Petersburg), February 20, 1974.
10. George Wyatt, "Malone Tops 2,000 Point Mark as Peterson Downs Colonial Heights," *Progress-Index* (Petersburg), February 24, 1974.
11. Larry Clark, "Petersburg Repeats as State Champs," *Progress-Index* (Petersburg), March 10, 1974.
12. Larry Clark, "Inside Sports," *Progress-Index* (Petersburg), March 12, 1974.
13. Koesters, discussion.
14. Early, "Recruiting Pressures."
15. Early, "Early Successes."
16. George Shirk, "NBA Star Malone May Join Sixers with Record-Setting Contract," *Philadelphia Inquirer*, September 3, 1982.
17. "Malone Paces Victory," *New York Times*, April 1, 1974.
18. Gutman, *Chairmen of Boards*, 125.
19. Mike Pollio, in discussion with the author, May 17, 2022.
20. Eddie Biedenbach, in discussion with the author, April 25, 2022.
21. Didinger, *One Last Read*, 114.
22. Dick Vitale (@DickieV), "Hey @espn had several tv ppl pick the best HS player they have ever seen. My MOUNT RUSHMORE OF The BEST in HS would be # 1 @KingJames 2 @MagicJohnson 3 @kobebryant 4 Moses Malone," Twitter, April 12, 2020, 2:33 p.m., https://twitter.com/dickiev/status/1249405407786930181?s=27&t=ovbog0rh2yf5r8u4upwriQ.
23. Gutman, *Chairmen of Boards*, 122–23.
24. George White, "They All Wanted Malone," *Houston Chronicle*, December 14, 1976.
25. Didinger, *One Last Read*, 115.
26. Kevin Wilson, in discussion with the author, April 10, 2023.
27. "Malone Slated to Say Friday," *Albuquerque Journal*, June 11, 1974.
28. "New Mexico Loses Malone," *Albuquerque Journal*, June 21, 1974.
29. Mark Whicker, "Moses Malone Went from High School to Pros and Rebounded His Way to the Hall of Fame," *Los Angeles Daily News*, last modified August 28, 2017, https://www.dailynews.com/2015/09/15/moses-malone-went-from-high-school-to-pros-and-rebounded-his-way-to-hall-of-fame/.
30. "New Mexico Loses Malone," *Albuquerque Journal*.
31. Locke and Ibach, *Caught in Net*, 87–88.
32. Rick Telander, "The Descent of a Man," *Sports Illustrated*, March 8, 1982, https://vault.si.com/vault/1982/03/08/the-descent-of-a-man.

33. Locke and Ibach, *Caught in Net*, 45.
34. Locke and Ibach, *Caught in Net*, 45–46.
35. Locke and Ibach, *Caught in Net*, 59, 64.
36. Telander, "Descent."
37. Telander, "Descent."
38. Locke and Ibach, *Caught in Net*, 89.
39. Locke and Ibach, *Caught in Net*, 89.
40. Locke and Ibach, *Caught in Net*, 90.
41. "New Mexico Loses Malone," *Albuquerque Journal*.
42. Bob Ibach, "Holy Moses! Terps Expect Investigation," *Evening Sun* (Baltimore), June 21, 1974.
43. Driesell, discussion.
44. Whicker, "Moses Malone."
45. Driesell, discussion.
46. Gordie Jones, "The Legend of Big Mo: Everyone Has a Moses Malone Memory, but His Legacy Lives On beyond the Court," *The Athletic*, March 25, 2019, https://theathletic.com/876572/2019/03/25/the-legend-of-big-mo-everyone-has-a-moses-malone-memory-but-his-legacy-lives-on-beyond-the-court/.
47. Locke and Ibach, *Caught in Net*, 90.
48. LeRoy Bearman, "Recruiting Malone Cost U. $10,000," *Albuquerque Journal*, June 26, 1974.
49. "Malone's Recruiters Being Probed," *The Capital* (Annapolis MD), June 24, 1974.
50. "Mrs. Malone Is Telling All: Clemson Offered Moses Cash," *The Capital* (Annapolis MD), July 2, 1974.
51. George Ferguson, "Roof Falls on Lobos," *Deseret News* (Salt Lake City UT), January 21, 1975.
52. Art Chansky, "Blame Put on Locke," *Herald-Sun* (Durham NC), October 8, 1975.

7. Stop Jivin' Me, Coach

1. Bucky Buckwalter, in discussion with the author, March 2, 2022.
2. Ernest Shaw, "Malone One of Many to Make Jump," *Progress-Index* (Petersburg), December 10, 2006.
3. "Hardship Cases Listed by NBA," *The Capital* (Annapolis MD), May 9, 1975.
4. "Royals Snap Up Lucas," *Sarasota Herald-Tribune*, May 27, 1962.
5. Joe Dowdall, "Harding at Best; Shamrocks, Too," *Detroit Free Press*, March 4, 1961.
6. "Pistons Can't Use 7-Foot Prep," *Lawrence (KS) Journal-World*, July 3, 1962.

7. "7-Foot Ex-Scholastic Star to Play Center for Pistons," *New York Times*, June 19, 1964.
8. "Shotgun Blast Fatal to Reggie Harding," *Bakersfield Californian*, September 5, 1972.
9. Pluto, *Loose Balls*, 141–42.
10. Spears and Washburn, *Spencer Haywood Rule*, 33, 35.
11. Spears and Washburn, *Spencer Haywood Rule*, 45.
12. Spencer Haywood, in discussion with the author, June 24, 2022.
13. Spears and Washburn, *Spencer Haywood Rule*, 93.
14. Spears and Washburn, *Spencer Haywood Rule*, 94.
15. Haywood, discussion.
16. Vince Boryla, interview by Bob Kuska, August 9, 2010, audio, Bob Kuska, private collection.
17. Boryla, interview.
18. George White, "They All Wanted Malone," *Houston Chronicle*, December 14, 1976.
19. Harry Marsh, "Malone Drafted in Third Round by Pro ABA Utah Stars; Kilbourne and Peal Think He Should Attend College First," *Progress-Index* (Petersburg), April 18, 1974.
20. "ABA Circus Tabs Malone," *Albuquerque Times*, April 18, 1974.
21. Sam Goldaper, "A.B.A. Goes for Broke in Draft," *New York Times*, April 18, 1974.
22. Pennington Greene, in discussion with the author, June 7, 2023; and Bernard Vaughan, in discussion with the author, May 13, 2023.
23. Dan Pattison, "Stars Formally Announce Sale," *Deseret News* (Salt Lake City UT), June 4, 1975.
24. Halberstam, *Breaks of the Game*, 193–94.
25. Buckwalter, discussion.
26. Halberstam, *Breaks of the Game*, 192–93.
27. Buckwalter, discussion.
28. Larry Keech, "NBA Agents Go Big Business: The Agents Who Represent Former Duke and UNC Basketball Players Hang Out in Executive Suites, Not on Street Corners," *News & Record* (Greensboro NC), last modified January 24, 2015, https://greensboro.com/nba-agents-go-big-business-the-agents-who-represent-former-duke-and-unc-basketball-players/article_e5183498-55fd-552e-8e20-643b773ab643.html.
29. Donald Dell, in discussion with the author, April 2, 2022.
30. Driesell, discussion.
31. Dell, discussion; and Lee Fentress, in discussion with the author, May 3, 2022.

32. Fentress, discussion.
33. Buckwalter, discussion.
34. Putnam, "Don't Send."
35. Pluto, *Loose Balls*, 328.
36. Leroy Cole, discussion.
37. "Will Moses Be Happy in the Promised Land?" *St. Louis Post-Dispatch*, September 1, 1974.
38. Gerald Eskenazi, "Schoolboy Accepts $3-Million Pro Offer," *New York Times*, August 30, 1974.
39. MacMullan, Bartholomew, and Klores, *Basketball*, 157.
40. Joe Gross, "Lefty Driesell Talks about Moses," *The Capital* (Annapolis MD), October 1, 1974.
41. "Moses Malone Signing Stirs Mixed Responses," *Los Angeles Times*, August 31, 1974.
42. Sam Goldaper, "Storm Gathering over Malone's Case," *New York Times*, August 27, 1974.
43. Mike Gold, "Kehoe Requesting Congressional Investigation," *The Diamondback*, September 6, 1974, https://digital.lib.umd.edu/student-newspapers/id/f14a0ac3-7688-41c5-9d2f-66dc45b6bae8?relpath=pcdm&query=Moses%20malone (article removed).
44. Taylor Branch, "The Shame of College Sports," *The Atlantic*, October 2011, https://www.theatlantic.com/magazine/archive/2011/10/the-shame-of-college-sports/308643/.
45. Dwight Chapin, "The Odyssey of Moses Malone," *Modesto Bee*, December 26, 1974.
46. Rod Sieb, "Did Moses' Crossing Open the Floodgates?" *Basketball Weekly*, February 13, 1975.
47. Sieb, "Did Moses' Crossing Open Floodgates?"
48. Chapin, "Odyssey of Moses."
49. Goldaper, "Storm Gathering."
50. Harry Marsh, "Malone Signs Pro Contract; Conference Set in New York," *Progress-Index* (Petersburg), August 29, 1974.

8. A Star Is Born

1. MacMullan, Bartholomew, and Klores, *Basketball*, 140–41; and Kuska, *Balls of Confusion*, 74.
2. *30 for 30*, season 2, episode 10, "Free Spirits," directed by Daniel H. Forer, aired October 8, 2013, on ESPN.
3. MacMullan, Bartholomew, and Klores, *Basketball*, 137.

4. MacMullan, Bartholomew, and Klores, *Basketball*, 139.
5. Freddie Lewis, in discussion with the author, February 21, 2023.
6. Pluto, *Loose Balls*, 200.
7. Craig Wirth, "Wirth Watching—Here Come the Stars, Here Come the Stars," ABC, May 22, 2017, https://www.abc4.com/news/wirth/wirth-watching-here-come-the-stars-here-come-the-stars/.
8. Pluto, *Loose Balls*, 213.
9. "Moses Malone: From Scared Prep Player to Confident Pro," *Lakeland (FL) Ledger*, March 30, 1975.
10. Willie Wise, in discussion with the author, April 19, 2023.
11. Ron Boone, in discussion with the author, August 30, 2022.
12. Bill Bean, in discussion with the author, June 22, 2022.
13. Boone, discussion; Randy Denton, in discussion with the author, September 1, 2022; and Wise, discussion.
14. Putnam, "Don't Send My Boy."
15. Howard Blatt, "Relentless Malone Still Getting It Done," *Daily News* (New York), December 25, 1993.
16. Denton, discussion; Jim Eakins, in discussion with the author, March 3, 2023; and Wali Jones, in discussion with the author, September 1, 2022.
17. Buckwalter, discussion.
18. Dan Pattison, "Stars, Moses Lose Debuts," *Deseret News* (Salt Lake City UT), October 4, 1974.
19. Sam Goldaper, "Garden Matchup: Reserve Centers," *New York Times*, October 8, 1974.
20. Pluto, *Loose Balls*, 326–27.
21. Dan Pattison, "Ferrin: Bring Moses along Slowly," *Deseret News* (Salt Lake City UT), August 30, 1974.
22. Dan Pattison, "Stars Face Nets—Minus Willie Wise," *Deseret News* (Salt Lake City UT), October 18, 1974.
23. Leonard Koppett, "Nets Overcome Stars, 95–91," *New York Times*, October 31, 1974.
24. Buckwalter, discussion; and Wali Jones, discussion.
25. Pluto, *Loose Balls*, 327.
26. "Malone Better Than Expected," *Albuquerque Journal*, December 24, 1974.
27. Dan Pattison, "Better Believe in Moses, Stars," *Deseret News* (Salt Lake City UT), December 9, 1974.
28. Steve Rudman, in discussion with the author, September 8, 2022.
29. Didinger, *One Last Read*, 116.

30. "Teen Night": advertisement, *Deseret News* (Salt Lake City UT), November 21, 1974.
31. Harvey Kirkpatrick, in discussion with the author, September 21, 2022.
32. Eakins, discussion.
33. Rudman, discussion.
34. Jim Hague, "Gerald Govan," *Hudson County Sports Podcast*, produced by Jim Hague, YouTube video, 1:20:16, November 19, 2020, https://www.youtube.com/watch?v=_aeEwG5Ak34.
35. Harry Xanthakos, "Moses Malone: No Miracles . . . Just Victories," *Black Sports*, January 1975, 38.
36. Rick Hummel, "Moses Vows to Stay with Spirits," *St. Louis Post-Dispatch*, January 11, 1976.
37. Steve Rudman, "Moses Malone Proves Talking Can Be Cool," *Salt Lake Tribune*, January 26, 1975.
38. Kirkpatrick, discussion.
39. Rudman, "Moses Malone Proves."
40. Kirkpatrick, discussion.
41. Jeff Gordon, "Moses Malone Stuns Cage Experts with Successful Jump to Pro League," *Stripes*, August 2, 1978, https://www.stripes.com/news/moses-malone-stuns-cage-experts-with-successful-jump-to-pro-league-1.55608; and Malone, "Playboy Interview," 52.
42. Rudman, discussion.
43. Malone, "Playboy Interview," 52.
44. Nathan Dickerson, in discussion with the author, May 12, 2022; and Fentress, discussion.
45. Wali Jones, discussion.
46. Wise, discussion.
47. Wise, discussion.
48. Ungrady, *Tales from Maryland Terrapins*, 156.
49. Mark Asher, "Moses Paves Easy Road for Mother," *Salt Lake Tribune*, February 7, 1975.
50. "From Scared Prep Player to Confident Pro," *Lakeland (FL) Ledger*.
51. Denton, discussion.
52. Wali Jones, discussion.
53. Boone, discussion.
54. Moses Malone, "Original Old School: First and Foremost," interview by Aaron Paul, *Slam*, November 10, 2010, https://www.slamonline.com/nba/original-old-school-first-and-foremost/.
55. Gerald Govan, in discussion with the author, August 30, 2022.

56. Buckwalter, discussion.
57. Brad Rock, "Moses Malone Owned It, Even with Utah Stars," *Deseret News* (Salt Lake City UT), September 15, 2015, https://www.deseret.com/2015/9/15/20572378/moses-malone-owned-it-even-with-utah-stars#moses-malone-seen-here-aug-29-1974-is-the-high-school-basketball-player-who-turned-pro-direct-from-high-school-he-was-selected-by-the-utah-stars-ap-photo-robert-houston.
58. Eakins, discussion.
59. Gutman, *Chairmen of Boards*, 135–36.
60. "Bucky Coaches Last Victory," *Deseret News* (Salt Lake City UT), February 11, 1975.
61. Rudman, discussion.
62. Eakins, discussion; and Leonard Shapiro, "Kupchak Duel with Malone Spices Series," *Washington Post*, April 26, 1977.
63. Deford, "Bounding."
64. Shapiro, "Kupchak Duel."

9. Bad News and the Spirits

1. Pluto, *Loose Balls*, 327.
2. Ken Gardner, in discussion with the author, February 10, 2023.
3. Denton, discussion; and Sam Goldaper, "Malone and Spirits Iron Out Problems," *New York Times*, January 8, 1976.
4. Kirkpatrick, discussion; and Earl Gustkey, "The King of Cable: Since 1952, U.S. Has Helped Bill Daniels Get the Picture," *Los Angeles Times*, September 8, 1986.
5. Dan Pattison, "Daniels Sells Four Key Stars," *Deseret News* (Salt Lake City UT), December 2, 1975.
6. Gustkey, "King of Cable."
7. Rudman, discussion.
8. "'Keep Stars' Is Concern of Chamber," *Deseret News* (Salt Lake City UT), January 16, 1974.
9. Dan Pattison, "Stars Formally Announce Sale," *Deseret News* (Salt Lake City UT), June 4, 1975.
10. Pattison, "Daniels Sells Four Key Stars."
11. Bean, discussion.
12. Gardner, discussion.
13. Steve Green, in discussion with the author, September 2, 2022.
14. Denton, discussion.
15. Del Harris, in discussion with the author, May 28, 2022.

16. Paul Montgomery, "Spirits Get Stars of Stars," *New York Times*, December 3, 1975.
17. Bill Livingston, "Player of the Year Moses Malone," *Basketball Digest*, June-July 1983, https://archive.org/details/sim_basketball-digest_june-july-1983_10_8/page/20/mode/2up?q=moses+malone.
18. Fentress, discussion.
19. Harry Marsh, "The Sports Scene," *Progress-Index* (Petersburg), December 7, 1975.
20. Lawrence F. O'Brien National Basketball Association Papers (MS 504), series 3, box 17c, folder 33, Springfield College Archives and Special Collections, Springfield MA.
21. "NBA's Hawks Hit Jackpot," *Salt Lake Tribune*, May 30, 1975.
22. O'Brien Papers, series 3, box 17c, folder 33.
23. "NBA Holds Special Draft of NBA Players," *The Capital* (Annapolis MD), December 31, 1975.
24. "Jazz to Pick Malone in N.B.A. Draft," *New York Times*, December 6, 1975.
25. Rick Hummel, "Will Moses Reach the Promised Spirits?," *St. Louis Post-Dispatch*, December 31, 1975.
26. Rick Hummel, "Malone Sought in NBA Draft," *St. Louis Post-Dispatch*, December 5, 1975.
27. *30 for 30*, "Free Spirits."
28. Barry Parkhill, in discussion with the author, September 15, 2022.
29. Matt Bonsteel, "The Greatest Marvin Barnes Stories Ever Told," *Washington Post*, September 10, 2014.
30. Lewis, discussion.
31. Gutman, *Chairmen of Boards*, 138–39.
32. Rick Hummel, in discussion with the author, October 27, 2022.
33. Rod Thorn, in discussion with the author, September 22, 2022.
34. Thorn, discussion.
35. Green, discussion.
36. Jeffrey Denberg, "MOSES—Moses Malone, at 34, Is the Prototype 'Blue-Collar' Center, but He Has the Same Hunger to Win as the Skinny Kid Who Went from High School to the ABA," *Atlanta Journal-Constitution*, April 25, 1989.
37. Lewis, discussion.
38. Gutman, *Chairmen of Boards*, 139.
39. Boone, discussion.
40. Pluto, *Loose Balls*, 387–88.
41. Sam Goldaper, "Pro Basketball Leagues Merge; New York to Retain Two Teams," *New York Times*, June 18, 1976.

42. Rick Hummel, "Spirits Can't See NBA Shunning Utah," *St. Louis Post-Dispatch*, March 31, 1976.

10. Wandering Moses

1. Robertson, *Big O*, 51–55.
2. Robertson, *Big O*, 184.
3. Sam Smith, *Hard Labor*, 20.
4. Sam Smith, *Hard Labor*, 103.
5. Sam Goldaper, "Robertson Ends Career: NBA Great Accepts CBS-TV Pact," *New York Times*, August 28, 1976.
6. Sam Smith, *Hard Labor*, 39.
7. Goldaper, "Pro Basketball Leagues Merge."
8. Goldaper, "Pro Basketball Leagues Merge"; and Quinn, *Don't Be Afraid*, 84.
9. Sam Smith, *Hard Labor*, 336.
10. Sam Goldaper, "A.B.A. Drops Squires for a Lack of Funds," *New York Times*, May 11, 1975.
11. O'Brien Papers, series 3, box 17c, folder 34.
12. Sam Smith, *Hard Labor*, 165.
13. Frank Deford, "One Last Hurrah in Hyannis," *Sports Illustrated*, June 28, 1976, https://vault.si.com/vault/1976/06/28/one-last-hurrah-in-hyannis.
14. Pluto, *Loose Balls*, 432.
15. Monte Burke, "The NBA Finally Puts an End to the Greatest Sports Deal of All Time," *Forbes*, January 7, 2014, https://www.forbes.com/sites/monteburke/2014/01/07/the-nba-finally-puts-an-end-to-the-greatest-sports-deal-of-all-time/?sh=4e7eced94f0b.
16. O'Brien Papers, series 2, box 16.
17. O'Brien Papers, series 3, box 17c, folder 34.
18. Larry Shaw, "Blazers Trade Petrie, Get Malone, Lucas," *The Oregonian*, August 6, 1976.
19. Halberstam, *Breaks of the Game*, 191.
20. MacMullan, Bartholomew, and Klores, *Basketball*, 182.
21. Bob Robinson, "'Play-Action' New Lifeblood of Blazer Attack; Walker Awaited," *The Oregonian*, September 26, 1976.
22. Halberstam, *Breaks of the Game*, 192.
23. Bob Robinson, "Malone Wins Believers as Blazers Bounce Seattle," *The Oregonian*, October 17, 1976; Robinson, "'Play-Action,'"; and Bob Robinson, "Running Blazers to Unveil New Look," *The Oregonian*, September 30, 1976.
24. Bill Walton, in discussion with the author, September 14, 2023.
25. Johnny Davis, in discussion with the author, February 27, 2023.

26. Walton, discussion.
27. Glickman, *Promoter*, 144.
28. Deford, "Bounding."
29. Halberstam, *Breaks of the Game*, 195–96.
30. Walton, discussion.
31. Robinson, "Malone Wins Believers."
32. Bob Robinson, "Malone Places Blazers' Brass in Dilemma Just by Playing Well," *The Oregonian*, October 18, 1976.
33. Halberstam, *Breaks of the Game*, 195–96.
34. Halberstam, *Breaks of the Game*, 196.
35. Lionel Hollins, in discussion with the author, August 16, 2023.
36. Williams and Jones, *Tales from Philadelphia*, 3.
37. Criblez, *Tall Tales*, 184–85.
38. Malone, "Playboy Interview," 52.
39. Wendel, *Buffalo*.
40. Claude Terry, in discussion with the author, February 2, 2023.
41. Wendel, *Buffalo*.
42. Shapiro, "Kupchak Duel."
43. Deford, "Bounding."

11. A Launch Pad

1. Steve Patterson, in discussion with the author, April 27, 2023.
2. Steve Patterson, discussion.
3. Steve Patterson, discussion.
4. "Owners, Fans Waited Years before Rockets Took Off," Chron (website), September 16, 2001, https://www.chron.com/life/article/Owners-fans-waited-years-before-Rockets-took-off-2045395.php.
5. "Owners, Fans Waited Years," Chron (website).
6. Steve Patterson, discussion.
7. Rudy Tomjanovich, in discussion with the author, May 25, 2022.
8. Tomjanovich and Falkoff, *Rocket at Heart*, 71.
9. George White, "From Snores to Final," *Houston Chronicle*, May 3, 1981.
10. "Controlling Interest in Rockets Sold," *New York Times*, December 13, 1973.
11. Curry Kirkpatrick, "Blasting Off in Houston," *Sports Illustrated*, January 17, 1977, https://vault.si.com/vault/1977/01/17/blasting-off-in-houston.
12. George White, "Rocket GM Weathered Dark Days Because Faith in the City Didn't Waver," *Houston Chronicle*, March 3, 1978.
13. Lucas and Moriarty, *Winning a Day*, 64.
14. Tomjanovich, discussion.

15. Campbell, discussion.
16. Tomjanovich and Falkoff, *Rocket at Heart*, 88.
17. Malone, "Original Old School."
18. Tomjanovich, discussion.
19. Kevin Kunnert, in discussion with the author, March 27, 2023; and Tomjanovich and Falkoff, *Rocket at Heart*, 79–80.
20. John Wilson, "Malone a Jumping Jack," *Houston Chronicle*, December 17, 1976.
21. Eakins, discussion.
22. "Rockets Win, Move into Top Spot," *Houston Chronicle*, December 27, 1976.
23. George White, "Rockets Team Up on the Lakers," *Houston Chronicle*, March 3, 1977.
24. Paul Montgomery, "Malone Powers Rockets in 99–91 Defeat of Nets," *New York Times*, March 7, 1977.
25. Leonard Shapiro, "From Early Defeat, Rockets Build Success," *Washington Post*, March 20, 1977.
26. Kevin Pelton, "Moses Malone by the Numbers: A Truly Unique Talent," ESPN, September 14, 2015, https://www.espn.com/nba/story/_/id/13655965/nba-moses-malone-truly-unique-talent-according-numbers.
27. George White, "Rockets Flout NBA Theory," *Houston Chronicle*, May 3, 1977.
28. George White, "76ers Disparage Rocket Defense, Lack of Speed," *Houston Chronicle*, May 7, 1977.
29. Kunnert, discussion.
30. Tomjanovich and Falkoff, *Rocket at Heart*, 82.
31. Mark West, in discussion with the author, December 9, 2022.
32. Bolling Hill, discussion.
33. Gholson, discussion.
34. Ronald O. Howell, "Moses Malone: Basketball's Million-Dollar Baby," *Ebony*, January 1980.
35. Mike Newlin, in discussion with the author, February 22, 2023.
36. Robert Reid, in discussion with the author, August 18, 2022.
37. Phillip Bond, in discussion with the author, April 5, 2023.
38. Tomjanovich and Falkoff, *Rocket at Heart*, 95.
39. Tomjanovich, and Falkoff, *Rocket at Heart*, 96.
40. C. J. Kupec, in discussion with the author, March 9, 2023.
41. George White, "Braves Roar Past Rockets," *Houston Chronicle*, November 17, 1977.
42. Calvin Murphy, "Rockets Hall of Famer Calvin Murphy and Rice Owls Icon Wayne Graham (Throwback Thursday)," interview by Robert Land, April 9, 2020, in *Houston Sports Talk*, produced by Robert Land and Stephen

Kerr, podcast, MP3 audio, 19:49, https://www.podomatic.com/podcasts/houstonsportstalkpod/episodes/2020-04-09T05_00_00-07_00.

12. Chairman of the Boards

1. Campbell, discussion.
2. Pamela Noel, "Wives of Sports Superstars," *Ebony*, September 1984, 148.
3. Delrick Brown, in discussion with the author, May 23, 2023.
4. "Louis Charles Gill Jr.," Legacy.com, obituary, October 22, 2019, https://www.legacy.com/obituaries/name/louis-gill-obituary?pid=194251072.
5. Kirk Williams, "Moses Malone Eulogy," Lakewood Church, Houston TX, September 19, 2015.
6. Deford, "Bounding."
7. Tomjanovich, discussion.
8. Deford, "Bounding."
9. Olden Polynice, in discussion with the author, March 23, 2023.
10. George White, "Malone at 23," *Houston Chronicle*, January 12, 1979.
11. Carroll Dawson, in discussion with the author, March 20, 2023.
12. White, "Malone at 23."
13. Deford, "Bounding."
14. White, "Malone at 23."
15. George White, "Young Giant Malone Makes Big Impression," *Houston Chronicle*, May 8, 1977.
16. Otto Moore, in discussion with the author, December 7, 2022.
17. J. A. Adande, "Moses Malone Was NBA's Most Underappreciated Great Player," ESPN, September 13, 2015, https://www.espn.com/nba/story/_/id/13647582/nba-moses-malone-was-nba-most-underappreciated-great-player.
18. White, "Malone at 23."
19. Dominique Wilkins, in discussion with the author, September 19, 2022.
20. Ron Rabena, in discussion with the author, November 2, 2022.
21. Gutman, *Chairmen of Boards*, 151.
22. Vitale, discussion.
23. George White, "For Rockets' Malone: 37 Caroms, 33 Points," *Houston Chronicle*, February 10, 1979.
24. White, "For Rockets' Malone."
25. Mychal Thompson, in discussion with the author, June 7, 2023.
26. Harris, discussion.
27. Rick Barry, in discussion with the author, June 27, 2022.
28. Dick Peebles, "Rick Barry: The Man for the Job," *Houston Chronicle*, June 21, 1978.

29. George White, "Nissalke: Lucas Loss in Compensation for Barry 'Stupid Decision,'" *Houston Chronicle*, February 12, 1979.
30. Barry, discussion.
31. George White, "Too Many Chiefs, Not Enough Indians—or Wins—for Rockets," *Houston Chronicle*, April 15, 1979.
32. Basketball Reference, "NBA & ABA Single Season Leaders and Records for Rebounds per Game," n.d., https://www.basketball-reference.com/leaders/trb_per_g_season.html; Basketball Reference, "Boston Celtics Stats—per Game (Totals)," n.d., https://www.basketball-reference.com/teams/BOS/stats_per_game_totals.html; Basketball Reference, "1960–61 Philadelphia Warriors Roster and Stats," n.d., https://www.basketball-reference.com/teams/PHW/1961.html; and Basketball Reference, "1978–79 Houston Rockets Roster and Stats," n.d., https://www.basketball-reference.com/teams/HOU/1979.html.

13. Four Guys from Petersburg

1. Gutman, *Chairmen of Boards*, 112–13.
2. George White, "Rockets Nail Down Malone, Four-Point Plan Nears Finish," *Houston Chronicle*, July 17, 1979.
3. "Moses Malone's Pact Puts Rocket in Hit Parade," *Odessa (TX) American*, July 17, 1979.
4. George White, "Malone Can't Miss at Track or on Court," *Houston Chronicle*, January 21, 1981.
5. Paul Mokeski, in discussion with the author, March 27, 2023.
6. Sam Williams, in discussion with the author, May 8, 2023.
7. Rumeal Robinson, in discussion with the author, May 5, 2023.
8. Mel Hughlett, in discussion with the author, December 7, 2022.
9. George White, "A Night for Murphy," *Houston Chronicle*, March 24, 1978.
10. Steve Patterson, discussion.
11. Phil Jasner, "Moses Malone: From 'Superkid' to Superstar," *Basketball Digest*, May 1985, https://archive.org/details/sim_basketball-digest_1985-05_12_7/page/20/mode/2up?q=moses+malone.
12. Reggie Theus, in discussion with the author, May 10, 2023.
13. Wilkins, discussion.
14. Thomas Bonk, in discussion with the author, January 25, 2023.
15. Ed Ratleff, in discussion with the author, February 23, 2023.
16. Major Jones, in discussion with the author, June 9, 2022.
17. Tomjanovich, discussion.
18. George White, "Intense Mo & Co. Blast West in OT," *Houston Chronicle*, February 4, 1980.

19. Mokeski, discussion.
20. White, "Malone Can't Miss."
21. George White, "Rockets Spank Blazers 126–104," *Houston Chronicle*, March 14, 1981.
22. George White, "Rockets' Paultz Will Play More," *Houston Chronicle*, November 14, 1980.
23. Tom Henderson, in discussion with the author, May 23, 2023.
24. George White, "Rockets, Spurs Ready to Wear Gloves Again," *Houston Chronicle*, April 10, 1981.
25. George White, "'M' for Moses Means Money for Every Win," *Houston Chronicle*, April 21, 1981.
26. George White, "Rockets Best in West, Gain NBA Final," *Houston Chronicle*, April 30, 1981.
27. Ed Fowler, "Underdog Rockets Are 'Good,' but Not at Celebrating," *Houston Chronicle*, April 30, 1981.
28. Harris, discussion.
29. Harris, discussion.
30. John Papanek, "Once More, with a Lot of Feeling," *Sports Illustrated*, May 25, 1981, https://vault.si.com/vault/1981/05/25/once-more-with-a-lot-of-feeling-love-hate-anger-and-some-inspired-play-by-two-young-forwards-series-mvp-cedric-maxwell-and-larry-bird-enabled-the-celtics-to-defeat-the-rockets-and-revive-a-boston-tradition-winning-the-nba-cham.
31. Mike Dunleavy Sr., in discussion with the author, April 26, 2023; and Harris, discussion.
32. Henderson, discussion.
33. Major Jones, discussion.
34. George White, "Why Did Malone Put Knock on Boston?," *Houston Chronicle*, May 14, 1981.
35. Papanek, "Once More."
36. George White, "It's Another Coronation for the Celtics," *Houston Chronicle*, May 15, 1981.
37. Mike Thomas, "Larry Bird Made His Feelings Known about Moses Malone with 4-Letter Word on Boston Celtics Day," SportsCasting (website), Oct. 7, 2021, https://www.sportscasting.com/larry-bird-made-feelings-known-moses-malone-4-letter-word-boston-celtics-day/.

14. King of Fonde

1. Olajuwon and Knobler, *Living the Dream*, 39–41, 43–45, 53–55.
2. Olajuwon and Knobler, *Living the Dream*, 62.

3. Olajuwon and Knobler, *Living the Dream*, 66.
4. Roy S. Johnson, "Olajuwon Charms and Dominates," *New York Times*, March 29, 1983.
5. Olajuwon and Knobler, *Living the Dream*, 99.
6. Corey Roepken, "Tripleheader to Welcome New Era at Fonde Rec," Chron (website), January 4, 2013, https://www.chron.com/sports/highschool/article/tripleheader-to-welcome-new-era-at-fonde-rec-4168991.php?forceWeb=1.
7. George White, "Fonde Center: 'The Best Little Basketball Gym in Texas,'" *Houston Chronicle*, June 4, 1979.
8. Mark McKee, *The History of Texas High School Basketball*, vol. 1, *1970–1974*, Texas High School Basketball History, http://www.txhighschoolbasketball.com/download/.
9. James Clayton, in discussion with the author, November 10, 2023.
10. White, "Fonde Center."
11. Fred Brown, in discussion with the author, October 19, 2022.
12. Herb Baker, in discussion with the author, October 19, 2022.
13. Polynice, discussion.
14. Harold "Moe" Vines, in discussion with the author, June 21, 2022.
15. Baker, discussion.
16. Olajuwon and Knobler, *Living the Dream*, 99, 101.
17. Hakeem Olajuwon, in discussion with the author, January 11, 2023.
18. Olajuwon, discussion.
19. Dunleavy, discussion.
20. "Olajuwon Credits Mentor Malone for His Success," *The Sporting News*, September 13, 2015, https://www.sportingnews.com/au/nba/news/olajuwon-credits-mentor-malone-for-his-success/15rsnjmq8lqc11bw7ddae3c2gm.
21. Reid, discussion.
22. "Olajuwon Credits Mentor," *The Sporting News*.
23. Olajuwon, discussion.
24. Eric Davis, in discussion with the author, January 19, 2023.
25. Fred Brown, discussion.
26. Polynice, discussion.
27. Vines, discussion.
28. Olajuwon and Knobler, *Living the Dream*, 123–24.
29. Vines, discussion.
30. Mike Jones, in discussion with the author, May 28, 2022.
31. Tony Dale, in discussion with the author, June 22, 2022.
32. Campbell, discussion.
33. Dale, discussion.

34. Fred Brown, discussion; and Reid, discussion.
35. Vines, discussion.
36. Ron Foster, in discussion with the author, September 8, 2022.
37. Campbell, discussion.
38. Bill Patterson, in discussion with the author, May 22, 2023.
39. Reid, discussion.
40. Major Jones, discussion; and Vines, discussion.
41. Price, *Earl Campbell*, 182, 226.
42. Campbell, discussion.
43. Major Jones, discussion; and Joe Torry, in discussion with the author, March 19, 2023.
44. Major Jones, discussion.
45. Malone, "Playboy Interview," 52.
46. Barry Warner, in discussion with the author, January 23, 2023.
47. Malone, "Playboy Interview," 52.
48. Polynice, discussion.

15. Straight Cash

1. "Bird, East All-Star Winners," *Houston Chronicle*, February 1, 1982.
2. Reid, discussion.
3. Neil Hohlfeld, "Sikma Brings a Real Challenge to Malone," *Houston Chronicle*, February 11, 1982.
4. George White, "Malone's Blistering Pace Puts Him at NBA Pinnacle," *The Sporting News*, February 27, 1982.
5. Ed Fowler, "Moses Malone: Player of the Year," *Basketball Digest*, June-July 1982, https://archive.org/details/sim_basketball-digest_june-july-1982_1_8/page/n21/mode/2up?q=moses+malone.
6. Ed Fowler, "Moses Malone: Houston's Private Property," *Houston Chronicle*, February 13, 1982.
7. George White, "Malone Hopes to Shun Free Agency," *Houston Chronicle*, October 27, 1981.
8. Steve Hershey, "Malone's Windfall: Many See It as NBA's Downfall," *Washington Post*, September 29, 1982.
9. "Nuggets, Rockets Are Sold," *New York Times*, June 16, 1982.
10. Fran Blinebury, "Malone Offered Nearly $2 Million per Year by Rockets," *Houston Chronicle*, June 5, 1982.
11. Fran Blinebury, "Re-Signing Moses Not a Cinch," *Houston Chronicle*, March 7, 1982.
12. O'Brien Papers, series 1, box 1A.

13. Croatto, *From Hang Time*, 58.
14. Croatto, *From Hang Time*, 49.
15. O'Brien Papers, series 1, box 1A.
16. Bella, *Barkley*, 128.
17. Mendelsohn, *The Cap*, 171.
18. Ed Fowler, "Buss Wants to Make Malone Richer," *Houston Chronicle*, September 20, 1981.
19. Mendelsohn, *The Cap*, 146; and Alan Hahn, "The 2012 Loophole," *Newsday*, January 18, 2011.
20. Mendelsohn, *The Cap*, 147, 148–49.
21. Mendelsohn, *The Cap*, 150, 201.
22. George White, "Lakers' Owner Declares He'll Sign Malone in '82," *Houston Chronicle*, April 7, 1981.
23. Fran Blinebury, "Bidding Hasn't Been Heavy for Mo's Expensive Services," *Houston Chronicle*, June 13, 1982.
24. Fran Blinebury, "Mo Speaks Out," *Houston Chronicle*, June 17, 1982.
25. Fran Blinebury, "Moses' Market Is Dwindling," *Houston Chronicle*, June 19, 1982.
26. Williams and Jones, *Tales from Philadelphia*, 25, 29–30.
27. John Nash, in discussion with the author, June 30, 2022.
28. John Nash, discussion.
29. Howard Eskin, in discussion with the author, December 1, 2022.
30. Williams and Jones, *Tales from Philadelphia*, 25.
31. Harold Katz, in discussion with the author, March 4, 2024.
32. John Nash, discussion.
33. Tim Malloy, in discussion with the author, February 15, 2022.
34. John Nash, discussion.
35. Billy Cunningham, in discussion with the author, May 13, 2022.
36. Cunningham, discussion.
37. Katz, discussion.
38. Katz, discussion.
39. Livingston, "Player of the Year."
40. Shirk, "Malone May Join Sixers."
41. John Nash, discussion.
42. Bradley Graham, "Malone Is Playing Basketball—and the Waiting Game," *Houston Chronicle*, September 7, 1982.
43. Erving and Greenfield, *Dr. J*, 365–66.
44. Deford, "Bounding."
45. Steve Patterson, discussion.
46. John Nash, discussion.

47. Neil Hohlfeld, "Rocket Owner Never Wavered in 76er Talks," *Houston Chronicle*, September 16, 1982.
48. Anthony Cotton, "I Can Do So Many Things," *Sports Illustrated*, November 1, 1982, https://vault.si.com/vault/1982/11/01/i-can-do-so-many-things.
49. Williams and Jones, *Tales from Philadelphia*, 7.
50. Bill Livingston, in discussion with the author, November 29, 2022.
51. George Shirk, "NBA Teams Greet 76ers' Deal with Shock, Anger," *Philadelphia Inquirer*, September 17, 1982.

16. Time to Go to Work

1. Williams and Jones, *Tales From Philadelphia*, 19.
2. Erving and Greenfield, *Dr. J*, 196.
3. Williams and Jones, *Tales from Philadelphia*, 19.
4. Williams and Jones, *Tales from Philadelphia*, 10–11, 99.
5. Erving, "Moses Malone's Basketball Hall of Fame."
6. George Shirk, "An Inner Drive Has Steered Malone to the Top," *Philadelphia Inquirer*, September 16, 1982.
7. Erving and Greenfield, *Dr. J*, 373.
8. Pete Croatto, "The Year We Won It All: A Behind-the-Scenes Oral History of the 76ers' Epic 1983 Championship," *Philadelphia*, April 22, 2023, https://www.phillymag.com/news/2023/04/22/76ers-1983-championship/.
9. Cotton, "I Can Do So Many Things."
10. Williams and Jones, *Tales from Philadelphia 76ers*, 49.
11. Bird, *Drive*, 88–89.
12. Hollins, discussion.
13. John Kilbourne, in discussion with the author, June 21, 2022.
14. Marc Narducci, "Malone's Arrival Finally Got 76ers over the Hump," *Philadelphia Inquirer*, May 29, 2008.
15. Livingston, discussion.
16. Erving and Greenfield, *Dr. J*, 371.
17. Gordie Jones, "Legend of Big Mo."
18. Williams, *Tales from Philadelphia*, 87.
19. Rivers and Brooks, *Those Who Love the Game*, 85–86.
20. Moyer, "How Moses 'Mumbles' Malone."
21. Sidney Moncrief, in discussion with the author, May 5, 2023.
22. Ira Berkow, "A Force That Could Stop Malone," *New York Times*, April 24, 1983.
23. Cunningham, discussion; and Charles Jones, in discussion with the author, May 1, 2023.
24. Erving, "Moses Malone's Basketball Hall of Fame."

25. Perry Moss, in discussion with the author, May 15, 2023.
26. Franklin Edwards, in discussion with the author, June 21, 2022.
27. Phil Jasner, "Sixers' Malone Hurting Himself," *Philadelphia Daily News*, April 20, 1983.
28. Frank Brickowski, in discussion with the author, May 23, 2023.
29. Gordie Jones, "Moses Malone: The Ultimate Hardhat and 1980s NBA Icon," CSN Philly, September 14, 2015, https://web.archive.org/web/20150915233525/http://www.csnphilly.com/basketball-philadelphia-76ers/fo-fo-fo-remembering-moses-malone-nba-symbol-80s.
30. Livingston, "Player of the Year."
31. Croatto, "Year We Won."
32. Earl Cureton, in discussion with the author, May 27, 2022.
33. Franklin Edwards, discussion.
34. Williams and Jones, *Tales from Philadelphia*, 87.
35. Shirk, "Malone Lives by Instincts."
36. George Shirk, "Moses Malone: What You See Is What You Get," *Philadelphia Inquirer*, May 8, 1983.
37. Cureton, discussion.
38. Williams and Jones, *Tales from Philadelphia*, 83–84.
39. Reid, discussion; Brickowski, discussion; and Arthur Triche, in discussion with the author, June 4, 2023.
40. Hollins, discussion.
41. Leo Rautins, in discussion with the author, May 5, 2023.
42. Julius Erving, "Dr. J's Best Moses Malone Story," interview by Bill Simmons, *The BS Report*, December 19, 2013, podcast, video, 1:50, https://www.dailymotion.com/video/x2npoin.
43. Roy S. Johnson, "Malone and Erving on 76ers: Is It the End of Frustration?," *New York Times*, October 17, 1982.
44. Williams and Jones, *Tales from Philadelphia*, 197.
45. Ron Dick, in discussion with the author, June 21, 2022.
46. Cureton, discussion.
47. Iavaroni, discussion.
48. Steve Hayes, in discussion with the author, December 1, 2022; and Iavaroni, discussion.
49. George Shirk, "76ers Place Three Players on All-Stars," *Philadelphia Inquirer*, January 31, 1983.
50. Williams and Jones, *Tales from Philadelphia*, 82.
51. Williams and Jones, *Tales from Philadelphia*, 98.
52. Cunningham, discussion.

17. The Promised Land

1. George Vecsey, "76ers Pay First Installment on Old Debt," *New York Times*, May 23, 1983.
2. Williams and Jones, *Tales from Philadelphia*, 9–10.
3. Roy S. Johnson, "Laker Leadership Split on Abdul-Jabbar," Pro Basketball Notebook, *New York Times*, June 3, 1983.
4. Bruce Newman, "This May Be One for the Books," *Sports Illustrated*, February 28, 1983, https://vault.si.com/vault/1983/02/28/this-may-be-one-for-the-books.
5. Cunningham, discussion.
6. Michael Lee, "With Jersey Retirement, Moses Malone and His Legendary Hustle Are Finally Immortalized in Philadelphia," *The Athletic*, February 8, 2019, https://theathletic.com/806358/2019/02/08/with-jersey-retirement-moses-malone-and-his-legendary-hustle-are-finally-immortalized-in-philadelphia/.
7. Cureton, discussion.
8. Cunningham, discussion.
9. Phil Jasner, "Pains Won't Bend Moses," *Philadelphia Daily News*, April 22, 1983.
10. Kilbourne, discussion.
11. Williams and Jones, *Tales from Philadelphia*, 116.
12. Gordie Jones, "Moses Malone Was an Influential Sixer, for Far More Than Fo' Reasons," *Forbes*, August 16, 2019, https://www.forbes.com/sites/gordiejones/2019/08/16/moses-malone-was-an-influential-sixer-for-far-more-than-fo-reasons/?sh=2c95fae2442e.
13. Peter Vecsey, in discussion with the author, December 5, 2023.
14. Williams and Jones, *Tales from Philadelphia*, 117.
15. Sessum, discussion.
16. Adrian Burgos Jr., "When It Comes to Latino Baseball Players, Writers Still Place Accent in Wrong Place," *The Sporting News*, May 30, 2016, https://www.sportingnews.com/us/mlb/news/latino-players-accents-carlos-gomez-adrian-gonzalez/byvcdmvabyq21uvadij3hc2p1.
17. Sam Goldaper, "76ers Try Again," *New York Times*, April 24, 1983.
18. George Shirk, "Malone Develops New Knee Problem," *Philadelphia Inquirer*, April 22, 1983.
19. Sam Goldaper, "Malone Leads 76ers Past Knicks in Opener, 112–102," *New York Times*, April 25, 1983.
20. George Shirk, "Malone Is Up and Jumping Again," *Philadelphia Inquirer*, April 24, 1983.
21. Cureton, discussion; and Williams and Jones, *Tales from Philadelphia*, 113.
22. Goldaper, "Malone Leads 76ers."

23. Frank Dolson, "King's Tender Ankle Steals the Medical Spotlight," *Philadelphia Inquirer*, April 25, 1983.
24. Williams, *Ahead of the Game*, 260.
25. Jaiden Campana, "Sixers Unveil Malone Statue," *Philadelphia Inquirer*, February 19, 2019.
26. Gordon Edes, "Riley Recalls the Bummer of '83: Laker Coach Has Painful Memories of Final Series Sweep by 76ers," *Los Angeles Times*, June 6, 1987.
27. Sam Goldaper, "76ers Take a 1-0 Lead over Lakers," *New York Times*, May 23, 1983.
28. Bruce Newman, "Better by Leaps and Bounds," *Sports Illustrated*, June 6, 1983, https://vault.si.com/vault/1983/06/06/better-by-leaps-and-bounds.
29. Fran Blinebury, "Too Much Malone for Too Little LA Muscle," *Houston Chronicle*, May 31, 1983.
30. Cunningham, discussion.
31. Mark Whicker, in discussion with the author, December 5, 2022.
32. Bruce Newman, "Thou Shalt Rejoice, Said Moses," *Sports Illustrated*, June 13, 1983, https://vault.si.com/vault/1983/06/13/thou-shalt-rejoice-said-moses.
33. Fred Carter, in discussion with the author, April 20, 2023.
34. Cureton, discussion.
35. Livingston, discussion.
36. Cureton, discussion.
37. Phil Jasner, "How Philly Blasted the Lakers!," *Basketball Digest*, November 1983, https://archive.org/details/sim_basketball-digest_1983-11_11_1/page/32/mode/2up.
38. Fentress, discussion.
39. Sam Goldaper, "Malone's Season Worth $2.9 Million," *New York Times*, June 8, 1983.
40. Bill Lyon, "Malone's Energy Recharged a Team," *Philadelphia Inquirer*, June 2, 1983.
41. Clayton Sheldon, in discussion with the author, February 23, 2023.

18. Reluctant Superstar

1. Williams and Jones, *Tales from Philadelphia*, 88–89.
2. Jim Lynam, in discussion with the author, January 26, 2023.
3. Moses Malone, "Moses Malone's Basketball Hall of Fame Enshrinement Speech," Naismith Memorial Basketball Hall of Fame Enshrinement, October 5, 2001, Springfield MA, video, 29:11, https://www.hoophall.com/hall-of-famers/moses-malone/.
4. Floy Johnson, in discussion with the author, August 22, 2022.

5. Dale, discussion.
6. Hughlett, discussion.
7. Franklin Edwards, discussion.
8. Johnson, discussion.
9. Gholson, discussion.
10. Major Jones, discussion.
11. Reid, discussion.
12. Fred Roberts, in discussion with the author, June 28, 2023.
13. Newlin, discussion.
14. Kupec, discussion.
15. Hughlett, discussion.
16. Shirk, "Malone Lives by Instincts."
17. Didinger, "Moses Makes His."
18. Didinger, "Moses Makes His."
19. Didinger, "Moses Makes His."
20. Didinger, "Moses Makes His."
21. McCallum, *Unfinished Business*, 249.
22. Shirk, "Moses Malone: What You See."
23. Croatto, *From Hang Time*, 194.
24. Croatto, *From Hang Time*, 71.
25. Croatto, *From Hang Time*, 154, 159.
26. Fentress, discussion.
27. Gary Stevenson, in discussion with the author, March 26, 2024.
28. Bengston, *History of Basketball*, 78.
29. Knight, *Shoe Dog*, 29, 183.
30. Aaron Dodson, in discussion with the author, June 3, 2023.
31. Thompson, *I Came as a Shadow*, 275.
32. Mychal Thompson, discussion.
33. Bengston, *History of Basketball*, 72.
34. Dodson, discussion.
35. Bengston, *History of Basketball*, 71, 72.
36. Elizabeth Wellington, "Sneakers That Soared," *Philadelphia Inquirer*, February 6, 2007.
37. Anthony Gilbert, in discussion with the author, May 31, 2023.
38. Dodson, discussion.
39. Wellington, "Sneakers."
40. Dodson, discussion.
41. Mitch Buonaguro, in discussion with the author, June 29, 2022.

42. Moses Malone Jr., "True Story: Every time Mike came in town to play against Pops, he'd be @ our house playing cards with my dad," Facebook, January 9, 2022 (account and post deleted; no URL available).
43. FanDuel Sports Network Ohio & Great Lakes, "LeBron James Shares Lasting Advice Given to Him by NBA Legend Moses Malone," video, 0:23, December 20, 2016, https://www.youtube.com/watch?v=eaIAy44pIXE.
44. Johnson, discussion.

19. Fat and Lazy

1. Brian Robb, "Cedric Maxwell Reflects on the Fights, Hatred (Food Was Left!) and Future of Celtics-Sixers Rivalry," Boston Sports Journal (website), May 1, 2018, https://www.bostonsportsjournal.com/2018/05/01/cedric-maxwell-reflects-fights-hatred-future-celtics-sixers-rivalry.
2. Phil Jasner, "Auerbach Has 76ers Seeing Red," *Philadelphia Daily News*, October 18, 1983.
3. Phil Jasner, "Cunningham Has Sixers in Morning," *Philadelphia Daily News*, November 11, 1983.
4. Phil Jasner, "Malone Limps to Sideline," *Philadelphia Daily News*, December 23, 1983.
5. Rautins, discussion.
6. Phil Jasner, "Katz Wants More from Moses," *Philadelphia Daily News*, March 3, 1984.
7. Rautins, discussion.
8. George Shirk, "Sixers Owner Criticizes Efforts of Malone and Team," *Philadelphia Inquirer*, March 3, 1982.
9. Shirk, "Sixers Owner."
10. Anthony Cotton, "Blood, Sweat and Cheers," *Sports Illustrated*, October 31, 1983, https://vault.si.com/vault/1983/10/31/blood-sweat-and-cheers.
11. Phil Jasner, "Summer of 76ers—Players Find Living Is Easy after Taking NBA Title," *Philadelphia Daily News*, October 5, 1983.
12. Shirk, "Sixers Owner."
13. Phil Jasner, "Richardson: Sixers Cool Needed," *Philadelphia Daily News*, March 7, 1984.
14. Noel, "Wives of Sports Superstars," 144.
15. Cunningham, discussion.
16. Cunningham, discussion.
17. Billy Cunningham, "Episode #39: A Humble Philadelphia Basketball Legend: Coach Billy Cunningham," interview by Stephanie Hayden, host, March

5, 2019, in *High Five Success Stories*, podcast, MP3 audio, 1:08:29, https://www.listennotes.com/podcasts/high-five-success/episode-39-a-humble-axUoOIsbcvm/; and Phil Jasner, "Everybody Else Hates a Winner," *Philadelphia Daily News*, October 27, 1983.

18. Williams, *Ahead of the Game*, 270.
19. Bella, *Barkley*, 128.
20. Bella, *Barkley*, 128.
21. *76ers Insider*, produced by Jon Gurevitch and J. David Kelliher, aired January 1992 on Prism, video, 30:13, https://www.youtube.com/watch?v=opIs5YpXKrY.
22. Bondy, *Tip Off*, 227.
23. Leon Wood, in discussion with the author, August 30, 2023.
24. Barkley and Johnson, *Outrageous!*, 26, 132.
25. Howard White, discussion.
26. Barkley and Johnson, *Outrageous!*, 212.
27. Bella, *Barkley*, 145.
28. Charles Barkley, "Moses Malone Eulogy," September 19, 2015, Lakewood Church, Houston TX.
29. Bella, *Barkley*, 145.
30. Jackie MacMullan, host, "Dr. J and the ABA," March 22, 2022, in *Icons Club: The Evolution of the NBA Superstar*, produced by Bobby Wagner, Noah Malale, Jonathan Kermah, Isaac Lee, Justin Verrier, and Vikram Patel, podcast, MP3 audio, 51:00, https://podcasts.apple.com/us/podcast/book-of-basketball-2-0/id1483525141?i=1000554837211.
31. Bella, *Barkley*, 144.
32. Mark Heisler, "Goodbye, Sir Charles, We'll Miss You," *Los Angeles Times*, December 10, 1999.
33. Bella, *Barkley*, 144.
34. Jackie MacMullan, "How Moses Malone Mentored a Young Charles Barkley," ESPN, September 13, 2015, https://www.espn.com/nba/story/_/id/13650802/nba-how-moses-malone-mentored-young-charles-barkley.
35. Jere Longman, "76ers Beat Pacers," *Philadelphia Inquirer*, April 13, 1985.
36. MacMullan, "Dr. J and ABA."
37. MacMullan, "Dr. J and ABA."

20. The Breakup

1. Cunningham, discussion.
2. Pat Williams, in discussion with the author, May 6, 2022.
3. Patrick Ewing, "Patrick Ewing," interview by Darius Miles and Quentin Richardson, hosts, May 28, 2020, in *Knuckleheads*, podcast, MP3 audio, 45:50,

https://www.listennotes.com/podcasts/knuckleheads-with/patrick-ewing-stay-yo-a-at-CxPIplFATiV/.

4. Mike Bruton, "Sixers End Trip on Note of Discord," *Philadelphia Inquirer*, February 3, 1986.
5. Jeffrey Denberg, "Jordan's Contention: Opponents Complain, Trying to Set Him Up," *Atlanta Journal-Constitution*, April 17, 1990.
6. Mike Bruton, "Malone and Guokas in Patch-Up Meeting," *Philadelphia Inquirer*, February 4, 1986.
7. John Nash, discussion.
8. Mike Bruton, "Malone Out for Two Weeks; Center Should Return for Playoffs," *Philadelphia Inquirer*, March 30, 1986.
9. Chuck Newman, "After Grim Prognosis, Malone Lost for Season," *Philadelphia Inquirer*, April 26, 1986.
10. "Erving: 'A Little Mismanagement' by Sixers Brass," *Philadelphia Inquirer*, June 4, 1986.
11. Mike Bruton, "What Has Happened to the Stability So Vital to the Sixers' Success?" *Philadelphia Inquirer*, June 8, 1986.
12. Williams and Jones, *Tales from Philadelphia*, 166.
13. Bob Ford, "Ten Years Later, Two Deals Still Haunting Sixers," *Philadelphia Inquirer*, June 16, 1996.
14. Ford, "Ten Years Later."
15. Pat Williams, discussion.
16. Ford, "Ten Years Later."
17. Ford, "Ten Years Later."
18. Williams, *Tales from Philadelphia*, 166.
19. Pat Williams, discussion.
20. John Nash, discussion.
21. Mike Bruton, "76ers Deal Malone and Top Pick, Net Hinson, Ruland," *Philadelphia Inquirer*, June 18, 1986.
22. Jayson Stark, "Prognosis Unknown: Nagging Questions on Ruland's Fitness," *Philadelphia Inquirer*, June 18, 1986.
23. Jeff Ruland, in discussion with the author, May 11, 2023.
24. Jere Longman, "Cavs Make Daugherty No. 1," *Philadelphia Inquirer*, June 18, 1986.
25. Lynam, discussion.
26. John Nash, discussion.
27. Ford, "Ten Years Later."
28. Matt Guokas, in discussion with the author, August 30, 2023; and Pat Williams, discussion.

29. Ford, "Ten Years Later."
30. Williams and Jones, *Tales from Philadelphia*, 173.
31. Mike Bruton, "Malone Lashes Out at Katz in Parting Shots," *Philadelphia Inquirer*, June 18, 1986.
32. "Malone Criticizes Katz, Vows Revenge on Court," *Philadelphia Inquirer*, June 25, 1986.
33. Williams and Jones, *Tales from Philadelphia*, 271.
34. Jere Longman, "Bird's the Same, Celtics Aren't, the Team, for Once, Has the Look of Being Mortal," *Philadelphia Inquirer*, November 25, 1986.
35. Sheldon, discussion.
36. Pat Williams, discussion.
37. Williams and Jones, *Tales from Philadelphia*, 281.

21. Come On Down!

1. Chuck Douglas, in discussion with the author, April 18, 2023.
2. Jere Longman, "Scrooge Malone Coming to Town," *Philadelphia Inquirer*, December 25, 1986.
3. Anthony Cotton, "Malone: Big One but No Grudge," *Washington Post*, December 25, 1986.
4. Longman, "Scrooge Malone."
5. Deniz Hardy, in discussion with the author, April 25, 2023.
6. Mark Alarie, in discussion with the author, May 1, 2023.
7. Ennis Whatley, in discussion with the author, May 9, 2023.
8. Alarie, discussion; and Darwin Cook, in discussion with the author, May 2, 2023.
9. Cook, discussion.
10. Anthony Cotton, "Moses Malone's 39 Lift Bullets over the 76ers," *Washington Post*, January 11, 1987.
11. Jack McCallum, "Back to Haunt the Sixers," *Sports Illustrated*, March 16, 1987, https://vault.si.com/vault/1987/03/16/back-to-haunt-the-sixers-moses-malone-the-big-one-philly-let-get-away-has-made-washington-a-winner-on-the-court-and-at-the-box-office.
12. Paul Coro, "Remembering Manute Bol and the Favorite of Many Tall Tales about Him," *Los Angeles Times*, March 18, 2018.
13. Blaine Harden, "The Long Lonely Journey of Manute Bol," *Washington Post*, March 22, 1987.
14. Coro, "Remembering Manute Bol."

15. Leigh Montville, "A Tall Story," *Sports Illustrated*, December 17, 1990, https://www.si.com/vault/1990/12/17/123285/a-tall-story-manute-bol-the-sixers-7-ft7-in-center-views-life-from-a-unique-perspective (page removed).
16. Douglas, discussion.
17. Thomas Golianopoulous, "The Fighter," *Slam*, November 25, 2010, https://www.slamonline.com/news/nba/the-fighter/.
18. Gordon Edes, "Moses and Manute: The Bullets' 'Old' Power and Young Tower," *Los Angeles Times*, February 8, 1987.
19. Archie Talley, in discussion with the author, November 22, 2022.
20. Uitti and Bogues, *Muggsy*, 27–28.
21. Garnett Slatton, in discussion with the author, April 26, 2023.
22. Muggsy Bogues, in discussion with the author, April 29, 2023.
23. Bogues, discussion.
24. Bogues, discussion.
25. Slatton, discussion.
26. Malone, "Playboy Interview," 52.
27. Lott Brooks, in discussion with the author, November 15, 2022.
28. Reid, discussion.
29. Tony Dale, in discussion with the author, June 22, 2022; and Kevin Vergara, in discussion with the author, May 17, 2022.
30. Slatton, discussion.
31. Mike Jones, discussion.
32. Gordie Jones, "Moses Malone: Ultimate Hardhat."
33. Dunleavy, discussion.
34. Fentress, discussion.
35. Terry Lefton, "On the Court and in the Business World, Moses Malone Stood Tall," *Sports Business Journal*, September 21, 2015, https://www.sportsbusinessjournal.com/Journal/Issues/2015/09/21/Marketing-and-Sponsorship/The-Lefton-Report.aspx?hl=nba&sc=0.
36. Fred Brown, discussion.
37. Gary Stevenson, in discussion with the author, March 26, 2024.
38. Vergara, discussion.
39. Cunningham, discussion.
40. Ronald O. Howell, "Moses Malone: Basketball's Million-Dollar Baby," *Ebony*, January 1980, 42.
41. Anthony Cotton, "Malone Yearns for the Ball," *Washington Post*, December 3, 1987.
42. Cotton, "Malone Yearns."

43. Anthony Cotton, "Moses Malone Firm: Bullets Need Him," *Washington Post*, February 19, 1988.
44. Tony Kornheiser, "It's Time for Moses and the Bullets to File Separation Papers," *Washington Post*, May 1, 1988.
45. Jeffrey Denberg, "Lakers Won't Rest on Their '87 Laurels in Quest to Repeat," *Atlanta Journal-Constitution*, February 28, 1988.
46. Anthony Cotton, "NBA Pact Cuts Draft, Aids Free Agency," *Washington Post*, April 27, 1988.
47. Kornheiser, "It's Time"; and Anthony Cotton, "Sunday May Tell Tale for Moses Malone," *Washington Post*, May 7, 1988.
48. Jeff Malone, in discussion with the author, May 13, 2023.
49. Slatton, discussion.
50. Leonard Shapiro, "Hawks Offer 3-Year Deal to Malone, Cut in '88 Pay," *Washington Post*, July 4, 1988.

22. Superstar in Decline

1. Reid, discussion.
2. Alarie, discussion.
3. Carter, discussion.
4. Jon Koncak, in discussion with the author, May 16, 2023.
5. Wilkins, discussion.
6. "Top Moments: Larry Bird, Dominique Wilkins Stage Classic Game 7 Duel," NBA.com, September 14, 2021, https://www.nba.com/news/history-top-moments-bird-wilkins-shootout.
7. "Top Moments: Larry Bird, Dominique Wilkins," NBA.com.
8. Jeffrey Denberg, "Players Welcome Chance to 'Thrive Under Pressure,'" *Atlanta Journal-Constitution*, August 17, 1988.
9. Jeffrey Denberg, "First, 'Nique Must Prove He'll Share," *Atlanta Journal-Constitution*, October 9, 1988.
10. Jeffrey Denberg, "Malone Has Made an Immediate Impact," *Atlanta Journal-Constitution*, November 7, 1988.
11. Jeffrey Denberg, "Malone Angered by Playoff Play Calling," *Atlanta Journal-Constitution*, May 17, 1989.
12. Koncak, discussion; and Theus, discussion.
13. Tom Enlund, "Malone Brings Brilliance, Questions," *Milwaukee Journal Sentinel*, October 27, 1991.
14. Rivers and Brooks, *Those Who Love the Game*, 73.

15. Steve Holman, in discussion with the author, May 9, 2023; and Jeffrey Denberg, "Hawks, Malone Pound Pacers," *Atlanta Journal-Constitution*, December 24, 1988.
16. Holman, discussion.
17. Theus, discussion.
18. Mark Bradley, "Time Running Down for Hawks to Ignite," *Atlanta Journal-Constitution*, March 21, 1989.
19. Jeffrey Denberg, "Malone's Rebounding the Best Since Bellamy," On the Beat, *Atlanta Journal-Constitution*, April 13, 1989.
20. Jeffrey Denberg, "Some Hawks Point to Theus as Root of Problem," *Atlanta Journal-Constitution*, April 2, 1989.
21. Holman, discussion.
22. Rivers and Brooks, *Those Who Love the Game*, 173.
23. Triche, discussion.
24. Gordie Jones, "Moses Malone Was Influential Sixer."
25. Whatley, discussion.
26. Roy S. Johnson, "Dr. Malone's Remedy for Hawks: Defense," *Atlanta Journal-Constitution*, February 14, 1989.
27. Koncak, discussion.
28. Jeffrey Denberg, "Bucks Score 1st-Round KO—Sloppy Hawks Fall 96–92 at The Omni," *Atlanta Journal-Constitution*, May 8, 1989.
29. Jeffrey Denberg, "An Inside Job: Hawks Beat Warriors 112–96," *Atlanta Journal-Constitution*, November 19, 1989.
30. Koncak, discussion; and Triche, discussion.
31. Spud Webb, in discussion with the author, March 20, 2024.
32. Koncak, discussion.
33. Ailene Voisin, "Lakers Play, Handle Their Problems, Like Champions," *Atlanta Journal-Constitution*, March 14, 1990.
34. Smith, *Talk of Champions*, 207.
35. Pete Babcock, in discussion with the author, May 10, 2023.
36. Jeffrey Denberg, "Wilkins Makes All-Star Team; Malone Left Off," *Atlanta Journal-Constitution*, January 31, 1990.
37. Jeffrey Denberg, "Hawks Need More Than a New Coach," *Atlanta Journal-Constitution*, April 25, 1990.
38. Jeffrey Denberg, "Malone Works on Image as Hawks Camp Opens," *Atlanta Journal-Constitution*, October 6, 1990.
39. Jeffrey Denberg, "Malone-for-Pierce Trade Talks Stall," *Atlanta Journal-Constitution*, June 22, 1990.

40. Jeffrey Denberg, "Koncak to Start; Malone Given 'McHale' Role," *Atlanta Journal-Constitution*, November 30, 1990.
41. Webb, discussion.
42. Johnny Davis, discussion.
43. Tim McCormick, in discussion with the author, May 9, 2023.
44. Moncrief, discussion; Rumeal Robinson, discussion; and Jeffrey Denberg, "Malone Has Years Left, but Will They Be with the Hawks?" *Atlanta Journal-Constitution*, February 27, 1991.
45. Ailene Voisin, NBA Notebook, *Atlanta Journal-Constitution*, July 14, 1991.
46. Jack McCallum, The NBA, *Sports Illustrated*, January 21, 1991, https://vault.si.com/vault/1991/01/21/the-nba.

23. Endings

1. Hardy, discussion.
2. Dick, discussion.
3. Noel, "Wives of Sports Superstars," 148.
4. Hughlett, discussion.
5. In the Matter of the Marriage of Alfreda Gill Malone and Moses Eugene Malone, No. 75023 (Fort Bend D., Tex. 1992).
6. Matter of Alfreda Gill Malone and Moses Eugene Malone.
7. Matter of Alfreda Gill Malone and Moses Eugene Malone.
8. "Judge Puts Restrictions on Malone," *Lawrence (KS) Journal-World*, June 4, 1992.
9. United Press International, "Malone Denies Wife's Claims of Abuse," September 10, 1992, https://www.upi.com/Archives/1992/09/10/Malone-denies-wifes-claims-of-abuse/6818716097600/.
10. Ralph Cooper, in discussion with the author, March 28, 2023.
11. "Malone Denies Charges," *Port Arthur (TX) News*, September 10, 1992.
12. Matter of Alfreda Gill Malone and Moses Eugene Malone.
13. Tom Enlund, "Malone Is Wondering Why He Was Arrested," *Milwaukee Journal Sentinel*, February 4, 1993.
14. Vergara, discussion.
15. Kirk Williams, "Moses Malone Eulogy," Lakewood Church, Houston, Texas, September 19, 2015.
16. Todd Day, in discussion with the author, May 23, 2023.
17. Brickowski, discussion.
18. Bob Wolfley, "Harris Vows Team Won't Lose to Win," *Milwaukee Journal Sentinel*, July 12, 1991.
19. Harris, discussion.

20. Fred Roberts, "The Fred Roberts Interview," interview by Michael McClellan, *Celtic Nation* (blog), n.d., https://www.celtic-nation.com/blog/the-fred-roberts-interview/.
21. Tom Enlund, "Back Injury May Limit Role of Bucks Center Malone This Season," *Milwaukee Journal Sentinel*, October 14, 1992.
22. Rick Braun, "Surgery to Put Malone Out at Least 3 Months," *Milwaukee Journal Sentinel*, November 7, 1992.
23. Blue Edwards, in discussion with the author, May 20, 2023.
24. Lester Conner, in discussion with the author, May 23, 2023.
25. Day, discussion.
26. Conner, discussion.
27. Day, discussion.
28. Brickowski, discussion.
29. Gwen Knapp, "Grand Old Sixer a Brand New Sixer," *Philadelphia Inquirer*, August 13, 1993.
30. Carter, discussion.
31. Warren Kidd, in discussion with the author, June 14, 2023.
32. Howard Blatt, "Relentless Malone Still Getting It Done," *Daily News* (New York), December 25, 1993.
33. Bob Ford, "Malone Hits Milestone as Sixers Leave Bucks Feeling Spent," *Philadelphia Inquirer*, December 12, 1993.
34. Frank Lawlor, "Hornets Trounce Sixers, 125–91," *Philadelphia Inquirer*, March 23, 1994.
35. Jerry Briggs, "Spurs Sign Malone, but Not a Head Coach," *San Antonio Express-News*, August 26, 1994.
36. Moses Malone, "Moses Malone on David Robinson and Michael Jordan," September 11, 2009, video, 5:14, https://www.youtube.com/watch?v=Y9OckM2fFmw.
37. Doc Rivers, "'Do You Believe . . . ?' NBA Edition with Doc Rivers," interview by Bill Simmons, December 12, 2023, in *The Bill Simmons Podcast*, produced by Kyle Crichton, podcast, MP3 audio, 1:28:59, https://www.theringer.com/the-bill-simmons-podcast/2023/12/12/23998794/do-you-believe-nba-edition-with-doc-rivers.
38. Spurs Notes, *San Antonio Express-News*, January 13, 1995.
39. Glenn Rogers, "Shooting to Seven Straight—Hornets Can't Handle Streaking Spurs," *San Antonio Express-News*, December 28, 1994.
40. Rivers and Brooks, *Those Who Love the Game*, 86–87.
41. Buck Harvey, "Moses' Farewell: Starless Goodbye," *San Antonio Express-News*, February 10, 1995.

42. Mike Jones, discussion.
43. Mike Harris, "Moses' Commandment: Anything but Retiring," *Richmond Times-Dispatch*, December 22, 1996.

24. Relentless Friend

1. Associated Press, "Hall of Famer Was Accused of Abusing Daughters," ESPN, December 6, 2004, https://www.espn.com/nba/news/story?id=1940008.
2. David Aldridge, "NBA 75: At No. 18, Moses Malone Was 'Absolutely Relentless' and Let His Prodigious Game Do the Talking," *The Athletic*, January 26, 2022, https://theathletic.com/3082138/2022/01/26/nba-75-at-no-18-moses-malone-was-absolutely-relentless-and-let-his-prodigious-game-do-the-talking/?source=user_shared_article.
3. Associated Press, "Hall of Famer Was Accused."
4. Belcher v. State, 661 S.W.2d 230 (Tex. App. 1984).
5. Carl Belcher, in discussion with author, August 22, 2022.
6. Carl Belcher, discussion.
7. Franklin Edwards, discussion.
8. Dale, discussion.
9. Johnson, discussion.
10. Cook, discussion; and Mokeski, discussion.
11. Johnson, discussion.
12. Dale, discussion.
13. Mike Jones, discussion.
14. Dale, discussion.
15. Sandra White, in discussion with the author, July 15, 2022.
16. Dale, discussion.
17. Campbell, discussion; and Major Jones, discussion.
18. Reid, discussion.
19. Sessum, discussion.
20. Johnson, discussion.
21. Lewis, discussion.
22. Joe Walker, in discussion with the author, November 7, 2023.
23. Mike Jones, discussion; and Vergara, discussion.
24. Dale, discussion.
25. Anthony Colbert Jr., in discussion with the author, August 17, 2022.
26. Jonathan Feigen, "Rockets, NBA Legend Moses Malone Remembered with Tears, Laughter," Chron (website), September 19, 2015, https://blog.chron.com/ultimaterockets/2015/09/rockets-nba-legend-moses-malone-remembered-with-tears-laughter/?photo=687867.

27. Moses Malone Jr., "People always ask me why I didn't name my son Moses.... Well, the honest answer is ... I wouldn't want him ..." Facebook, March 1, 2021 (account and post deleted; no URL available).
28. Moses Malone Jr., "FYI Pops Made Sure Me He Took Me Too Starting In 7th Grade Till My Sophomore Year In High School," Facebook, November 22, 2021 (account and post deleted; no URL available).
29. Cooper, discussion.
30. Johnson, discussion.
31. Cunningham, discussion; Harris, discussion; and Mike Jones, discussion.
32. Vergara, discussion.
33. Clayton, discussion.
34. NBA.com, "75 Stories: Moses Malone."
35. Major Jones, discussion.
36. Hayes, discussion.
37. Haywood, discussion.
38. Mike Jensen, "Chaney Elected to Hall of Fame—Former 76ers Great Moses Malone Was the Only Player Selected," *Philadelphia Inquirer*, May 31, 2001.
39. Erving, "Moses Malone's Basketball Hall of Fame."
40. Malone, "Malone's Basketball Hall of Fame."
41. Fultz, discussion.
42. William Lawson, in discussion with the author, August 23, 2023.
43. Bolling Hill, discussion.
44. Miles, discussion.
45. Williams and Jones, *Tales from Philadelphia*, 163.
46. Joe Juliano, "Malone Provides Crash Course in Rebounding," *Philadelphia Inquirer*, December 7, 2005.
47. Joe Juliano, "Malone Shows Dalembert a Passion for the Rebound," *Philadelphia Inquirer*, February 7, 2007.
48. Donyell Marshall, in discussion with the author, August 22, 2023.
49. Marcus Hayes, "How Moses Led Allen Iverson from the Wilderness," *Philadelphia Inquirer*, February 9, 2019.
50. Gilbert, discussion; and Guy Torry, in discussion with the author, March 21, 2023.
51. John Nash, discussion.
52. Lynam, discussion.
53. Leah Nash, in discussion with the author, July 23, 2022.
54. Joe Walker, discussion.
55. Leah Nash, discussion.
56. Leah Nash, discussion.

57. Leah Nash, discussion; and Mike Jones, discussion.
58. Cureton, discussion.
59. Tony Brothers, in discussion with the author, August 30, 2023.
60. Haywood, discussion.
61. Barry, discussion; and Walton, discussion.
62. Johnnie White, in discussion with the author, November 8, 2023.
63. Sandra White, discussion.
64. Vergara, discussion.
65. Brothers, discussion.
66. Leah Nash, discussion.
67. Gordie Jones, "The Strange and Tragic Case of Retired Sixers Big Men Suffering Heart-Related Issues," Liberty Ballers, November 17, 2022, https://www.libertyballers.com/2022/11/17/23464783/the-strange-and-tragic-case-of-retired-sixers-big-men-suffering-heart-related-issues.
68. Aldridge, "At No. 18."
69. Johnson, discussion.
70. Barkley, "Moses Malone Eulogy."
71. Leah Nash, discussion.

Epilogue

1. Michael Lee, "With Jersey Retirement, Moses Malone and His Legendary Hustle Are Finally Immortalized in Philadelphia," *The Athletic*, February 8, 2019, https://theathletic.com/806358/2019/02/08/with-jersey-retirement-moses-malone-and-his-legendary-hustle-are-finally-immortalized-in-philadelphia/.
2. Vergara, discussion.
3. Scott O'Neil, email message to author, April 8, 2023.
4. Clayton, discussion.
5. Franklin Edwards, discussion.
6. O'Neil, discussion.
7. Hayes, "How Moses Led Allen Iverson."
8. Franklin Edwards, discussion.

BIBLIOGRAPHY

Abrams, Jonathan. *Boys among Men: How the Prep-to-Pro Generation Redefined the NBA and Sparked a Basketball Revolution*. New York: Crown Archetype, 2016.

Barkley, Charles, and Roy S. Johnson. *Outrageous! The Fine Life and Flagrant Good Times of Basketball's Irresistible Force*. New York: Simon & Schuster, 1992.

Bella, Timothy. *Barkley: A Biography*. New York: Hanover Square Press, 2022.

Benedict, Jeff. *LeBron*. New York: Avid Reader Press, 2023.

Bengston, Russ. *A History of Basketball in Fifteen Sneakers*. New York: Workman Publishing, 2023.

Bird, Larry. *Drive: The Story of My Life*. New York: Doubleday, 1989.

Bondy, Filip. *Tip Off: How the 1984 NBA Draft Changed Basketball Forever*. Cambridge MA: Da Capo, 2007.

Criblez, Adam J. *Tall Tales and Short Shorts: Dr. J, Pistol Pete, & the Birth of the Modern NBA*. New York: Rowman & Littlefield, 2017.

Croatto, Pete. *From Hang Time to Prime Time: Business, Entertainment, and the Birth of the Modern-Day NBA*. New York: Simon & Schuster, 2020.

Cureton, Earl, and Jake Uitti. *Earl the Twirl: My Life in Basketball*. Jefferson NC: McFarland, 2023.

Dawkins, Darryl, and Charles Rosen. *Chocolate Thunder: The Uncensored Life and Times of Darryl Dawkins*. N.p.: Sports Media Publishing, 2003.

Didinger, Ray. *One Last Read: The Collected Works of the World's Slowest Sportswriter*. Philadelphia: Temple University Press, 2007.

Drexler, Clyde, and Kerry Eggers. *Clyde the Glide: My Life in Basketball*. New York: Sports Publishing, 2011.

Erving, Julius, and Karl Taro Greenfield. *Dr. J: The Autobiography*. New York: HarperCollins, 2013.

Feinstein, John. *The Punch: One Night, Two Lives, and the Fight That Changed Basketball Forever*. New York: Back Bay, 2002.

Garnett, Kevin, and David Ritz. *KG A to Z: An Uncensored Encyclopedia of Life, Basketball, and Everything in Between*. New York: Simon & Schuster, 2021.

Glickman, Harry. *Promoter Ain't a Dirty Word*. Portland OR: Timber Press, 1978.

Gutman, Bill. *Chairmen of the Boards: Erving, Bird, Malone, Johnson.* New York: Tempo Books, 1980.

Halberstam, David. *The Breaks of the Game.* New York: Alfred A. Knopf, 1981.

Harmon, F. Martin. *Charles "Lefty" Driesell: A Basketball Legend.* Macon GA: Mercer University Press, 2014.

Knight, Phil. *Shoe Dog: A Memoir by the Creator of Nike.* New York: Scribner, 2015.

Kuska, Bob. *Balls of Confusion: Pro Basketball Goes to War.* Sheperdstown WV: From Way Downtown, 2024.

Lazenby, Roland. *Showboat: The Life of Kobe Bryant.* New York: Little, Brown and Company, 2016.

Locke, Tates, and Bob Ibach. *Caught in the Net.* New York: Leisure Press, 1982.

Lucas, John, and Joseph Moriarty. *Winning a Day at a Time.* Center City MN: Hazelden Foundation, 1994.

MacMullan, Jackie, Rafe Bartholomew, and Dan Klores. *Basketball: A Love Story.* New York: Broadway Books, 2018.

McCallum, Jack.. *Unfinished Business: On and Off the Court with the 1990–91 Boston Celtics.* New York: Summit Books, 1992.

McKee, Mark. *The History of Texas High School Basketball.* Vol. 1, *1970–1974.* Texas High School Basketball History. http://www.txhighschoolbasketball.com/download.

McMullen, Paul. *Maryland Basketball: Tales from Cole Field House.* Baltimore: Johns Hopkins University Press, 2002.

Mendelsohn, Joshua. *The Cap: How Larry Fleisher and David Stern Built the Modern NBA.* Lincoln: University of Nebraska Press, 2020.

Montville, Leigh. *Manute: The Center of Two Worlds.* New York: Simon & Schuster, 1993.

Olajuwon, Hakeem, and Peter Knobler. *Living the Dream: My Life and Basketball.* New York: Little, Brown and Company, 1996.

Pearlman, Jeff. *Showtime: Magic, Kareem, Riley, and the Los Angeles Lakers Dynasty of the 1980s.* New York: Avery Publishing, 2014.

Pluto, Terry. *Loose Balls: The Short, Wild Life of the American Basketball Association.* New York: Simon & Schuster, 1990.

Price, Asher. *Earl Campbell: Yards after Contact.* Austin: University of Texas Press, 2019.

Quinn, Jim. *Don't Be Afraid to Win: How Free Agency Changed the Business of Pro Sports.* New York: Radius Book Group, 2019.

Rivers, Doc, and Bruce Brooks. *Those Who Love the Game: Glenn "Doc" Rivers on Life in the NBA and Elsewhere.* New York: HarperTrophy, 1993.

Robertson, Oscar. *The Big O: My Life, My Times, My Game.* New York: Rodale, 2003.

Runstedtler, Theresa. *Black Ball: Kareem Abdul-Jabbar, Spencer Haywood, and the Generation That Saved the Soul of the NBA*. New York: Bold Type Books, 2023.

Ryan, Bob. *The Pro Game: The World of Professional Basketball*. New York: McGraw-Hill, 1975.

Ryan, Michael. *Five Star: Celebrating 25 Years of History, Legends, and Instruction from the Nation's Premier Basketball Camp*. Grand Rapids MI: Masters Press, 1990.

Shaughnessy, Dan. *Wish It Lasted Forever: Life with the Larry Bird Celtics*. New York: Scribner, 2001.

Simmons, Bill. *The Book of Basketball: The NBA According to the Sports Guy*. New York: Ballantine Books, 2009.

Smith, Kenny. *Talk of Champions: Stories of the People Who Made Me: A Memoir*. New York: Doubleday, 2023.

Smith, Sam. *Hard Labor: The Battle That Birthed the Billion-Dollar NBA*. Chicago: Triumph, 2017.

Spears, Marc J., and Gary Washburn. *The Spencer Haywood Rule: Battles, Basketball, and the Making of an American Iconoclast*. Chicago: Triumph, 2020.

Thompson, John. *I Came as a Shadow: An Autobiography*. New York: Henry Holt & Company, 2020. Kindle.

Tomjanovich, Rudy, and Robert Falkoff. *A Rocket at Heart: My Life and My Team*. New York: Simon & Schuster, 1997.

Uitti, Jake, and Tyrone "Muggsy" Bogues. *Muggsy: My Life from a Kid in the Projects to the Godfather of Small Ball*. Chicago: Triumph, 2022.

Ungrady, Dave. *Tales from the Maryland Terrapins: A Collection of the Greatest Terrapin Stories Ever Told*. New York: Sports Publishing, 2014.

Vitale, Dick, and Dick Weiss. *It's Awesome, Baby!: 75 Years of Memories and a Lifetime of Opinions on the Game I Love*. Overland Park KS: Ascend Books, 2014.

Wendel, Tim. *Buffalo, Home of the Braves*. Read by Tim Wendel and Pete Weber. Traverse City MI: Sun Bear Press, 2009. Audio ed., 4 hr., 25 min.

Williams, Pat. *Ahead of the Game: The Pat Williams Story*. Ada MI: Revell, 2014.

Williams, Pat, and Gordon Jones. *Tales from the Philadelphia 76ers Locker Room: A Collection of the Greatest Sixers Stories from the 1982–83 Championship Season*. New York: Sports Publishing, 2007.

INDEX